# The Memory Wars

# The Memory Wars

## FREUD'S LEGACY
## IN DISPUTE

*Frederick Crews*

*and*

Harold P. Blum

Marcia Cavell

Morris Eagle

Matthew Hugh Erdelyi

Allen Esterson

Robert R. Holt

James Hopkins

Lester Luborsky

David D. Olds

Mortimer Ostow

Bernard L. Pacella

"Penelope"

Herbert S. Peyser

Charlotte Krause Prozan

Theresa Reid

James L. Rice

J. Schimek

Marian Tolpin

**Granta Books**
London

Granta Publications, 2/3 Hanover Yard, London N1 8BE.

First published in the USA and Canada by *The New York Review of Books*, 250 West 57th Street, New York, NY 10107, 1995.

First published in Great Britain by Granta Books 1997.

A CIP catalogue record for this book is available from the British Library.

1 3 5 7 9 10 8 6 4 2

Printed and bound in Great Britain by
Mackays of Chatham PLC, Chatham, Kent

*Frederick Crews dedicates his portion of this book to*
*Peter Swales*
*demon researcher, free spirit, loyal friend*

# CONTENTS

# ACKNOWLEDGMENTS

This book is heavy in indebtedness. To begin with, it would not have come into existence at all without the prompting of the editors of *The New York Review of Books*, who saw an edifying debate where others, including me, saw only the smoke of battle. The teeny-bopper adjective "awesome" borders on understatement when applied to Robert Silvers's editorial acumen, courage, and all-around wisdom. And as the book project's editor, Ann Kjellberg has been astute, resourceful, reliable, and cordial. I will miss working with her.

Special thanks are due the correspondents who agreed to have their critical letters to *The New York Review of Books* reprinted here, knowing full well that I would get the first and last words. That is sportsmanship! But I also want to thank the other correspondents who are represented only in summary. Understandably, they did not wish to contribute actively to a book whose main emphasis struck them as mistaken. Nevertheless, they earned my gratitude by engaging important issues in a lively manner. Although no intention could have been farther from their minds, they, too, played an essential role in making *The Memory Wars* a reality. I should mention as well the many concerned readers whose letters never saw publication. Few of those letters were complimentary, but most of them were thoughtful and challenging.

Several factual errors in my own work have been silently corrected; the changes have no bearing on the letters reproduced and summarized here. For having pointed out inaccuracies, I am grateful to Rolando A. Amador, Ross Cheit, Marie Kann, Cyrille Koupernik, John Richardson, Anthony Stadlen, and Robert Wilcocks. At Professor Cheit's request, his letters to *The New York Review* and my replies have been omitted.

For various kinds of encouragement and/or information, I owe thanks to Robyn Dawes, D. A. Begelman, Henry Cohen, Joseph C. Doherty, Borden Elniff, Barbara Epstein, Edward Erwin, Allen Esterson, Pamela Freyd, Peter Freyd, Brina Gehry, Alison Gopnik, Phyllis Grosskurth, Adolf Grünbaum, Han Israëls, Bart Johnson, Michael G. Kenny, John F. Kihlstrom, Ronald Lehrer, Elizabeth Loftus, Malcolm Macmillan, Gary Saul Morson, Richard Ofshe, James Okerblom, Mark Pendergrast, Russell A. Powell, Paul Preuss, James L. Rice, Barbara Riebling, Bernard Rimland, Jim Schnabel, Daniel Simon, Richard Skues, Frank J. Sulloway, Catherine Tice, Peter van Sommers, Richard Webster, and Robert Wilcocks. I was unacquainted with most of those people before writing the essays that appear below; my contact with them has been enriching.

Two other individuals must be singled out for praise. Elizabeth Crews has been, for thirty-six years now, my best critic as well as my dearest friend. And Peter Swales, to whom my share of *The Memory Wars* is dedicated, gave me extraordinary help when "The Unknown Freud" was under attack from many sides. Freud scholars, but too few others, know that Peter is a living treasure. I look forward to the day when his unique essays on the early Freud are available within one set of covers.

Finally, I thank the editors of *The* [London] *Times Higher Education Supplement* for permission to reuse the essay that forms the afterword to this book.

FREDERICK CREWS

# A NOTE ON NOTES

To avoid redundancy, the original citations that appeared in the following essays and letters have undergone some consolidation. Shortened parenthetic references, as follows, will be used for the two most commonly cited texts:

SE: *The Standard Edition of the Complete Psychological Works of Sigmund Freud*, 24 volumes, translated by James Strachey (Hogarth Press, 1953–1974)

Freud-Fliess Letters: *The Complete Letters of Sigmund Freud to Wilhelm Fliess, 1887–1904*, translated and edited by Jeffrey Moussaieff Masson (Harvard University Press, 1985)

# INTRODUCTION

No book was ever less premeditated than this one. Its germ, back in December of 1992, lay in my proposal to *The New York Review of Books* that I review James L. Rice's useful source study, *Freud's Russia*, which a Berkeley colleague had passed along to me in manuscript. Although other works pertinent to psychoanalysis then kept coming to my notice, expanding the scope of what, in November 1993, became "The Unknown Freud," I myself had no eventual book in mind. My intention, as it crystallized, was simply to convey a sense of how radically our idea of Freud and psychoanalysis has been changing under the pressure exerted by surprising biographical revelations on the one hand and rigorous methodological critiques on the other. I sensed, of course, that my article would arouse controversy, but not that it would make my name a household epithet among Freudians across the United States and elsewhere.

Later, it was *The New York Review*'s idea that I write a second piece discussing several new books that examined the practice of so-called recovered memory, a therapeutic innovation that, since the mid-1980s, had been producing major social effects in a number of English-speaking countries. By then I was fully aware of the attention aroused by "The Unknown Freud." When my new review essay, "The Revenge of the Repressed," appeared as a two-part article in November and December of 1994, I knew what kind of reaction to expect. But only after several heated rounds of published correspondence, representing just a sampling of the passions aroused by my articles of 1993 and 1994, did the editors of *The New York Review* suggest that the whole protracted debate might constitute the makings of a book. By then, little remained for me to do but write this introduction and append a personal afterword about the Freud uproar, originally commissioned by *The* [London] *Times Higher Education Supplement*.

This is not to say, however, that my portion of *The Memory Wars* lacks a unifying perspective. As a one-time Freudian who had decided to help others resist the fallacies to which I had succumbed in the 1960s, I had long before articulated the critique of psychoanalysis that undergirds "The Unknown Freud."[1] Nor was I ever in doubt about the perniciousness of the recovered memory movement—a frenzy that is now deluding countless patients (mostly women) into launching false charges of sexual abuse against their dumbfounded and

---

1. See especially the first five chapters of my book *Skeptical Engagements* (Oxford University Press, 1986). Relevant essays from an earlier period, when I was still attempting to see what I could retain of the Freudian heritage, appeared in *Out of My System: Psychoanalysis, Ideology, and Critical Method* (Oxford University Press, 1975).

mortified elders—or about the ultimate origin of that movement in Freudian assumptions. In my view, the relatively
patent and vulgar pseudoscience of recovered memory rests in
appreciable measure on the respectable and entrenched pseudoscience of psychoanalysis. Thus, even though "The Revenge of
the Repressed" was not even a gleam in my eye when I was
writing "The Unknown Freud," the closing paragraphs of the
latter essay sound like a preview of its successor.

As a debate, however, *The Memory Wars* is necessarily a
vortex of dissension. In introducing that debate, I cannot pretend to be speaking for its other participants—some of whom
are represented only in summary, since they declined the
opportunity to have their letters reprinted here. And I feel a
reluctance, in any case, to take the measure of a multifaceted
quarrel that continues to expand and evolve even as this book
goes to press. As I will show, crucially pertinent events have
occurred since the last exchange recorded here, placing both
my articles and some of the letters in a significantly new light.
What follows will thus be less an introduction than an update
that is intended to advance the existing dialogue from the only
perspective I can honestly represent, my own.

First, however, it may be useful to summarize the ways
in which my articles on Freud and on recovered memory therapy—hereafter designated by the acronym RMT—have proved
controversial, not just within the covers of this book but well
beyond it. The areas of conflict are these six:

1. Freud's character and career. "The Unknown Freud"
maintains that Freud's drive for renown repeatedly goaded
him to generalize from an inadequate or even imaginary base
of observation and to rule his international movement more

like a petty generalissimo than like a discoverer of replicable knowledge. Did I represent him fairly, and do my conclusions, if they are to be accepted, have any bearing on questions of theory that are still at issue?

2. The credibility of contemporary psychoanalysis. Has Freud's movement by now evolved into a genuine discipline whose knowledge claims deserve our respect? Or, as I believe, does psychoanalysis merely adapt itself resourcefully to changes in public sentiment, meanwhile remaining enmired in the same deep methodological errors that attended its birth in the 1890s?

3. The nature of RMT. Is it the disgrace that I take it to be, the most destructive episode in the entire history of professional psychotherapy? Or, at the opposite extreme of perception, is it a needed balm for "survivors"—real victims of childhood sexual molestation who previously found no one to elicit and believe the dreadful stories they had hidden even from themselves?

4. The share of responsibility, if any, that Freudianism bears for the rise and rapid spread of RMT. Isn't it willfully foolish on my part to blame the errors of one psychological school on an earlier one that has taken a directly opposite view of children's sexuality and the causes of adult neurosis?

5. My qualifications for making pronouncements about psychoanalysis and psychotherapy without benefit of analytic training or even of a personal analysis, or of experience in administering therapy of any kind. And

6. The extent to which my critique of psychoanalysis can be dismissed as a personal vendetta against a system of thought that I once found intellectually attractive.

On points 1 through 3, the main body of *The Memory Wars* provides ample material, pro and con, for readers to form opinions of their own. But I will necessarily revert in this introduction to point 4, the relationship between RMT and psychoanalysis, since that is where new evidence has come to my attention. As for points 5 and 6, which boil down to whether my criticisms need to be taken seriously at all, I may as well deal with them here at the outset.

The issue of my lack of professional experience tends to be raised not by recovered memory therapists, many of whom could not withstand much scrutiny of their own credentials, but by psychoanalysts, and it takes a form that has been usual since Freud himself first began trying to one-up his detractors. Those who haven't been analyzed, the argument goes, simply don't know enough about the therapeutic process to criticize it, and those who haven't accumulated clinical experience as therapists necessarily lack the solid basis of observation on which Freudian tenets reside.

My response to this argument is that it is altogether question begging—the question being whether "clinical experience" constitutes a trustworthy test of the clinician's theoretical armamentarium. It is easy to show that this couldn't possibly be the case. Literally hundreds of psychotherapeutic schools propound mutually incompatible theories about the causes and cure of neuroses, yet each school finds its theory "confirmed" in dealings with patients. Thus clinical experience, standing alone, is not a probative tool but an inducement to complacency and tunnel vision. For testing and evaluating psychological theories, a point of vantage outside the consulting room is required. Likewise, it won't do to say that only the analyzed can judge whether psychoanalysis offers its clients veridical insight or merely the illusion of it. Though difficult to resolve, such matters lie in the public domain; and members of the public had better address them, because it will be a long while before analysts and other psychotherapists are ready to do so without prejudice.

It is equally question begging for Freudians to say, as they do both publicly and (much less politely) among themselves, that my animadversions against psychoanalysis can be set down to neurotic traits and scarring experiences—a personal analysis that went awry, a rejected application for candidacy to become a lay analyst, and so forth. The fact that those rumors are false is only part of what is the matter with them; the larger failing is the evasion of criticism by recourse to ad hominem gossip. Let me say for the record, however, that my loss of intellectual trust in psychoanalysis came about in the most mundane way, through reading, and that other readers of the same texts might well find them compelling in just the way that I did.

Back in the late Sixties and early Seventies, a collision with the writings of philosophers such as Michael Polanyi, Karl Popper, Sidney Hook, and Ernest Nagel brought me to the painful realization that Freudianism in its self-authenticating approach to knowledge constitutes not an exemplification of the rational-empirical ethos to which I felt loyal, and to which Freud himself had professed allegiance, but a seductively mythic alternative to it.[2] Only much later did it dawn on me

_____

2. See Michael Polanyi, *Personal Knowledge: Towards a Post-Critical Philosophy*, revised edition (Routledge and Kegan Paul, 1962); Karl R. Popper, *Conjectures*

that psychoanalysis is the paradigmatic pseudoscience of our epoch—one that deserves to be addressed not in the thrifty spirit of "What can we salvage from Freud?" but rather with principled attention to its faulty logic, its manufacturing of its own evidence, and its facile explanation of adult behavior by reference to unobservable and arbitrarily posited childhood fantasy. This belief on my part may be mistaken, but it was reached after much uncomfortable deliberation, and it is shared by others who cannot be accused of lurching compulsively from one extreme position to its opposite.

Indeed, there is nothing especially original in my apprehension of Freud and psychoanalysis. I have done little more than synopsize the work of herculean scholars like Henri Ellenberger, Frank Sulloway, and Malcolm Macmillan and of persistent philosophical inquirers like Adolf Grünbaum and Frank Cioffi.[3] To be sure, some of those authors—Ellenberger,

---

*and Refutations: The Growth of Scientific Knowledge* (Basic Books, 1962); *Psychoanalysis: Scientific Method and Philosophy; A Symposium,* edited by Sidney Hook (New York University Press, 1959); and Ernest Nagel, "Methodological Issues in Psychoanalytic Theory," in Hook, pp. 38–56.

3. See Henri F. Ellenberger, *The Discovery of the Unconscious: The History and Evolution of Dynamic Psychiatry* (Basic Books, 1970); Frank J. Sulloway, *Freud, Biologist of the Mind: Beyond the Psychoanalytic Legend* (1979; revised edition, Harvard University Press, 1992); Malcolm Macmillan, *Freud Evaluated: The Completed Arc* (North–Holland, 1991); Adolf Grünbaum, *The Foundations of Psychoanalysis: A Philosophical Critique* (University of California Press, 1984); and the following articles among others by Frank Cioffi: "Wittgenstein's Freud," in *Studies in the Philosophy of Wittgenstein,* edited by Peter Winch (Routledge and Kegan Paul, 1969), pp. 184–210; "Freud and the Idea of a Pseudo-Science," in *Explanation in the Behavioural Sciences,* edited by Robert Borger and Frank Cioffi (Cambridge University Press, 1970), pp. 471–499; and "Wollheim on Freud," *Inquiry,* Vol. 15 (1972), pp. 171–186.

Sulloway, and Grünbaum—initially couched their findings more tentatively and tactfully than I have done. It has gone largely unremarked, however, that their later development has been toward greater adamancy.[4] As for Cioffi and Macmillan, my judgment of Freud's work concurs with theirs in every detail.

Note, for example, the finale to Macmillan's exhaustive and learned *Freud Evaluated*, the most recently published of the major studies in the field:

> Should we therefore conclude that psycho-analysis is a science? My evaluation shows that at none of the different stages through which it evolved was Freud's theory one from which adequate explanations could be generated. From the very beginning, much of what passed as theory was found to be description, and poor description at that.... In every one of the later key developmental theses, Freud assumed what had to be explained.

---

4. Compare, for example, Ellenberger's chapter on Freud in *The Discovery of the Unconscious* with his subsequent article, "The Story of 'Anna O': A Critical Review with New Data," *Journal of the History of the Behavioral Sciences*, Vol. 8 (1972), pp. 267–279. Note, too, the preface to the 1992 edition of *Freud: Biologist of the Mind*, where Sulloway, citing his agreement with my own critique of his book, concludes that "the whole process" of Freudian interpretation "was essentially circular" (p. xiv) and that Freud's cliquish approach to knowledge has been "largely fatal" to the scientific standing of psychoanalysis (p. xv). Even Grünbaum, whose logical allowance for a "serendipitous" future confirmation of unspecified Freudian ideas is often held up as a rebuke to my own premature cynicism, now poses the key question and offers a somber prediction: "Does Psychoanalysis Have a Future? Doubtful," *Harvard Mental Health Letter*, Vol. 11, No. 4 (October 1994), pp. 3–6.

...None of his followers, including his revisionist critics who are themselves psycho-analysts, have probed any deeper than did Freud into the assumptions underlying their practise, particularly the assumptions underlying "the basic method"—free association. None question whether those assumptions hold in the therapeutic situation; none has attempted to break out of the circle.[5]

This is exactly my own position—but it is supported in Macmillan's case by the most meticulous scholarship ever bestowed on Freud's claims.

Again, readers who examine Frank Cioffi's trenchant papers dating back to 1969 will perceive that what critics have called my "absolutist" and "vindictive" brief against Freud is only a long footnote to his own conclusions. As a matter of fact, my assessment of Freud's perverse achievement could be regarded as a gloss on just two sentences of Cioffi's:

It seems that Freud stood to his patients' associations, dreams, symptoms, reminiscences and errors more as a painter to his pigments than as the sleuth to his traces of mud and cigar ash.

The implications of this are that instead of seeing in "condensation," "displacement," "representation by the opposite," etc., etc., laws governing unconscious processes,

5. Macmillan, *Freud Evaluated*, pp. 610–612.

we recognize them as recipes for the construction of associative chains to preselected termini; not mechanisms by whose operation the symptom, dream, etc., was constructed, but rules for "working a piece of fancy into it."[6]

In this view, entities like the psychic troika of id, ego, and superego deserve to be regarded not as discoveries like radium or DNA, nor even as mistakes like ether or animal magnetism, but as pure inventions like Esperanto, Dungeons & Dragons, or, closer yet, Rube Goldberg algorithms for making something happen with maximum complication. In short, Freudian theory is a display of ingenuity unencumbered by recalcitrant data. As Cioffi cryptically puts it, "What a psychoanalytic explanation tells us is itself."[7]

Cioffi's insight, once fully absorbed, alters the landscape of Freud studies beyond recognition, even mooting a good deal of negative commentary that grants Freud his pose as a sincere empirical psychologist. We begin to grasp that the deviser of psychoanalysis was at bottom a visionary but endlessly calculating artist, engaged in casting himself as the hero of a multivolume fictional opus that is part epic, part detective story, and part satire on human self-interestedness and animality. This scientifically deflating realization, not my personal

---

6. Cioffi, "Wittgenstein's Freud," p. 205.
7. "Wittgenstein's Freud," p. 194. See also, in this connection, Edward Erwin, *A Final Accounting: Philosophical and Empirical Issues in Freudian Psychology* (MIT Press, 1995, forthcoming) and the extraordinary debunking effort by Max Scharnberg, *The Non-Authentic Nature of Freud's Observations*, 2 volumes (Uppsala, 1993). Scharnberg promises further studies under the same title.

urge to broadcast it, is what the Freudian community needs to challenge if it can.[8]

Diverse though it is in authorship, subject matter, and perspective, *The Memory Wars* does amount to a coherent debate that makes certain issues stand out boldly. From my point of view, the hostile letters republished and summarized here are themselves an integral, if dialectical, element in a larger demonstration. Beyond their usefulness in pressing me to clarify my position and meet objections that will have occurred to other readers, the letters illustrate some of my contentions more vividly than I could have done myself. Thus the briefs for Freud show, by their marked inconsistency with one another, that contemporary psychoanalysis possesses neither a core of accepted doctrine, nor an agreement over Freud's hits and misses, nor a common goal of treatment, nor a cogent account of why the therapy sometimes "works" but sometimes doesn't. Such disarray points unmistakably toward my main contention about

---

8. The most recent and most promising development in Freud studies is the articulation of just this understanding of Freud as a self-dramatizing rhetorician. Not surprisingly, it is literary critics who are leading the way. See, e.g., Robert Wilcocks, *Maelzel's Chess Player: Sigmund Freud and the Rhetoric of Deceit* (Rowman and Littlefield, 1994); Alexander Welsh, *Freud's Wishful Dream Book* (Princeton University Press, 1994); and John Farrell, *Freud's Paranoid Quest: Psychoanalysis and Modern Suspicion* (New York University Press, 1996, forthcoming). One prototype for such efforts, and a cause for hope that professors of literature will finally develop qualms about swallowing Freudian theory as a laxative for the unobstructed flow of their discourse, can be found in Stanley Fish's *Times Literary Supplement* essay of August 29, 1986, "Withholding the Missing Portion: Power, Meaning, and Persuasion in Freud's 'The Wolf-Man,'" revised (to its detriment) in *Doing What Comes Naturally: Change, Rhetoric, and the Practice of Theory in Literary and Legal Studies* (Duke University Press, 1989), pp. 525–554.

psychoanalysis: that it lacks any semblance of a shared empirical basis for resolving differences of theory and interpretation, and thus that its pretensions to tested knowledge are hollow.

An even wider divergence of judgment characterizes the included and summarized letters about the recovered memory movement. Of course, this is hardly surprising, since some correspondents want to defend that movement while others merely claim that its defects owe nothing to Freudianism. Yet the letters are nevertheless of a piece in their failure to cope with the central liability of RMT: that the therapist's presupposition that childhood sexual abuse is the likeliest cause of adult misery may issue in specious "memories" on the suggestible patient's part. That error partakes of a much wider insensitivity to suggestion —a shortcoming whose roots can be found in Freud's stubborn faith, in defiance of explicit challenges on the point, that messages from the unconscious are by and large incorruptible. If my portion of a book as miscellaneous as *The Memory Wars* can be said to have a main focus, it is precisely the carry-over, from Freudianism to its stepchild RMT, of blindness to the role of therapy itself in producing behavior that gets mistaken for the residue of long-buried trauma from the patient's early years.[9]

The linkage between these two styles of psycho-therapy—point 4 in my list above—is what now demands a

---

9. Analysts do, of course, recognize that a patient's thoughts and feelings will be warped by "transference" toward the therapist. Yet that very name *transference* points to the problem: an unwarranted assumption that the patient's needs, demands, and "resistance" have been imported from a much earlier stage of life and that the therapist serves chiefly as a stand-in for more primordial objects of lust, love, and aggression. Thus the "analysis of the transference" tends to

revised accounting, for the essays and letters in *The Memory Wars* tell only part of an appalling story that continues to unfold. My own contributions below all rested on the assumption that psychoanalysis stands largely in a genealogical, not a participatory, relation to the hunt for missing scenes of sexual abuse. But one published letter (see the summary on pp. 233–235 below), signed by no fewer than twenty-nine "psychoanalytically trained clinicians who work with adults who were sexually molested and abused as children," opened up another vista that has subsequently proved to be all too enlightening.

Although those twenty-nine therapists deplored "the worst elements within the recovery movement," they also appeared broadly hospitable to the movement's ruling premises. One of those premises, which has rapidly come to the fore as "repressed memory" has been shown to be scientifically uncorroborated, is that early sexual trauma typically gets processed not through repression but through *dissociation*, or the withdrawal of the victim's sense of self from the very scene of a trauma. These days, reference to dissociated experiences of abuse tends to indicate a relatively canny but still zealous commitment to RMT. Yet dissociation was precisely the watchword of these otherwise Freudian correspondents.

It was especially suggestive that my critics were prepared to hint that dissociated trauma could eventuate in the formation of multiple personalities. "Multiple personality disorder," now officially renamed "dissociative identity disorder," is the

---

underrate the immediate source of the patient's irritability: the contemporary behavior of the therapist, an unequal partner in dialogue who deflects every legitimate complaint about his own needling manner onto the patient's enduring fixations. For further discussion, see pp. 119–121 below.

strangest fruit of the recovered memory movement—the most extreme outcome, depending on one's perspective, either of repeated and horrific childhood sexual abuse or of psychotherapeutic malpractice in the here and now.[10] To be told, then, as I was in their letter, that I had failed to appreciate the trauma victim's "multiple experiences of self and others" struck me as a deeply ominous sign. Moreover, I was directed to educate myself in what the authors called "a growing and rich psychoanalytic literature" about the distant aftereffects of forgotten molestation, including such works as Jody Messler Davies and Mary Gail Frawley's *Treating the Adult Survivor of Childhood Sexual Abuse: A Psychoanalytic Perspective* (Basic Books, 1994) and Howard B. Levine's anthology *Adult Analysis and Childhood Sexual Abuse* (Analytic Press, 1990).

Pressed for time, I had only begun to scan that body of texts when I replied in *The New York Review* to the abuse-oriented Freudians, suggesting to them that an entente with RMT would hardly serve to shore up the crumbling respectability of psychoanalysis. But the advice was belated: my twenty-nine adversaries, I am now left to conclude, simply *are* recovered memory practitioners who have convinced themselves that "psychoanalytic knowledge" somehow authorizes their reversion to Freud's pre-psychoanalytic "seduction theory" of 1896, whereby the muffled but unextinguished memory of having been sexually abused in childhood was deemed

---

10. A middle path, to be sure, is traced by the philosopher Ian Hacking in *Rewriting the Soul: Multiple Personality and the Sciences of Memory* (Princeton University Press, 1995). Unfortunately, Hacking's account is vitiated by insufficient vigilance against cases of fraud, malingering, and iatrogenesis, or therapist-induced symptomatology.

the source of every "hysteria." I soon learned that the home base of all but eight of the signers, the William Alanson White Institute, has transformed itself from a center of relatively pragmatic psychoanalysis to a magnet for RMT enthusiasts who, in fact, were shortly to hold a one-sided symposium validating "Memories of Sexual Betrayal."[11] Further, I myself was then magnanimously invited to comment in writing on two of the papers presented there; they would form the nucleus of a special issue of the journal *Psychoanalytic Dialogues* devoted precisely to the intended merger of psychoanalysis and RMT.[12]

In preparing that critique, I have by now acquainted myself with many writings that prove how vastly I had under-rated the ties between those two movements. There is no longer room for doubt that a considerable number, if still a minority, of nominal Freudians are ready to toss out infantile sexuality and the Oedipus complex in favor of the "survivor psychology" I had castigated in "The Revenge of the Repressed."[13] As it

---

11. The symposium was held at the New York Hilton on March 18, 1995.

12. This will be volume 6, number 2 (1996), of *Psychoanalytic Dialogues*.

13. See, e.g., Judith L. Alpert, "Analytic Reconstruction in the Treatment of an Incest Survivor," *Psychoanalytic Review*, Vol. 81 (1994), pp. 217–235; Philip M. Bromberg, "'Speak That I May See You': Some Reflections on Dissociation, Reality, and Psychoanalytic Listening," *Psychoanalytic Dialogues*, Vol. 4 (1994), pp. 517–547; C. Brooks Brenneis, "Belief and Suggestion in the Recovery of Memories of Childhood Sexual Abuse," *Journal of the American Psychoanalytic Association*, Vol. 42 (1994), pp. 1027–1053; Bertram J. Cohler, "Memory Recovery and the Use of the Past: A Commentary on Lindsay and Read from Psychoanalytic Perspectives," *Applied Cognitive Psychology*, Vol. 8 (1994), pp. 365–378; Jody Messler Davies and Mary Gail Frawley, "Dissociative Processes and Transference-Countertransference Paradigms in the Psychoanalytically Oriented Treatment of Adult Survivors of Childhood Sexual Abuse," *Psycho-analytic Dialogues*, Vol. 2 (1992), pp. 5–36; Paul A. Dewald, "Effects on an

happens, this development within psychoanalysis is occurring at a time when RMT itself, after a meteoric rise between 1988 and 1993, has been rapidly losing favor in the courts, the professional journals, and even the mass media of the United States and other infected countries.[14] Perhaps, then, most ana-

---

Adult of Incest in Childhood: A Case Report," *Journal of the American Psychoanalytic Association*, Vol. 37 (1989), pp. 997–1014; Judith L. Herman and Emily Schatzow, "Recovery and Verification of Memories of Childhood Sexual Trauma," *Psychoanalytic Psychology*, Vol. 4 (1987), pp. 1–14; Dori Laub and Nanette C. Auerhahn, "Knowing and Not Knowing Massive Psychic Trauma: Forms of Traumatic Memory," *International Journal of Psycho-Analysis*, Vol. 74 (1993), pp. 287–302; Ethel Spector Person and Howard Klar, "Establishing Trauma: The Difficulty Distinguishing between Memories and Fantasies," *Journal of the American Psychoanalytic Association*, Vol. 42 (1994), pp. 1055–1081; Mark Trewartha, "On Post-analytic Amnesia," *Annual of Psychoanalysis*, Vol. 18 (1990), pp. 153–174; Scott E. Wetzler and John A. Sweeney, "Childhood Amnesia: A Conceptualization in Cognitive-Psychological Terms," *Journal of the American Psychoanalytic Association*, Vol. 34 (1986), pp. 663–685; Miriam Williams, "Reconstruction of an Early Seduction and Its Aftereffects," *Journal of the American Psychoanalytic Association*, Vol. 35 (1987), pp. 145–163; and Elizabeth K. Wolf and Judith L. Alpert, "Psychoanalysis and Sexual Abuse: A Review of the Post-Freudian Literature," *Psychoanalytic Psychology*, Vol. 8 (1991), pp. 305–327. Some of these writers express a degree of caution about RMT, but all attest to the turn toward it within American psychoanalysis. Note that such a trend is different from—indeed, fundamentally antithetical to—attention to the here-and-now mistreatment of children.

14. The changing American legal climate is reflected in the Supreme Court's crucial ruling in *Daubert* v. *Merrell Dow Pharmaceuticals, Inc.*, 113 S. Ct. 2786 (1993). Although not without its ambiguities, the Daubert precedent has already tightened standards for the admissibility of expert testimony. Under the previous "Frye rule," the "general acceptance" of an idea within the relevant informed community was deemed adequate for admissibility. Now, however, the idea must have been "derived by the scientific method" and "supported by appropriate validation." Scrupulously applied, *Daubert* will exclude from federal court trials an expert witness's testimony about the alleged retrieval of repressed or dissociated memories. In this connection, see note 6 on page 244.

18

lysts will prove reluctant to book passage on a vessel whose deck is already discernibly listing toward the waterline. But meanwhile, the fact that some Freudians can so readily accommodate themselves to a diagnostic outlook that Freud himself came to consider an absurdity is pregnant with implication for the issues debated in this book.

One such issue is that of alleged progress in the evolution of psychoanalytic theory. Freudians often scold me and other critics for failing to note that "[p]sychoanalysis as a field has moved far beyond Freud. We have learned much in the past 80 years."[15] Such a boast imputes to psychoanalysts a collective rationality that can reliably discriminate between nonsense and actual knowledge. As I have already noted, however, the existence of assorted orthodox, deviant, neo-, and post-Freudian schools that all regard themselves as psychoanalytic points unmistakably to an absence, within the movement at large, of any clear path connecting facts to suppositions. Now we have been offered the most scandalous and sobering instance of that condition.

Again, anyone who believes that mutations of psychoanalysis typically thrive because of their scientific cogency will be discomfited by the new clinical literature that grafts *The Courage to Heal* onto *The Interpretation of Dreams*. To be sure, that literature does marshal research to support its claims. It does so, however, in a self-interested spirit, drawing largely on the tendentious work of fellow RMT partisans, ignoring

---

15. Glen O. Gabbard, Sheldon M. Goodman, and Arnold D. Richards, "Psychoanalysis after Freud: A Response to Frederick Crews and Other Critics," *Psychoanalytic Books*, Vol. 6 (1995), pp. 155–173; the quotation is from p. 156.

contrary reports, and deriving dubious conclusions from cognitive and neurophysiological studies that were never intended to provide justification for RMT.[16] This last stratagem fits all too neatly within the tradition—illustrated by more than one of the letters republished in this book—of attempts to make hand-me-down articles of Freudian faith look like inferences from replicated research. The dogmas change according to cultural whim, but the work of packaging them as "findings" marches on.

In some respects, however, I myself need to alter my position in view of the surprising rapprochement between RMT and psychoanalysis. I have maintained until now, for example, that Freudianism has been losing its capacity to wreak social harm as it has gradually forsaken its most ambitious pretensions and retreated toward hermeneutic perspectivism—that is, toward abandoning truth claims and recasting the therapeutic goal as mere reconciliation of the client to a less self-punitive myth about his or her identity. But I should have realized that there is nothing binding about this anemic reduction of the Freudian program. Insofar as psychoanalysis succumbs to the temptation of rejuvenating itself through RMT, all bets are off about social harm.

Thus, too, I now feel less inclined to credit commonly reported research indicating that nearly all extant psychotherapies yield approximately the same modest degree of benefit. Such a state of affairs points to the relatively uniform operation of placebo factors—benefits conferred by the sheer

---

16. See Crews, "Forward to 1896? Commentary on Harris and Davies," forthcoming in *Psychoanalytic Dialogues*, Vol. 6, No. 2 (1996), pp. 231–250.

receiving of professional attention—from one style of therapy to another. But the attention of someone who convinces you that you were sexually brutalized by your father, now reconceived as a monster who has escaped justice all these years, is a different story altogether. To judge from the ravages already caused by the recovered memory movement, Freudians who join that movement may bring about not just the "survivor paranoia" of disoriented patients but also, in some instances, the bankruptcy and even imprisonment of their accused family members.

Whatever its social effects may prove to be, the RMT initiative within American psychoanalysis constitutes a significant-looking challenge to the Freudian old guard. In two related senses, that initiative is transparently ideological in character. First, a marked "feminization" of psychodynamic theory and therapy is under way. Analysts like Adrienne Harris, Mary Gail Frawley, and Jody Messler Davies alter the Freudian model of the mind to enshrine at its core the "introject" of an abused little girl—the child-self that was allegedly split off from the ego when the sexual abuse began, and that must now be reunited with the conscious adult self.[17] Accordingly, the analysts reconceptualize treatment as an exercise of womanly empathy with that furtive and dissociated inner child. The resulting vision may be no more gender biased than Freud's, but it is more unguardedly and militantly so.

---

17. These writers do not claim, of course, that everyone is female or has been molested. They simply invest all of their interest in the "abuse model" of mental development, putting the rest of Freudian theory into limbo.

And second, the feminist commitment to locating and emotionally bonding with women survivors inevitably spills over into hostility toward a largely male Freudian establishment that is still inclined to honor such patriarchal dogmas as "analytic neutrality," penis envy, the Oedipus complex, and its practical corollary, an automatic distrust of any patient's conscious "screen memory" of molestation. Whether or not old-line Freudians realize the fact, a war of psychoanalytic succession is under way, with the issue of forgotten child abuse as its casus belli. At this point it would be premature to venture a guess as to the outcome.

The potentiality for reversion to a theory centered on claims of real-life childhood victimization, we can now make out, has always lain just beneath the surface of mainstream psychoanalysis. When, in 1897, Freud launched his movement as we now recognize it, he abandoned one unviable theory about the causation of hysteria (the experience of "seduction" by an elder) for a less intuitively plausible one (repression of forbidden sexual wishes). If early events are to be regarded as causes of later neurosis, it is easier to picture them as physical assaults on the child than as mere imaginings about penisectomy at the hand of a father who, the toddler supposedly reasons, must adopt that means of keeping him from realizing his goal of fornicating with his mother.

It is little wonder, then, that Sándor Ferenczi in 1932, breaking loose at last from Freud's suffocating control, founded a one-man recovered memory movement, reinstating the seduction theory in all its fanatical narrowness. The psychoanalytic RMT of our own era was very largely anticipated in Ferenczi's practice, including his boldest heresy, scrapping analytic coldness in favor of hands-on supportiveness toward patient-survivors. Ferenczi's rebellion was doomed by Freud's implacable opposition and by the absence of a facilitating feminist ambiance. But in the mid-1980s, with women's causes on the march and with nothing to fear from Freud's ghost, the same undertaking encountered no obstacles. Significantly, one contribution to the launching of RMT as we know it was Jeffrey Masson's emotionally charged rehabilitation of the late Ferenczi in his best seller of 1984, *The Assault on Truth*.[18]

The interesting question, then, is not whether psychoanalysis helped to bring on the recovered memory movement —of course it did, both directly and dialectically—but whether we are now witnessing a hostile takeover of the older therapeutic business by the younger. The mere specter of such a result is already causing adjustments of a predictable kind. When challenged by earlier countertrends, the conservative guardians of Freud's legacy have usually muddled through by recourse to a halfway measure: adding new and sometimes opposite concepts and explanations to the old ones, thus rendering the theory a bewildering but handsomely ecumenical palimpsest of accommodative gestures. The same process remains at work today.

Listen, for example, to three non-RMT analysts recently disparaging "The Unknown Freud":

---

18. Jeffrey Moussaieff Masson, *The Assault on Truth: Freud's Suppression of the Seduction Theory* (Farrar, Straus and Giroux, 1984), pp. 145–187. See also Lewis Aron and Adrienne Harris, editors, *The Legacy of Sándor Ferenczi* (Analytic Press, 1993).

Crews has thoroughly misunderstood the modern usage
of repression in psychoanalytic discourse. Ever since
Freud departed from his view that all neuroses were
caused by actual seduction of children, repression
evolved in a different direction. Today it is used to refer
to the banishment from consciousness of unacceptable
wishes arising from *within*. Severe childhood trauma,
such as sexual abuse, overwhelms the ego's capacity for
repression and more commonly produces a different set
of defensive operations involving denial, disavowal, and
disassociation [sic].[19]

This passage certainly does bring us up to date with
"today's" amending of traditional Freudian theory. What are we
witnessing here, if not a smoking of the peace pipe with the
RMT faction among fellow analysts? Repression, the very heart
of psychoanalysis as Freud conceived it, is being asked to cede
half its realm to the current watchword of the recovered memory movement, dissociation. ("Disassociation" is archaic in this
sense.) The authors do not even bother to pretend that dissociation has come into prominence by virtue of objective discoveries about authenticated cases of sexual abuse. Repression
and dissociation are here being assigned different terrain for the
same reason (and perhaps with the same success) that Goneril
and Regan were, to forestall civil war and the total loss of an
already tottering authority.

---

19. Gabbard et al., "Psychoanalysis after Freud," p. 169. Incidentally, Freud
*never* maintained that "all neuroses were caused by actual seduction of children."

These writers are at least correct, however, in implying that I myself have hitherto paid little regard to dissociation. It is not easy to keep pace with the shell game whereby critics of Freudianism are always told that new breakthroughs render their strictures obsolete. What matters, however, is that the innovations prove no better grounded than the ideas they have displaced. In this case the novelty is not, of course, the mere descriptive concept of dissociation; indeed, its nineteenth-century originator, Pierre Janet, believed that Freud's repression was plagiarized from it. The contemporary wrinkle is that dissociation is now assigned a powerful *causal* role in the newly elaborated operation of recovered memory. In that capacity it emits, if anything, an even more insubstantial aura than repression does.

In the words of one psychoanalyst who has become a wholehearted convert to RMT, dissociation is the mind's way of processing "memories of traumatic childhood abuse which cannot be forgotten in the usual way, because they never succeeded in being fully known in the first place."[20] It is hard not to admire the fittingness of such a notion to the legerdemain of the recovered memory movement. By its very ineffability, dissociation is ideally adapted to dignifying the "memory" of illusory events that the therapist nevertheless feels duty bound to credit.[21] If no awareness of the alleged trauma was originally registered, then its

20. Jody Messler Davies, "Dissociation, Repression, and Reality Testing in the Countertransference: The Controversy over Memory and False Memory in the Psychoanalytic Treatment of Adult Survivors of Childhood Sexual Abuse," forthcoming in *Psychoanalytic Dialogues*, Vol. 6, No. 2 (1996).

21. As Davies puts it, the therapist must "validate the patient's belief that abuse occurred, or risk reenacting the role of denying parent, which may have enabled the abuse in the first place." It is important to grasp that Davies's point, which

"reconstruction" in therapy needn't be tested against any conscious recollections. The therapist's and the patient's joint biographical artifact becomes, as it were, the perfect crime—but with the patient also serving as victim of her own concoction.

It would appear, then, that by popular internal demand, a bustling dissociation wing is being added to the conceptual mystery house of psychoanalysis. Let us take careful note of what this means for the already minuscule believability of Freudian theory. Since molestation-minded analysts typically strive for, and achieve, "the recovery and disclosure of as many memories of early sexual abuse as possible"[22]—dozens of rapes, for example, from which the child was instantaneously and serially able to detach her conscious mind—the newly favored concept is, de facto, not mere dissociation but a virulent strain of it that operates habitually, even routinely, whenever trauma is encountered. This is an exact counterpart of the "robust repression" whose implausibility I do discuss in this book.[23] Both phenomena went unremarked in the entire human record before the 1980s, but one or both are now needed to lend respectability to the staggering claims of recov-

---

faithfully echoes *The Courage to Heal*, covers "beliefs" that the RMT specialist herself has coaxed into being. Compare this complete abdication of judgment by a psychoanalyst with the claim of Gabbard, Goodman, and Richards that "[p]sychoanalysts scrupulously avoid persuading the patient to remember things that did not happen. . . . Analysts are trained to be skeptical about the veridicality of memories" ("Psychoanalysis after Freud," p. 169).
22. Davies and Frawley, "Dissociative Processes . . . ," p. 23.
23. The name "robust repression" was coined by Richard Ofshe, who found the concept implicit in the teachings of RMT practitioners. It is explained and exposed to withering criticism in Richard Ofshe and Ethan Watters's *Making Monsters*, discussed on pages 200–203 below.

ered memory practitioners. Such is the psychoanalytic progress since Freud that I have been chided for leaving out of account.

Amid the befogging of evidential common sense, one point that seems all too clear is the futility of waiting for psychoanalytic professional associations to acknowledge the folly of RMT and to expunge it from current practice. Given the politics of Freudian territorialism, such a reform can probably occur only after the now ascendant purveyors of memory retrieval have become objects of general public disgrace. Other psychological and medical guilds, at least formally committed to disgorging fraud, have recently been crafting pronouncements that, though diplomatic to a fault, make manifest their discomfort with RMT.[24] But with honorable individual exceptions, Freudians appear more outraged by cost-efficient "brief therapy" than by recourse among some of their colleagues to reckless tampering with their patients' psychic equilibrium.

If Freudian reformers were to condemn RMT, moreover, on what principled basis could they do so? A checklist for quackery would have to ask the therapist such questions as these: How do you know that a particular class of early ordeals is always lastingly traumatic? Can you locate, and validate the traumaticity of, a particular unrecalled event by means that an independent investigator would find believable? By what means can you reliably tell the difference between delayed effects of early trauma and immediate effects of your own

---

24. Such statements have been issued by, among others, the American Psychiatric Association, the Council on Scientific Affairs of the American Medical Association, the American Psychological Association's Working Group on the Investigation of Memories of Childhood Abuse, and a working party of the British Psychological Association.

interference? Do your ministrations typically leave your patients emotionally dependent on you? Do many of those patients deteriorate even further during treatment, contracting a despair that leads to "abrupt terminations, escalating self-abuse, or suicidal behaviors"?[25] And has your therapy passed independent tests of relative effectiveness and relative freedom from the risk of disaster to your clients and other affected parties? Such a questionnaire would embarrass every "archaeological" and "transference-based" regimen—every one, in other words, that "provisionally" infantilizes its clients in the interest of recovering early material whose repression or dissociation allegedly made them ill. But this is simply a characterization of the classical Freudian program, which cannot offer reassurance on a single one of the named criteria.

Let us suppose, finally, that the "retraumatizing" of psychoanalysis by means of a revived seduction theory is only an ephemeral threat after all. The fact remains that psychoanalysis and RMT are profoundly alike and that their resemblance is anything but fortuitous. It was Freudianism that taught the recovered memory movement to regard not just the dream but also the human body itself as a readable note pad of the unconscious—a tablet whose symptom-hieroglyphics (tics, sores, rashes, lameness, stammering, etc.) could be faithfully retranslated into the otherwise unutterable thoughts that etched them. In their shared predilection for fixed symbolic meanings, dogmatic explanations, split selves, and quasi-demonic "introjects," and in their common affinity for what Freud once praised as "the obscure but indestructible surmises

---

25. Davies and Frawley, *Treating the Adult Survivor* . . . , p. 138.

of the common people against the obscurantism of educated opinion" (SE, 18:178), both systems stand closer to animistic shamanism than to science.[26] Both must be discarded if, once and for all, we are to bring psychotherapy into safe alignment with what is actually known about the mind.

---

26. Indeed, for sheer gnostic zaniness there is nothing in the recovered memory literature that quite approaches Freud's belief, which he and Ferenczi considered expounding in a book, that "[Lamarck's] concept of 'need,' which creates and modifies organs, is nothing else than the power unconscious ideas have over the body of which we see the remains in hysteria—in short, the 'omnipotence of thoughts.'" See Ernest Jones, *The Life and Work of Sigmund Freud*, 3 volumes (Basic Books, 1953–1957), Vol. 3, p. 312.

# THE UNKNOWN FREUD

# I.

That psychoanalysis, as a mode of treatment, has been experiencing a long institutional decline is no longer in serious dispute. Nor is the reason: though some patients claim to have acquired profound self-insight and even alterations of personality, in the aggregate psychoanalysis has proved to be an indifferently successful and vastly inefficient method of removing neurotic symptoms. It is also the method that is least likely to be "over when it's over." The experience of undergoing an intensive analysis may have genuine value as a form of extended meditation, but it seems to produce a good many more converts than cures. Indeed, among the dwindling number of practicing analysts, many have now backed away from any medical claims for a treatment that was once touted as the only lasting remedy for the entire spectrum of disorders this side of psychosis.

Freud's doctrine has been faring no better, in scientifically serious quarters, as a cluster of propositions about the mind. Without significant experimental or epidemiological support for any of its notions, psychoanalysis has simply been left behind by mainstream psychological research. No one has been able to mount a successful defense against the charge, most fully developed in Adolf Grünbaum's meticulous *Foundations of Psychoanalysis*, that "clinical validation" of Freudian hypotheses is an epistemic sieve; as a means of gaining knowledge, psychoanalysis is fatally contaminated by the inclusion, among its working assumptions and in its dialogue with patients, of the very ideas that supposedly get corroborated by clinical experience. And Grünbaum further showed that even if Freud's means of gathering evidence had been sound, that evidence couldn't have reliably yielded the causal constructions that he placed on it. We cannot be surprised, then, by Malcolm Macmillan's recent exhaustive demonstration that Freud's theories of personality and neurosis—derived as they were from misleading precedents, vacuous pseudo-physical metaphors, and a long concatenation of mistaken inferences that couldn't be subjected to empirical review— amount to castles in the air.[1]

Nevertheless, Freudian concepts retain some currency in popular lore, the arts, and the academic humanities, three arenas in which flawed but once modish ideas, secure from the menace of rigorous testing, can be kept indefinitely in play. There psychoanalysis continues to be accepted largely on faith—namely, a faith in Freud's self-description as a fearless

---

1. See Adolf Grünbaum, *The Foundations of Psychoanalysis: A Philosophical Critique* (University of California Press, 1984), and Malcolm Macmillan, *Freud Evaluated: The Completed Arc* (North–Holland, 1991).

explorer, a solver of deep mysteries, a rigorously objective thinker, and an ethically scrupulous reporter of both clinical data and therapeutic outcomes. That is the image that his own suave texts, aided by the work of loyalist biographers from Ernest Jones through Peter Gay, have managed to keep before our eyes for many decades now. Surely, the average reader of such works infers, a man who has widened our horizons so decisively must have bequeathed us some irreversible gains in our understanding of the mind.

Not surprisingly, however, the tradition of hero worship is now being challenged as vigorously as are the claims of Freudian therapy and theory. Since the 1970s, a rapidly growing number of independent scholars—including among others Henri Ellenberger, Paul Roazen, Frank Cioffi, Frank J. Sulloway, Peter J. Swales, E. M. Thornton, Morton Schatzman, Han Israëls, and Phyllis Grosskurth—have been showing us a different Freud, darker but far more interesting than the canonical one. According to their revisionist view, our would-be Prometheus was highly cultivated, sophisticated, and endowed with extraordinary literary power, sardonic wit, and charm, but he was also quite lacking in the empirical and ethical scruples that we would hope to find in any responsible scientist, to say nothing of a major one.

Now we are beginning to discern a notably willful and opportunistic Freud who appears to have thrown together his magisterial-looking claims from various unacknowledged sources—some of them more folkloric than scientific—while passing them off as sober inferences from the data of his clinical practice. Once having arrived at those claims, we see, he adhered to them with a blind, combative stubbornness—

though not without willingness to expand the system on an ad hoc basis to encompass newly perceived difficulties. And he promoted that conceptually overstuffed system by means of devious rhetorical maneuvers that disarmed criticism without obliging Freud himself to take the criticism into material account. Through all his conduct, at least from the 1890s onward, runs a note of existential daring and high disdain that could hardly be more remote from ordinary scientific prudence. Fiercely believing in his general vision yet stooping to low tricks in defense of it, this Freud is a saturnine self-dramatizer who defies us to see through his bravado and provides us with tantalizing autobiographical clues for doing so.

Such a figure differs so radically from the Freud we thought we knew that readers may understandably wonder which version comes closer to the truth. But it is really no contest. Until recently, most people who wrote about Freud in any detail were open partisans of psychoanalysis who needed to safeguard the legend of the scientist-genius-humanitarian, and many of the sources they used had already passed through the censorship of a jealously secretive psychoanalytic establishment, whose leaders have been so fearful of open historical judgment that they have locked away large numbers of Freud's papers and letters in the Library of Congress for periods extending as far ahead as the twenty-second century. But as some sensitive documents, having already served their Sleeping Beauty sentences, make their way into the light, and as serendipity turns up others from outside sources, the more improvisational and fallible Freud will necessarily come into ever sharper focus.

Two examples may help to show this link between emergent primary materials and the revisionist portrait of Freud.

When the orthodox analysts Marie Bonaparte, Anna Freud, and Ernst Kris first edited Freud's correspondence with his one-time friend Wilhelm Fliess in 1950, they omitted everything that, in their announced judgment, lacked "scientific" interest. Republication, under different editorship, of the unbowdlerized letters in 1985 showed that the dismissible "unscientific" category had included everything from Freud's cavalier approach to clinical sessions—his writing to Fliess while an early patient was under hypnosis, for example, and his habit of napping while his later psychoanalytic ones were free-associating on the couch—to his naive acceptance of Fliess's dubious theories of periodicity and nasal-genital correspondence.[2] The full letters also put on view the now notorious case of Emma Eckstein, whom Freud had grotesquely diagnosed as "bleeding for love" of himself, whereas she was actually suffering from a half-meter of gauze that Fliess had accidentally left within the remains of her nose after a mad-scientist operation to thwart a supposed "nasal reflex neurosis." We will see that the Eckstein story, which Freud's heirs were so anxious to hide from posterity, is no aberration in the wider record; it constitutes an entirely typical instance of Freud's rashness in always preferring the arcane explanation to the obvious one.

As for the second example, the following scarcely believable events may illustrate how previously unexamined (not

2. The 1950 German edition of the Freud–Fliess letters became *The Origin of Psycho-Analysis, Letters to Wilhelm Fliess, Drafts and Notes: 1887–1902*, edited by Marie Bonaparte, Anna Freud, and Ernst Kris, translated by Eric Mosbacher and James Strachey (Basic Books, 1954). The revelations about letter writing and napping appear on pp. 21 and 303 of the 1985 Freud–Fliess Letters.

suppressed) documents can transform our image of Freud. Thanks to a long-neglected and rediscovered cache of letters that avoided becoming time capsules in the Library of Congress, we can now reconstruct the history of Freud's relations with one Horace Frink, a married American patient and protégé who, like many another psychoanalyst of the 1920s, was having an affair with a patient of his own, the bank heiress Angelika Bijur.[3] Despite this redundant testimony to his sexual orientation, Frink was told by Freud that he was a latent homosexual who stood in great peril of becoming an overt one. To avoid that fate, Freud prescribed, Frink would have to divorce his wife and marry Bijur, whom he also urged to divorce her husband, even though Freud had never met either of the allegedly unsuitable spouses.

Freud's transparent aim was to get his own hands on some of the heiress Bijur's money. As he brazenly if perhaps semifacetiously wrote to Frink in steering him toward divorce and remarriage to Bijur, "Your complaint that you cannot grasp your homosexuality implies that you are not yet aware of your phantasy of making me a rich man. If matters turn out all right let us change this imaginary gift into a real contribution to the Psychoanalytic Funds."[4] The divorce and remarriage did occur—soon followed by the deaths of both of the abandoned, devastated spouses, an early suit for divorce by Frink's new wife, and the decline of the guilt-ridden Frink himself into a psychotic depression and repeated attempts at suicide.

---

3. See Lavinia Edmunds, "His Master's Choice," *Johns Hopkins Magazine*, Vol. 40 (April 1988), pp. 40–49.
4. Edmunds, "His Master's Choice," p. 45.

It is not recorded whether Freud ever expressed regret for having destroyed these four lives, but we know that it would have been out of character for him to do so. Advancing the fortunes of his movement was for him an imperative that overrode all others. As many casual remarks in his correspondence reveal, he was indifferent to his patients' suffering and quite dismissive of their real-world dilemmas, which struck him as a set of pretexts for not getting down to the repressed fantasies that really mattered. Nor did he care very much, except from a public relations angle, whether those patients improved as a result of his treatment. As he sarcastically wrote to Carl Jung in 1912 about a woman who had been in and out of his care since 1908, "she is beyond any possibility of therapy, but it is still her duty to sacrifice herself to science."[5] Frink, it seems, also had to be sacrificed—in this instance to Freud's working capital rather than to his intellectual passions.

What the Eckstein and Frink episodes have most in common is a perfect match between Freud's diagnoses and his immediate self-interest. That fit is obvious in Frink's case. As for Eckstein, by designating her bleeding as psychosomatic Freud was exculpating both his surgeon friend Fliess and himself for having recommended the gruesome and pointless operation. Such stories can only lead us to wonder whether Freud's powers of observation and analysis ever functioned with sufficient independence from his wishes. That, in brief, is the paramount issue confronting Freud studies today.

---

5. William McGuire, editor, *The Freud–Jung Letters: The Correspondence between Sigmund Freud and C. G. Jung*, translated by Ralph Manheim and R. F. C. Hull (Princeton University Press, 1974), pp. 473–474.

This is not to say that every Freud scholar is obliged to tackle that issue head on. Among the recent round of revisionist books I will discuss here, only one (Allen Esterson's) takes Freud's scientific incompetence as its central theme. In varying degrees, the others all convey mixed feelings about Freud's stature and the legitimacy of psychoanalytic claims. But for that very reason, it is instructive to see how convergent their accounts of Freud's imperious style of reasoning prove to be.

Take, to begin with, James L. Rice's informative and subtle study, *Freud's Russia: National Identity in the Evolution of Psychoanalysis*.[6] For Rice, Freud is anything but the objective scientific investigator who insulates himself from cultural impulses and discovers only later, as he maintained, that imaginative writers had anticipated his findings. Instead, he is fully a man of his own time, one whose sensibility, intellect, and specific ideas about the mind were crucially shaped by his reading. And he is also, as Rice puts it, "one of the great egos of our age" (p. 26).

Behind Freud's physicianly manner and his solemnity about the libidinal sacrifices exacted by civilized mores, Rice discerns, lay the nihilism of a disillusioned revolutionary who had deemed the species not worth saving after all. Insofar as it has been noticed, this quality has understandably called to mind the figure of Nietzsche, whose writings Freud disingenuously claimed to have encountered after the psychoanalytic system had been fully shaped.[7] Rice understands, however,

6. Transaction Publishers, 1993.
7. *Later:* The Nietzsche connection has now been thoroughly explored by Ronald Lehrer, *Nietzsche's Presence in Freud's Life and Thought* (State University of New York Press, 1995).

that nihilism and spiritual extremism in general had another strong correlate in Freud's imagination: Russia. Freud's family roots lay in Lithuania, where he retained many kin, and where his imagination turned when he thought, as he continually did, about the persecution of Jews and about their efforts to strike back. Up to the early years of Stalin's rule, Rice shows, Freud thrilled to revolutionism and looked to Russia for a political equivalent to his own assault on the tyranny of the despotic superego. Indeed, the Stalinist debacle had much to do with bringing on the futilitarian mood that dominates that most bathetic of "classics," *Civilization and Its Discontents* (1930).

Long before the accession of Stalin, however, Freud feared Russian extremism as strongly as he was drawn to it. As Rice convincingly argues, Freud's notion of ambivalence owed much to his idea of the Russian national character, featuring a supposed savage repressiveness which always gets reimposed after sadistic and erotic uprisings. This creaky formula became his master key to understanding Dostoevsky, about whom he published a celebrated monograph in 1928, "Dostoevsky and Parricide." That essay in turn, as Rice coolly anatomizes it, deserves our attention here as an especially clear instance of the apriorism that vitiates all of Freud's psychoanalytic work, both clinical and belletristic. The fact that we know so much about Dostoevsky from other sources affords us a rare opportunity to compare the record to what Freud self-indulgently made of it.

As Rice explains, in most respects "Dostoevsky and Parricide" is a derivative effort, indebted to views of the novelist that had been popular ever since his enormous Germanic vogue began in 1906. In one key respect, however, Freud's essay was original: its rejection of the idea that Dostoevsky suffered from epilepsy and its substitution of hysteria originating from a primal scene, or a child's discovery of "female castration" through witnessing an act of parental intercourse. Although other analysts within Freud's circle had already made the diagnosis of hysteria on Dostoevsky's part, it is obvious that they were doing so with the blessing of Freud, who had decreed in 1908 that "all those illnesses called hystero-epilepsies are simply hysterias" (Rice, p. 186).

Today, thanks to Rice's own work in *Dostoevsky and the Healing Art* (1985), there is no room for doubt that Dostoevsky, who endured seizures approximately once a month, waking and sleeping, for the last thirty-four years of his life, was a genuine epileptic. As Rice concedes, however, the state of medical knowledge in the 1920s allowed for some uncertainty on that point. In "Dostoevsky and Parricide" Freud advances his erroneous view with a typically guileful show of tentativeness; but then, just as typically, he goes on to treat it as firmly settled. Only with the hindsight granted by the general decline of psychoanalytic authority can we perceive, as Rice does, the perfect circularity of Freud's argumentative procedure. Dostoevsky's epilepsy is brushed aside in order to leave an opening for acts of non-neurological oedipal decoding, acts whose consilience with one another then "proves" that Dostoevsky was never epileptic.

This was by no means the only point of obtuseness in Freud's assessment of Dostoevsky, against whom he bore a gratuitous ill-will. As he wrote to Theodor Reik in 1929, he disliked Dostoevsky because he had already seen too many "pathological natures" in his clinical practice. "In art and life," he reported, "I am intolerant of them" (Rice, p. 159). In "Dostoevsky and Parricide" this intolerance takes the form of saddling the novelist with the political cynicism of the Grand Inquisitor and, more remarkably still, with the criminal temperament of Stavrogin. As Rice makes clear, Freud's whole indictment of Dostoevsky as humanity's jailer is built on prosecutorial animus and is buttressed by elementary misunderstanding of the difference between an author and his created characters. We need only add that such misunderstanding is facilitated by psychoanalytic theory, which teaches us to peel away defensive sublimations and to regard as primary whatever psychic materials appear most base.

Dostoevsky was an unlucky man in several ways, but he did have the good fortune to have died without presenting his troubles in person to Sigmund Freud and his epigones. Not so the other notable Russian featured in Rice's study, Sergei Pankeev, or the "Wolf Man," who, beginning in 1910, received some five years' worth of Freud's professional attention. Thanks to the suspenseful case history of 1918 in which Freud claimed to have removed all of his symptoms and inhibitions, the Wolf Man became the most celebrated of all Freud's alleged cures.[8] Freud knew perfectly well, however, that psychoanalysis had not helped the depressed and obsessive Pankeev at all. By reminding us of this discrepancy and by going into the specifics of Freud's bungling of the case, Rice brings us to the verge of a more general critique of Freudian logic.

---

8. See "From the History of an Infantile Neurosis" (SE, 17:3–122; the claim of cure is made on p. 11).

Just as he was later to do for Dostoevsky, Freud perceived Pankeev through the distorting lens of "Russian national character." The concept of *Russische Innerlichkeit*, or Russian spiritual inwardness, was especially comforting in Pankeev's case because it served Freud as a private excuse for the Wolf Man's recalcitrance to treatment. But Dostoevsky was already very much on Freud's mind when he first began treating Pankeev in 1910. Indeed, one of the main contributions of *Freud's Russia* is its demonstration that Pankeev and Dostoevsky were curiously interchangeable in Freud's mind. If, for example, a reader of "Dostoevsky and Parricide" wonders why Freud perversely insists on the murderousness of the haunted and harmless novelist, who had been permanently traumatized by a czarist firing squad, Rice suggests that the answer can probably be found in the severely relapsed Pankeev's announced intention of shooting Freud at the time when the Dostoevsky paper was being composed (p. 191). For the phylogenetically minded Freud, what one Russian was acting out in 1926–1927 must be what another Russian had secretly harbored in his unconscious fifty years earlier.

The full career of Sergei Pankeev, who was in and out of psychoanalytic treatment for almost seventy years, makes up one of the strangest chapters in the history of Freud's movement. Having lost a millionaire's fortune when (on Freud's advice) he neglected to return to Russia and rescue his estate from the ascendant Bolsheviks, Pankeev adopted the vocation of celebrity charity patient. As the protagonist of Freud's triumphant case history, he allowed himself to be passed from one awestruck analyst to another and even took to signing his letters "*Wolfsmann*." Later, however, his conspicuous debilitation caused him to be regarded as a bomb that could blow up in the face of psychoanalysis, and he was strongly encouraged, by "pension" payments as well as exhortations, not to tell his story to outsiders.[9] But he eventually did so anyway, spilling his grievances to the Austrian journalist Karin Obholzer in the 1970s and lamenting that, in the final stage of his long Freudian odyssey, "the whole thing looks like a catastrophe. I am in the same state as when I first came to Freud, and Freud is no more."[10]

Yet Pankeev's thralldom to Freud was no greater than that of the analytic community at large, which left the contradictions and implausibilities in Freud's published account of the Wolf Man case entirely unchallenged from 1918 until the 1970s. Even with the aging Pankeev on hand as living evidence that his announced cure was bogus, no Freudian dared to ask whether Freud had tampered with the record to make himself appear a master detective and healer. Rice understands, however, that that is exactly what Freud did.

Involved as he was in a fierce battle against the schismatics Carl Jung and Alfred Adler, each of whom had denied the importance of infantile sexuality in the etiology

9. See Frank J. Sulloway, "Reassessing Freud's Case Histories: The Social Construction of Psychoanalysis," *Isis*, Vol. 82 (June 1991), pp. 245–275; the quotation is from p. 260. The article has been reprinted in *Freud and the History of Psychoanalysis*, edited by Toby Gelfand and John Kerr (Analytic Press, 1992).
10. Karin Obholzer, *The Wolf-Man Sixty Years Later: Conversations with Freud's Controversial Patient*, translated by Michael Shaw (Routledge and Kegan Paul, 1982), p. 172.

of neurosis, Freud was determined to find a primal scene to serve as the fountainhead of Pankeev's symptoms. He made it materialize through a transparently arbitrary interpretation of a remembered dream of Pankeev's, from the suspiciously early age of four, about six or seven white wolves (actually dogs, as Freud was later compelled to admit) sitting in a tree outside his window. The wolves, Freud explained, were the parents; their whiteness meant bedclothes; their stillness meant the opposite, coital motion; their big tails signified, by the same indulgent logic, castration; daylight meant night; and all this could be traced most assuredly to a memory *from age one* of Pankeev's mother and father copulating, doggy style, no fewer than three times in succession while he watched from the crib and soiled himself in horrified protest.

Because he has absorbed the revisionist spirit in Freud scholarship, Rice stands in no danger of being taken in by Freud's posited primal scene. With acknowledgment, he builds upon a trenchant study by the singularly critical psycho-analyst Patrick Mahony, who, though he remains a loyal Freudian, has exposed much of Freud's inventiveness in this instance.[11] For Mahony and Rice alike, the Wolf Man's primal scene lacks all verisimilitude. Freud elsewhere reports that Pankeev's mother disliked sex, for example, yet here he has the wedded pair going at it repeatedly like teen-agers on speed, with a one-year-old kibitzer precociously keeping score while observing, from across the room, both his mother's "castrated" genitals and her rapt but suitably passive facial expression—a feat of observation, as Mahony has remarked, that "would

---

11. Patrick Mahony, *Cries of the Wolf Man* (International Universities Press, 1984).

exceed the ingenious staging of any pornographic film producer."[12]

More tellingly, and more portentously for a final judgment of psychoanalytic claims in general, Freud was never able to convince Pankeev himself that this "terribly farfetched" episode, as Pankeev later called it, had ever occurred (Obholzer, p. 35). "These scenes from infancy," Freud admits, "are not reproduced during the treatment as recollections, they are the products of construction" (SE, 17:50–51). That is to say, all such "memories," including the Wolf Man's, were proposed by Freud himself without necessarily involving the patient's cooperation or assent.

Yet having admitted that Pankeev had no recollection of a primal scene, Freud twice reports specific memories on the Wolf Man's part that "confirm" that scene with volunteered details. How strange this is, in view of Pankeev's assurance to Karin Obholzer that, given the customs of his social class, he could hardly have found himself in the parental bedroom where Freud insistently placed him! (Obholzer, p. 36) And to make matters more bizarre, in the course of revising his paper Freud himself came to deny the reality of the primal scene and then to reassert its genuineness, leaving all three propositions to jostle one another in the text. The illogic of Freud's presentation is matched, for absurdity, only by the inherent ridiculousness of the fabricated tale itself.

If the Wolf Man never presented Freud with the required primal scene, from which depths was it hauled up? Rice argues that it was the child Freud, not Pankeev, who slept

---

12. Mahony, *Cries of the Wolf Man*, p. 52.

in his parents' bedroom and who later fancied that he recalled a traumatically enlightening act of intercourse. And it was Freud who was demonstrably obsessed with copulation from the rear and with yet another pivotal feature of the Wolf Man analysis, sexual initiation at the hands of servant girls. One might add the suggestive fact that little Sigismund, according to *The Interpretation of Dreams*, was permanently scarred by a paternal rebuke after he had relieved himself in his parents' bedroom (SE, 4:16), thus anticipating, and perhaps determining, what would later be ascribed to the Wolf Man's infancy.

## 2.

What necessarily falls beyond Rice's purview is the relation of the Wolf Man case, with its fanatical misconstructions and its pathetic outcome, to Freud's normal practice. For a concise sense of that relation, readers can consult an important 1991 article by Frank Sulloway that reviews all of the major case histories and infers that they compose a uniform picture of forced interpretation, indifferent or negative therapeutic results, and an opportunistic approach to truth.[13] We can go further and ask whether, strictly speaking, Freud can be said to have ever practiced psychoanalysis in the sense that he commended to others. Freud generally lacked the equanimity to act on his key methodological principle, that the patient's free associations would lead of their own accord to the crucially repressed material. Some of his accounts and those of his ex-patients reveal that, when he was not filling the hour with

---

13. Sulloway, "Reassessing Freud's Case Histories."

opinionated chitchat, he sought to "nail" the client with hastily conceived interpretations which he then drove home unabatingly. As a distinguished American psychiatrist, Joseph Wortis, recalled from his own training analysis, Freud "would wait until he found an association which would fit into his scheme of interpretation and pick it up like a detective at a line-up who waits until he sees his man."[14]

Revisionist students of psychoanalysis agree that one case history in particular illustrates that tendentiousness with especial clarity. This is the 1905 "Fragment of an Analysis of a Case of Hysteria" (SE, 7:3–122), a work that forms the topic of Robin Tolmach Lakoff and James C. Coyne's new study, *Father Knows Best: The Use and Abuse of Power in Freud's Case of Dora*.[15] Even though "Dora" (Ida Bauer) severed relations with Freud after just three months of tempestuous sessions, Freud's portrait of her has been used as a model in psychoanalytic training—as, in Erik H. Erikson's words, "the classical analysis of the structure and genesis of hysteria."[16] But by today the Dora case is more often regarded as one long indiscretion on Freud's part. As the first of his fully psychoanalytic cases to be written up, it is relatively candid and vivid in its portrayal of his behavior—so much so that it filled his nonpsychoanalytic contemporaries with alarm. The immediate scandal aroused by the Dora report taught Freud to be

---

14. Joseph Wortis, "Fragments of a Freudian Analysis," *American Journal of Orthopsychiatry*, Vol. 10 (1940), p. 844.
15. Teachers College Press, 1993.
16. Erik H. Erikson, "Reality and Actuality," *Journal of the American Psychoanalytic Association*, Vol. 10 (1962), p. 455.

more circumspect in subsequent writings, but there is no sign that it altered his peremptory clinical style.

*Father Knows Best* resembles many another recent study of Dora in approaching the case from a manifestly feminist perspective. It distinguishes itself from most other accounts, however, by showing concern for Dora the actual person, whose escape from Freud's orbit may not have been as free of consequence as other observers have assumed. Though the eighteen-year-old Bauer went to Freud unwillingly, he did represent her final hope of establishing a relationship of trust and mutual respect with an authoritative adult. By betraying that hope in a singularly bullying way, Lakoff and Coyne maintain, Freud helped to ensure Bauer's later unhappiness.

Whether or not this is so, there can be no doubt that, even by the standards of 1901, Freud's treatment of Bauer constituted psychiatric malpractice. Granted, Freud could not have realized what now seems obvious, the sexual aggressiveness of his own behavior in attempting to force prurient suggestions upon his virginal teen-age patient. But as Lakoff and Coyne understand, what matters most is the larger picture, namely, that Freud withheld all sympathy from Bauer and assailed her self-esteem at every turn. Abetted by the bias of psychoanalytic theory away from real-life factors and toward sexual fantasy, he tried to convince Bauer that she herself, by virtue of having repressed her latent homosexuality, her fantasies of pregnancy and oral sex, and her memories of childhood masturbation and of the obligatory primal scene, was to blame for a distress that clearly had much to do with the current ugly situation into which she had been plunged by others. But that was not the worst of it, for he also tacitly sought her acquiescence in a scheme that can only be characterized as monstrous.

Lakoff and Coyne offer an exceptionally clear account of Bauer's situation when she consulted Freud. The key facts are these:

1. Her syphilitic father was having an affair with the wife of a close family friend, "Herr K."

2. Herr K himself had taken a sexual interest in Bauer since she was fourteen years old and was now pressing his attentions on her once again.

3. Bauer's father evidently found those attentions convenient, since Herr K's proposed misconduct seemed no worse than his own and might distract Herr K from his role as cuckolded husband, thus leaving the father a free hand with Frau K.

4. When Bauer complained to her father about this, he rebuffed her and sent her off to Freud to be cured not just of her numerous tics and suicidal thoughts but also of her insubordination.

Freud was only too happy to oblige. In Lakoff and Coyne's summary, he demanded that Bauer "become aware of her responsibility for her predicament and on the basis of that awareness, modify her reactions, bringing them into conformity with the wishes of her milieu" (p. 74). Prominent among those wishes was a desire that Bauer give up her antagonism to the pedophilic Herr K, whose intentions toward her had been made plain by a forced kiss when she was fourteen and a direct verbal invitation to sexual activity when she was sixteen, as well as by daily gifts and flowers. Accordingly, Freud labored to show Bauer not only that it had been hysterical on her part to spurn Herr K's original kiss but also that she had been in love with him all along.[17]

It is a pity, Freud tells us, that Dora spitefully cut off the treatment before he could bring her to this useful realization. If Herr K had learned "that the slap Dora gave him by no means signified a final 'No' on her part," and if he had resolved "to press his suit with a passion which left room for no doubts, the result might very well have been a triumph of the girl's affection for him over all her internal difficulties" (SE, 7:109–110). In short, a sexually and morally uninhibited Bauer, rounded into psychic trim by Freud, would have been of service to both her father and Herr K, the two predatory males who, unlike any of the women in the story, basked in the glow of Freud's unwavering respect.

It is this last aspect of gender bias that especially catches the interest of Lakoff and Coyne. Using the tools of their academic specialties—Lakoff's is "linguistic pragmatics," and Coyne's is "interpersonal systems theory"—the coauthors take turns exploring the nonreciprocity between Freud and Dora. Freud, they show, overmastered and dehumanized the patient with his badgering. In doing so, Lakoff and Coyne maintain,

---

17. "I should without question consider a person hysterical," writes Freud about the fourteen-year-old girl who had been grabbed and kissed in a darkened room by her family's married friend, "in whom an occasion for sexual excitement elicited feelings that were preponderantly or exclusively unpleasurable . . ." (SE, 7:28). Apart from its sheer dementedness, this statement is of interest for the light it throws not just on Freud's conception of female psychology but also on the itchiness of his diagnostic trigger finger. No wonder that he decided, in the critical year 1897, that several of his sisters, his brother, and he himself were all hysterics, or that people who disagreed with him, including Fliess, Adler, and even Jung, were suddenly found to be paranoiacs.

he was redoubling the age-old subjection of women to masculine will by exploiting a power imbalance already inherent in the clinical setting.

Lakoff and Coyne suggest that all psychotherapy relies to some extent on such an imbalance, and they consider it indispensable to therapeutic progress. But psychoanalysis, they feel, tips the scales egregiously, and doubly so when the analyst is male and the analysand female. Freud's personal quirks aside, Lakoff and Coyne argue, psychoanalysis as an institution—with its deliberate coldness, its cultivation of emotional regression, its depreciation of the patient's self-perceptions as inauthentic, its reckless dispensation of guilt, its historic view of women's moral inferiority and destined passivity, and its elastic interpretative license, allowing the analyst to be "right every time"—seems ideally geared to assaulting the very selfhood of insecure female patients.

The point is worth pondering, but the Dora case, precisely because it is one of the worst instances on record of sexist hectoring by a reputed healer, is not representative enough to convey it. If Lakoff and Coyne's primary target is really psychoanalysis rather than Freud personally, they would have done better to show how the standard analytic "power imbalance" warps the conduct of cases in which the therapist behaves more rationally and humanely than Freud did with Bauer. Contemporary analysts, faced with Lakoff and Coyne's critique, will have no trouble disowning this archaic example and maintaining that *Father Knows Best* overlooks the improved modern state of their craft.

Odd as it may seem, this book must also be judged insufficiently skeptical toward Freud himself. Because their interest stops at Freud's tyrannizing over Bauer and his dismissal of her real-life predicament in favor of "an inspection of [her] internal, pre-existing conflicts" (p. 74), Lakoff and Coyne rashly concede the accuracy of what he asserted about those conflicts. There is, they declare, "no clear reason to dispute any of Freud's interpretations of the material" (p. 41); he is "precisely on target with every interpretation that reflects poorly on Dora's motives" (p. 128); and in general, he "often displays a remarkably subtle analytic ear for language as his patients use it" (p. 44), presumably in this case as well as in others. But these compliments defy the by now well-established fact that Freud's hypersensitive ear was chiefly attuned to his own fanciful associations, not to Bauer's. And his reconstructions of Bauer's infantile habits, traumas, and repressions are, transparently, a tissue of flimsy preconceived ideas. As he aptly said in a letter to Fliess when he had known Bauer for scarcely a week, the case "has smoothly opened to the existing collection of picklocks" (Freud–Fliess Letters, p. 427).

There is, finally, the neglected but overarching issue of whether Bauer was ever a hysteric in the first place. Lakoff and Coyne casually assume that she was, but her immediate family featured a rich array of disorders, from asthma to tuberculosis to syphilis, that would have set off alarms in the mind of a responsible physician. We will probably never know whether Bauer suffered from an organic disease, because Freud made no attempt to find out. Instead, he followed his customary diagnostic procedure, which we have already seen at work with the Wolf Man and in the armchair case of Dostoevsky. That is, he leapt immediately to a conclusion that would permit him to put his trademark suppositions into play and then held to them like a pit bull—later, however, portraying himself as having gradually solved the case with all the prudent objectivity and uncanny astuteness of his favorite literary character, Sherlock Holmes.

<h1 style="text-align:center">3.</h1>

Lakoff and Coyne's hesitation about taking too adversary a position toward Freud and psychoanalysis illustrates the continuing resilience of the Freud legend, which tends to snap back into shape at every point that is not under immediate pressure. To a lesser extent, even James Rice's steadily lucid book on Freud and Russia exhibits the same phenomenon. And so, as we shall see, does another revisionist effort, John Kerr's otherwise superb *A Most Dangerous Method.* All four authors could have profited from scanning still another recent book, Allen Esterson's *Seductive Mirage: An Exploration of the Work of Sigmund Freud.*[18] By concisely surveying the whole Freudian enterprise with a skeptical eye, Esterson dispels any impression that some parts of that enterprise have passed beyond controversy.

Except for an incisive discussion of the Wolf Man case establishing that Freud must have invented one of its key figures, the servant girl Grusha, *Seductive Mirage* does not add to our factual knowledge about Freud. Rather, it closely scrutinizes his ethics and rhetoric, his original "seduction theory" and its putative correction, his major case histories, his theories of neurosis and dream formation, his several reformulations of

---

18. Open Court, 1993.

metapsychology, and his clinical technique and its results. Esterson's book, I should emphasize, is not a polemic written by a long-time foe of psychoanalysis. It is a piece of careful and sustained reasoning by a mathematician who happens to be offended by specious means of argumentation. And its eventual verdict—that every notion and practice peculiar to psychoanalysis is open to fundamental objection—rests on evidence that any reader can check by following up Esterson's cited sources.[19]

Because people do have such a hard time perceiving the nakedness of Emperor Freud, *Seductive Mirage* will prove especially illuminating for the attention it gives to Freud's seduction theory and its sequel, the founding of psychoanalysis per se. After all, to take note of Freud's unsuccess with individual patients like Dora and the Wolf Man leaves the working assumptions of psychoanalysis largely uncompromised. There is always the possibility that Freud simply had little aptitude for therapeutically applying his perfectly sound principles. But if, with Esterson, we uncover grave flaws of reasoning or even outright fraudulence behind the cases that supposedly compelled Freud to adopt those principles, the stakes of the game are considerably raised.

As Esterson relates, up until a certain day in 1897 there was no such thing as psychoanalysis. The method of investigation was in place, but it was producing "findings" of an opposite purport—namely, that hysteria and obsessional neurosis were caused by the repression of actual sexual

---

19. Regrettably, however, Esterson's bibliography contains some errors, and it fails to cite all of the works referenced in the main text. I hope that a second printing will remove this defect.

abuse in childhood. Psychoanalysis came into existence when Freud reinterpreted the very same clinical data to indicate that it must have been his patients themselves, when scarcely out of the cradle, who had predisposed themselves to neurosis by harboring and then repressing incestuous designs of their own. Every later development of psychoanalytic theory would crucially rely upon this root hypothesis, which spared Freud the embarrassment of having to discard his most cherished concept, that of repression. But had he actually discovered anything, and if so, where was his evidence for it?

As Esterson reminds us, the controversy over Freud's seduction theory has concentrated on whether the accusatory tales recounted by his patients were believable. Some feminists and defenders of children follow Jeffrey Masson in holding that those stories were true and that Freud showed a failure of nerve in renouncing them.[20] Freudians, by contrast, take it for granted that the stories were false. In Peter Gay's words, "for a time [Freud] continued to accept as true his patients' lurid recitals," until he reluctantly concluded that he had been told "a collection of fairy tales."[21] But Esterson, drawing on pioneering studies by Frank Cioffi and Jean G. Schimek among others, demonstrates that both parties have been drastically misled.[22] The question they should have posed to themselves is not, Were those stories true? but rather, *What* stories?

20. Jeffrey Moussaieff Masson, *The Assault on Truth: Freud's Suppression of the Seduction Theory* (Farrar, Straus and Giroux, 1984).
21. Peter Gay, *Freud: A Life for Our Time* (Norton, 1988), pp. 94, 96.
22. See Frank Cioffi, "Wollheim on Freud," *Inquiry*, Vol. 15 (1972), pp. 171–186; "Was Freud a Liar?," *The Listener*, Vol. 91 (February 7, 1974), pp. 172–174; "'Exegetical Myth-Making' in Grünbaum's Indictment of Popper

It was Freud himself who taught both his followers and his adversaries to take the seduction narratives seriously as productions of his patients' minds. Beginning in 1914, some twenty years after his work on the pivotal cases, he repeatedly asserted that "almost all my women patients told me that they had been seduced by their father" and that he had innocently believed those narratives until their cumulative unlikelihood became too apparent (SE, 22:120; see also 14:17 and 20:33–34). But as Esterson makes unavoidably clear, Freud's papers from the Nineties expose this claim as a cover-up for a very different state of affairs.

"Before they come for analysis," Freud declared in 1896, "the patients know nothing about these scenes.... Only the strongest compulsion of the treatment can induce them to embark on a reproduction of them" (SE, 3:204). "The principal point," he revealed, "is that I should guess the secret and tell it to the patient straight out" (SE, 2:281). And he confessed that even after his patients had been "induced" to join in the storymaking, "*they have no feeling of remembering the scenes*" thus concocted (SE, 3:204; italics added). Here is the heart of the matter. As in the case of the Wolf Man's and

and Exoneration of Freud," in *Mind, Psychoanalysis and Science*, edited by Peter Clark and Crispin Wright (Blackwell, 1988), pp. 61–87; and Jean G. Schimek, "Fact and Fantasy in the Seduction Theory: A Historical Review," *Journal of the American Psychoanalytic Association*, Vol. 35 (1987), pp. 937–965. Esterson's conclusions were largely anticipated by an article published when his book was in press, Morton Schatzman's "Freud: Who Seduced Whom?" *New Scientist*, March 21, 1992, pp. 34–37. For a still more far-reaching study, upon which I rely below, see Han Israëls and Morton Schatzman, "The Seduction Theory," *History of Psychiatry*, Vol. 4 (1993), pp. 23–59.

Dora's primal scenes, Freud himself laid down the outlines of the seduction plots, which were then fleshed out from "clues" supplied by his bewildered and frightened patients, whose signs of distress he took to be proof that his constructions were correct.[23]

Freud's motive, in later years, for trying to hide his principal authorship of his patients' "scenes" is easy to discern. The myth of the birth of psychoanalysis required that *some* sexual material have been presented to Freud for explanation. Otherwise, even a simpleton would be able to detect the fallacious means by which Freud segued from the seduction theory to psychoanalysis proper. In Esterson's words, "having decided that his *own* constructions [about childhood sexual abuse] are untrue he concludes that they are not genuine occurrences, but are phantasies *of his patients!*" (p. 133). That was exactly the indefensible leap Freud had taken, but it disappeared from view as soon as he convinced his critics, and perhaps himself as well, that his patients had come to him with "lurid recitals."

Given Freud's severe problem with reality testing, it may seem wonderful that he was able to let go of his seduction theory at all. But here again, dishonesty and cowardice played

---

23. Freud's early papers make it clear why he felt entitled to dictate what must have happened to his patients decades earlier. For him, each presented symptom bore a message about a homologous sexual trauma. Thus, vomiting pointed infallibly to oral violation, painful defecating to anal violation, and so on (e.g., SE, 3:214). This allegorizing tendency, whereby a symptom is regarded as the charade of an unconscious memory, survived the seduction theory and found a happy home within psychoanalysis; it is, for example, a prominent feature of the Dora case.

a larger role than rationality. In the spring of 1896 he had already delivered a talk announcing the seduction theory to Viennese neurologists and psychiatrists, claiming that his views had been borne out by "some eighteen cases of hysteria," treated on the whole with "therapeutic success" (SE, 3:199). We now know from the uncensored Freud–Fliess letters that, at the time, Freud had not resolved a single one of his *thirteen* cases; nor, despite increasingly frantic efforts, did he ever do so. As the months dragged on and his patients wandered away, disillusioned, each of them became a potential refuter of his seduction claims. Somehow he had to minimize his exposure to the revelation that those people had been neither sexually abused nor cured of their symptoms. His means of doing so was to slap together a new theory whereby it *no longer mattered* what had happened to patients in their infancy, since in their fantasy life they and every other child who ever breathed had been the would-be seducers—namely, of their opposite-sex parents.

Freud had a plain medical and scientific obligation to retract his seduction theory as soon as he realized its implausibility in 1897. Instead, he publicly reaffirmed it in the following year (SE, 3:263). By 1905, in the Dora case history, he was taking the desperate tack of pretending that his published conclusions of 1895 and 1896 had already been fully psychoanalytic; the Dora case, he maintained, would "substantiate" those findings (SE, 7:7). And even when he felt secure enough to admit his seduction mistake and turn it to rhetorical advantage, he continued to adulterate the facts. In 1896 the alleged seducers of infants were said to have been governesses, teachers, servants, strangers, and siblings, but in later descriptions

Freud retroactively changed most of them to *fathers* so that a properly oedipal spin could be placed on the recycled material. At every stage, earlier acts of fakery and equivocation were compounded by fresh ones. And this pattern, as Esterson shows in devastating detail, holds for the entirety of Freud's psychoanalytic career.

Dissembling aside, it was no coincidence that the key amendment enabling psychoanalysis to begin its colorful history was one that placed Freud altogether beyond the reach of empirically based objections. Thenceforth, he and his successors could claim to be dealing with evidence that was undetectable by any means other than his own clinical technique—the same technique, as Esterson emphasizes, that had generated the false tales of seduction. Instead of spelling out that technique for the sake of the medically solicitous or the scientifically curious, Freud chose to keep it a mystery that he would unveil only to disciples whom he trusted to accept his word without cavil.

In a word, then, Freud had launched a pseudoscience—that is, a nominally scientific enterprise which is so faulty at the core that it cannot afford to submit its hypotheses for unsparing peer review by the wider community, but must instead resort to provisos that forestall any possibility of refutation. And, despite some well-intentioned efforts at reform, a pseudoscience is what psychoanalysis has remained.[24] Such a doctrine can accrue any number of theoretical niceties as it

---

24. The movement's anti-empirical features are legion. They include its cult of the founder's personality; its casually anecdotal approach to corroboration; its cavalier dismissal of its most besetting epistemic problem, that of suggestion; its

continually trims its sails to the Zeitgeist, but it can never confront the nullity of its knowledge claims, since to do so would be institutional suicide.

## 4.

It is precisely the institutional emergence of psychoanalysis—its metamorphosis from Freud's personal crusade to a contentious and internally riven movement—that occupies John Kerr's *A Most Dangerous Method: The Story of Jung, Freud, and Sabina Spielrein.*[25] As its subtitle indicates, this impressive work is essentially a narrative, one that spans the crucial years (1904–1914) of Freud's volatile collaboration and eventual falling out with Jung. But the narrative is informed at all points by Kerr's discriminating awareness of methodological issues. The story he tells is not just a dramatic tale of professional empire building, ethnic mistrust, erotic complications, and vendettas; it is also an account of the haphazard way in which psychoanalytic doctrine acquired some of its major lin-

---

habitual confusion of speculation with fact; its penchant for generalizing from a small number of imperfectly examined instances; its proliferation of theoretical entities bearing no testable referents; its lack of vigilance against self-contradiction; its selective reporting of raw data to fit the latest theoretical enthusiasm; its ambiguities and exit clauses, allowing negative results to be counted as positive ones; its indifference to rival explanations and to mainstream science; its absence of any specified means for preferring one interpretation to another; its insistence that only the initiated are entitled to criticize; its stigmatizing of disagreement as "resistance," along with the corollary that, as Freud put it, all such resistance constitutes "actual evidence in favour of the correctness" of the theory (SE, 13:180); and its narcissistic faith that, again in Freud's words, "applications of analysis are always confirmations of it as well" (SE, 22:146).
25. Alfred A. Knopf, 1993.

eaments. For Kerr, the deeply antiscientific character of Freudianism—with its unformalized procedures, its gratuitous causal assertions, and its appeal to evidence consisting of unobservable buried wishes—left a rational void that could only be filled by exercises of personal power.

Thus readers of *A Most Dangerous Method* who grasp the complex interactions between Jung, Freud, and Sabina Spielrein, the hitherto underappreciated woman who inadvertently sharpened the co-leaders' differences and precipitated their split, will find that they have also acquired insight into the surprisingly negotiable content of psychoanalysis itself. Because Freud was reluctant to say just what he meant by psychoanalysis, and because he was principally concerned to launch an international movement that would leave behind his hapless circle of misfits and drudges in Vienna, it appeared for a while that Jung, his chosen heir, could bend the emerging "science" to spiritualizing purposes of his own. Eventually, of course, Freud proved adamant on large and small points of dogma—but not before he and Jung had freely traded speculations and turned psychoanalytic theory building into a tense dialogue of coded thrusts and parries.

In several respects, *A Most Dangerous Method* serves as an invaluable corrective to received views about the Jung–Freud relationship. Kerr establishes, for example, that in prestige Jung was by no means the supplicant "son" to the authoritative "father," Freud. Because the Zurich contingent commanded a psychiatric clinic and had already published well-regarded research, "it was Jung and [Eugen] Bleuler who put Freud on the scientific map, not the other way around" (p. 9). Similarly, the common assumption that Jung was the less empirically minded of the two thinkers cannot survive Kerr's penetrating discussion. Freud was more suspicious of idealizations than Jung, but the latter, for all his woolly emphasis on a guiding subliminal self, adhered to hypotheses about conflict and regression that required fewer leaps of faith than Freud's.

Whereas Jung believed, plausibly, that the failure of patients to cope with present dilemmas caused them to act regressively, Freud saddled himself with a counterintuitive structure of inextinguishable, polymorphously perverse wishes and repressions that were supposed to become suddenly virulent many years after their formation, dwarfing the patient's contemporary sources of trouble and requiring a mode of analysis that demeaned those sources as trivial. Thus, while Freud treated the patient's unconscious as an obscure and devious text to be deciphered through the cracking of resistances, Jung saw the unconscious as a potential ally that deserved to be courted and activated. Jung may have been naive in his optimism and reckless (as Freud was) about the transmission of ancestral impulses, but his supportive and enabling attitude forestalled the kind of injury that Freud wrought on Dora, the Wolf Man, and others as he prodded them for "memories" that would shore up his dubious premises.

We are often admonished that Freud's work should not be held accountable to stricter standards than those prevailing in his own day. As Kerr shows, however, Freud's peers understood both the man and his errors more clearly than have the generations that came of age after psychoanalysis had acquired its transatlantic vogue. Freud, observed William James in 1909, is "obsessed with fixed ideas" (Kerr, p. vi); in the words of Poul Bjerre, he possessed "an infelicitous tendency to drive one-sidedness to absurdity" (p. 347). His refusal to provide extensive case data to support his notions aroused generally unfavorable comment (pp. 91, 117). As for his therapeutic regimen, James Jackson Putnam remarked in 1906 that it established a "dependence of the patient upon the physician which it may, in the end, be difficult to get rid of" (p. 233). And Putnam added that such unhealthy closeness allows the therapist to impose his sexual preoccupations through suggestion (p. 233). As Albert Moll astutely observed,

> Much in the alleged histories has been introduced by the suggestive questioning of the examiner.... The impression produced in my mind is that the theory of Freud and his followers suffices to account for the clinical histories, not that the clinical histories suffice to prove the truth of the theory. (Kerr, p. 245)

Above all, *A Most Dangerous Method* is useful for the light it throws on the ossification of psychoanalysis, during the period of the Freud–Jung struggle, into what Kerr calls "a totalizing worldview" (p. 9). Kerr is at his best when showing how inevitable it was that psychoanalysis would be plagued by sectarianism and, in its reconstituted core, patched together by enforced ideological conformity. Running through this book, subtly but insistently, is a parallel between psychoanalysis and a modern totalitarian regime in which propaganda campaigns and heresy trials come to preempt free debate. That analogy becomes inescapable when Kerr recounts the activity of Freud's top-secret "Committee," convened in 1912 by none other than Freud's official biographer-to-be Ernest Jones, and taking as its mission the shielding of Freud from criticism by promulgating whatever his latest line might be and by heaping ridicule on his opponents. This Orwellian project, which continued until 1926 and remained undisclosed until 1944, guaranteed that the sounding board for Freud's newest fancies, like those of any insecure dictator, would be an echo chamber.

Unsettling though it is, Kerr's discussion of the inquisitorial "Committee" will not be considered either his most original or his most shocking contribution to revisionist Freud scholarship.[26] That distinction belongs to two "love stories," one solidly documented and the other quite speculative, that Kerr regards as having crucially affected Freud's and Jung's perception and treatment of each other. The less certain of those stories shouldn't affect our picture of Freud unless it is borne out by further research. But in the better-established case of Sabina Spielrein's affair with Jung, at least, we gain some valuable insight into the sexual ethics of the earliest psychoanalysts and the sexual politics that affected the shaping of both Freudian and Jungian theory.

Briefly, Sabina Spielrein began as Jung's patient in Zurich, became his soul friend and mistress, drifted into Freud's orbit when the already married Jung deemed her a liability, and gained equivocal acceptance as a Freudian analyst in Vienna, thereafter returning to her native Russia to introduce and champion psychoanalysis until Stalin closed it down as

---

26. For a full narrative of the Committee's activities, see Phyllis Grosskurth, *The Secret Ring: Freud's Inner Circle and the Politics of Psychoanalysis* (Addison–Wesley, 1991).

counterrevolutionary.[27] In the course of that career—brought to a barbaric end when Spielrein and the other Jews of Rostov-on-Don were herded into a synagogue and shot by Nazi troops in 1942—Spielrein worked not just with Freud and Jung but also with such other luminaries as Jean Piaget, A. R. Luria, and Lev Vygotsky. The latter two were for a while her protégés in Moscow.

As Kerr is at some pains to argue, the one point on which Spielrein has hitherto received general credit, that of having anticipated Freud's concept of a death instinct, is largely a misapprehension. On the other hand, Kerr shows, Spielrein has not been properly acknowledged as the prototype of Jung's "anima," the female presence that supposedly occupies a command post within a man's unconscious. But that attenuated form of immortality looks like small recompense for Spielrein's suffering as a result of Jung's sexual hypocrisy and the icy misogyny with which she was greeted by Freud's small-minded cadre in Vienna.

Freud had heard directly from Spielrein about her involvement with her psychiatrist Jung, and he knew that the aspirations of the paterfamilias and hospital officer Jung in Protestant Zurich could have been considerably thwarted by word of that affair.[28] As he incurred more and more of

---

27. Spielrein began to come into modern historical focus with the publication of the Freud–Jung letters in 1974, and much of her importance was grasped by Aldo Carotenuto in *A Secret Symmetry: Sabina Spielrein between Freud and Jung* (1982; revised edition, Pantheon, 1983). Since then, however, two further discoveries of unedited documents have permitted the fuller understanding that is registered in *A Most Dangerous Method*.

28. Given the norms of conduct in Freud's circle, however, he could hardly have

Freud's intellectual displeasure, Jung trembled before the prospect of exposure by Freud, who had a well-known record of dealing unscrupulously with former friends.[29] But if Kerr is right, Jung held a higher card that could be played if necessary: Freud himself was the potential subject of an even more damaging story, one about a sexual involvement with his own sister-in-law.

It was Peter Swales—by all odds the canniest and most dogged, as well as the most irrepressible, of Freud historians— who first systematically argued that Freud, during the decades spanning the turn of the century, may have consoled himself for his then sexless, intellectually sterile marriage by sleeping with his usual traveling companion and confidante, Minna Bernays.[30] The idea has been summarily dismissed by Freudians, who find it incompatible with the high-mindedness they associate with the discoverer of ubiquitous

---

been morally outraged by the news. As Kerr relates, "Gross's exploits were legendary, Stekel had long enjoyed a reputation as a 'seducer,' Jones was paying blackmail money to a former patient, and even good Pastor Pfister was lately being entranced by one of his charges. Indeed, the most extraordinary entanglement was Ferenczi's, the amiable Hungarian having taken into analysis the daughter of the woman he was having an affair with and then falling in love with the girl" (pp. 378–379).

29. See, e.g., Kerr's recounting of how Freud vindictively leaked Fliess's unpublished theory of bisexuality to Otto Weininger, who mysteriously committed suicide after pirating that theory in his international best seller, *Sex and Character* (1903). Freud lied to Fliess in denying his own instigation of the plagiarism, but by 1906, thanks to a widely publicized lawsuit, his true role in the affair was common knowledge.

30. See Swales, "Freud, Minna Bernays, and the Conquest of Rome: New Light on the Origins of Psychoanalysis," *New American Review*, Vol. 1 (1982), pp. 1–23.

incest wishes.[31] But Swales's essay on the topic abounds in arresting circumstantial evidence. And we do know for certain that Jung confidentially told a number of people that the morally distressed Bernays herself had revealed the secret to him in person. It is equally clear that something induced Freud and Jung alike to step back from mud-slinging and to end their collaboration on relatively civil terms. To put it mildly, the jury is still out on the Freud–Bernays question.

Meanwhile, of course, there remains the less sensational but more important issue of whether anything is salvageable from a once respected body of theory whose evidential grounds have proved so flimsy. On this point, I must say, John Kerr is not always helpful or consistent. At moments he forgets his own powerful account of the psychoanalytic movement's early and decisive break with the scientific ethos—as, for example, when he refers to Freud as "a systematic thinker of the highest rank" (p. 101), or when he characterizes the typically self-flattering Rat Man case as "a stunning demonstration of the method and a matchless psychological study in its own right" (p. 184). Kerr also seems occasionally inclined to lay all the subsequent troubles of the psychoanalytic movement at the door of the Jung–Freud clash. Freudians who are willing to come to grips with the shameful side of their history,

---

31. See, e.g., the limp rebuttal by Peter Gay, "Sigmund and Minna? The Biographer as Voyeur," *The New York Times Book Review*, January 29, 1989, pp. 1, 43–45. Having examined the newly available cache of Freud–Bernays letters in the Library of Congress, Gay reports with relief that there is no suspicious evidence suggesting an affair; letters 95 through 160, those covering the exact years at issue, are unaccountably missing!

he tells us, may yet be able to "renovate [psychoanalysis] or build extensions" upon it (p. 14).

It may be pertinent to note here that *A Most Dangerous Method* began as a dissertation directed by a psychoanalyst, though a relatively critical one, Robert Holt. In a concluding bibliographical essay, Kerr tells us that Holt's (distinctly waffling) book of 1989, *Freud Reappraised*, has served as one of his essential guides to the scientific standing of psychoanalysis. Has Kerr, like the Frank Sulloway of the unrevised 1979 *Freud, Biologist of the Mind*, written a major study of psychoanalysis that is still residually under the spell of the Freud legend? If so, I would like to think that his further development will also follow Sulloway's. For now, I am left wondering which wing of the ramshackle Freudian edifice could be deemed solid enough to "build extensions" on.

## 5.

*A Most Dangerous Method* does make a case for psychoanalysis as having been a progressive force at the turn of the century, when psychiatry was burdened with sinister theories of hereditary degeneration and racial inferiority. We should be grateful to the early Freudians, Kerr tells us, for their candor about sex, their cultivation of a developmental perspective, their addressing of the problems and opportunities posed by transference, and their belief in deep and intricate continuities among a patient's disparate productions of symptom and language. Though one could retort that the Freudian craze postponed investigative approaches that have proved more fruitful than psychoanalysis, this perspective has some merit. To be deemed progressive, after all, a psychological movement needn't put forward accurate hypotheses; it need only raise useful new questions and attract followers who are eager to put aside the older dispensation.

Let us not remain in doubt, however, about whether psychoanalysis remains a vanguard influence today. Incorrect but widely dispersed ideas about the mind inevitably end by causing social damage. Thanks to the once imposing prestige of psychoanalysis, people harboring diseases or genetic conditions have deferred effective treatment while scouring their infantile past for the sources of their trouble. Parents have agonized about having caused their children's homosexuality, and gays have been told that their sexual preference is a mental disorder. And women have accepted a view of themselves as inherently envious, passive, and amoral.

Most recently, moreover, even our criminal justice system has suffered episodes of delusion that would have been impossible without the prior diffusion of Freud's ideas. As I write, a number of parents and child-care providers are serving long prison terms, and others are awaiting trial, on the basis of therapeutically induced "memories" of child sexual abuse that never in fact occurred.[32] Although the therapists in question

---

32. See, e.g., Lawrence Wright, "Remembering Satan," *The New Yorker*, May 17, 1993, pp. 60–81; May 24, 1993, pp. 54–76; Richard Ofshe and Ethan Watters, "Making Monsters," *Society*, Vol. 30, No. 3 (March/April 1993), pp. 4–16; Martin Gardner, "The False Memory Syndrome," *Skeptical Inquirer*, Vol. 17 (Summer 1993), pp. 370–375; and Ofra Bikel's documentary, "Innocence Lost: The Verdict" (PBS *Frontline*, July 20–21, 1993). It is necessary to add that I do not mean to impugn the integrity or minimize the suffering of actual incest survivors. They, too, have a stake in our ability to discriminate between real and delusional reports of childhood experience.

are hardly Park Avenue psychoanalysts, the tradition of Freudian theory and practice unmistakably lies behind their tragic deception of both patients and jurors.

This claim will, I know, strike most readers as a slur on Freud and his movement. Didn't psychoanalysis arise precisely from a *denial* that certain alleged molestations were veridical? But we have seen earlier that it was Freud's technique of breaking down resistance that brought those charges into being in the first place, and we have further seen that the same technique, unaltered in any way, saddled Dora and the Wolf Man with initially unremembered primal scenes. By virtue of his prodding, *both before and after* he devised psychoanalytic theory, to get his patients to "recall" nonexistent sexual events, Freud is the true historical sponsor of "false memory syndrome." Indeed, the modern cases hinge absolutely on Freud's still unsubstantiated notion that children routinely repress anxiety-producing memories—for how else could their initial denial of having been molested be so blithely set aside? Moreover, our incest Pied Pipers are following the most basic, if also the least noted, of all Freudian precedents, a discounting of the suggestibility of patients under emotional stress.[33]

---

33. It may seem calumnious to associate the skeptical, thoroughly secular founder of psychoanalysis with the practice of Bible-thumping incest counselors who typically get their patient-victims to produce images of revolting satanic rituals. Yet in the annus mirabilis 1897, Freud wrote a stunning letter to Wilhelm Fliess reporting that he had obtained from his patient Emma Eckstein "a scene about the circumcision of a girl. The cutting off of a piece of the labium minor...sucking up the blood, after which the child was given a piece of the skin to eat.... I dream, therefore, of a primeval devil religion with rites that are carried on secretly, and understand the harsh therapy of the witches' judges"

Freud's net legacy, then, may not be quite so positive as the conventional wisdom assumes. While we are assessing it, we can only applaud the efforts of revisionist scholars to restore to us the historical Freud who, before his own promotional efforts and those of his clandestine "Committee" rendered him sacrosanct, used to be regarded with healthy skepticism. The new Freud studies are having the salutary effect of putting the deviser of psychoanalysis back where he stood at the turn of the century, possessed of a hobbyhorse about the infantile-sexual roots of neurosis and having to win over a sophisticated audience of doubters. The first time around, Freud prevailed by snubbing his most acute critics and posturing before lay readers who knew only that he stood in the forefront of the anti-Victorian camp. This time, it seems, he will not be so lucky.

*November 18, 1993*

---

(Freud–Fliess Letters, p. 227). As Peter Swales has shown, what Freud meant here was not that he believed in literal witchcraft but that he shared the clerics' belief that a thematically pointed application of duress could evince from the subject genuine psychic material, uncompromised by suggestion. See Swales, "A Fascination with Witches," *The Sciences*, Vol. 27, No. 8 (November 1982), pp. 21–25. The principle of internal psychic determinism was so fixedly rooted in Freud's mind that he discounted not only the influence of his own insistent coaching but even that of theologically crazed interrogators, centuries earlier, who were extracting information by means of the rack and thumbscrew.

# EXCHANGE

J. SCHIMEK is Professor of Clinical Psychology at New York University and a training analyst at the Institute for Psychoanalytic Training and Research in New York City. He writes:

In *The New York Review* issue of November 18, F. Crews ("The Unknown Freud") makes a reference to an article of mine. In this article I showed that Freud's later accounts of his "seduction theory" ("all my female patients told me they had been seduced by their father") does not fit with the way he presented his theory and data originally in 1896.

An examination of Freud's texts of 1896 suggests that the early sexual trauma was not based directly on the patients' recovered memories but was reconstructed by Freud, by interpreting a variety of data in the light of his theoretical assumptions. This is not a startling or damning conclusion, since a few years later Freud readily admitted that many of the crucial experiences of childhood were never directly remembered but only inferred and reconstructed by the analyst, through the interpretation of dreams, fantasies, transference, etc.

I believe my findings have been taken out of context and misused by Crews and Esterson. To conclude from my arguments that Freud made up all the sexual material he got from his patients, and that his theories were dominated by "dishonesty and cowardice," is arbitrary, farfetched, and remote from my intent. I want hereby to dissociate myself completely from such indiscriminate and ill informed Freud bashing. ✳

JAMES HOPKINS is the author of a number of articles on the philosophy of psychoanalysis, and the editor (with Richard Wollheim) of *Philosophical Essays on Freud* and (with Anthony Savile) of *Psychoanalysis, Mind and Art: Perspectives on Richard Wollheim*. He is also Assistant Editor of the philosophical journal *Mind* and Lecturer in Philosophy at King's College in London. He writes:

In "The Unknown Freud" Frederick Crews puts forward a new interpretation of Freud's "seduction theory" of neurosis, and the events surrounding it, based on a number of recent studies by Cioffi, Schimek, Schatzman, Israëls, and others (see his footnote 22). Thus Crews writes:

> even when [Freud] felt secure enough to admit his seduction mistake, he continued to adulterate the facts. In 1896 the alleged seducers of infants were said to have been governesses, teachers, servants, strangers, and siblings, but in later descriptions Freud retroactively changed most of them to *fathers* so that a properly oedipal spin could be placed on the recycled material. At every stage, earlier acts of equivocation and fakery were compounded by fresh ones.

To assess this claim it is necessary to compare it with the historical data, which include both Freud's published work and his private correspondence from the time with his friend Wilhelm Fliess, to which Crews refers in his footnote 2. As Crews says, in 1896 Freud put forward the view that neurosis was caused by childhood seduction (or abuse), and that the seducers included governesses, teachers, and so forth. Also, as Crews stresses, these papers show Freud employing a technique which might well be supposed to have contaminated his observations by suggestion.

During 1897, however, as his letters to Fliess make clear, Freud framed a different theory, according to which the principal abuser in the case of women was the father; and he also tried to take account of the role of suggestion, in relation to the data upon which this theory was based. Thus on January 3, 1897, Freud exclaims "*Habemus papam!*" in reference to what he takes to be a clear case of paternal abuse; and on February 11, he records his belief that his own father's perversion is responsible for hysterical symptoms in his brother and several younger sisters remarking that "the frequency of this circumstance often makes me wonder." On April 28, he speaks explicitly of "a fresh confirmation of paternal etiology," describing a dialogue with a young woman whose "supposedly otherwise noble and respectable father regularly took her to bed when she was from eight to twelve years old and misused her without penetrating ('made her wet,' nocturnal visits)," to which he appends "QED."

As this indicates, the data upon which Freud's theories were based included his patients' recollections of "sexual scenes" or "seduction stories"; and it seems clear that the 1897 paternal seduction theory had the same basis, for Freud wrote on December 17, 1897, that his "confidence in paternal etiology" had risen greatly, because

[Emma] Eckstein deliberately treated her patient in such a way as not to give her the slightest hint of what would emerge from the unconscious and in the process obtained from her, among other things, the identical scenes with the father.

Here Freud was apparently using one of Mill's methods of causal enquiry, in order to see whether his data—evidently recollected scenes, involving the father—might be due to some influence of his own. Since the same scenes arose also in the case of a different therapist, of a different sex, who gave not "the slightest hint" as to what would be forthcoming, Freud evidently concluded that they were a relatively robust phenomenon, and not to be accounted for by suggestion on his part.

Although Freud clearly held this theory in 1897, he abandoned it without publishing it. He cited some related therapeutic and scientific reasons for this in his letter to Fliess of September 21, 1897. These included:

> The continual disappointment in my efforts to bring a single analysis to a real conclusion; the running away of people who for a period had been most gripped [by analysis]; the absence of the complete success on which I had counted; the possibility of explaining to myself the partial successes in other ways, in the usual fashion.... Then the surprise that in all cases, *the father*, not excluding my own, had to be accused of being perverse—the realisation of the unexpected frequency of hysteria, with precisely the same conditions prevailing in each, whereas surely such widespread perversions against children are not very probable.... Then, third,

the certain insight that there are no indications of reality in the unconscious, so that one cannot distinguish between truth and fiction that has been cathected with affect. (Accordingly, there would remain the solution that the sexual phantasy invariably seizes upon the theme of the parents.)

As is well known, Freud was to adopt the alternative hypothesis indicated in the last quoted sentence. The next letters contain the first specific formulations of the theory of the Oedipus complex, applied in his own case, as well as that of his patients.

This material makes quite clear that Crews's claim in the paragraph quoted above is false. Freud's writing in 1897 of "paternal etiology," "perversion against children," the fact that "in every case" the father had to be accused, etc., make clear that during 1897 he held a theory of paternal abuse. His continual references to scenes or stories of seduction, and in particular that to Eckstein above, show that the theory was in part based on scenes or stories produced by his patients, which scenes were liable to arise without suggestion. Since Freud's descriptions in 1897 were written in private correspondence which Freud himself did not see again, there can be no question of their having been "retroactively changed" in any manner for any purpose. In particular there can be no question of retroactive "oedipal spin," since Freud's letter formulating some of the main ideas of the Oedipus complex simply follows that about abandoning the paternal abuse theory quoted above. And since Freud's later accounts of the seduction episode are in close correspondence with the material in his letters from the time, there is no reason to suppose that they involve fakery, etc., either.

It seems from what he writes that Crews has made two related mistakes: (1) he has conflated Freud's unpublished paternal seduction theory of 1897 with the earlier and less specific theory published in 1896, and (2) he has supposed that Freud's later accounts of the seduction episode are meant to be accounts of the material in his 1896 publications, rather than accounts of the work which he did in 1897, and did not publish, but wrote about to Fliess. It is easy to see why the two theories might be confused, since the later developed out of the earlier in 1896–1897. Still the differences are fairly clearly indicated, for example in Freud's remarks about confirmation. Thus in the "*Habemus papam*" letter of January 3, Freud also records how a past male patient "travelled to his hometown in order to ascertain the reality of the things he remembered, and that he received full confirmation from his seducer, who is alive (his nurse, now an old woman). He is said to be doing very well." This is confirmation and follow-up relating to the earlier theory. By contrast, when Freud speaks in April of "a fresh confirmation of paternal etiology"—that is, a further (fresh) confirmation of a theory which he has already previously taken as confirmed—he is concerned with the later theory. Although Freud had been given accounts of paternal seduction from as early as the case of "Catherine" in *Studies in Hysteria* (1895), he seems to have concentrated on "scenes involving the father," and to have tried to control for effects of suggestion on these, only in 1897; and these are points relevant to Crews's charges.

Now of course if you mistake which theory a man is talking about, then even if what he says is true you are liable to think that he is speaking falsely or even incoherently. Since Crews is apparently taking Freud's later descriptions of his unpublished theory of paternal seduction as descriptions of something quite different, published work containing a distinct theory, he naturally thinks that what Freud says is false or worse. In this Crews is not alone. The same mistake, apparently stemming from the work of Frank Cioffi, is clearly also to be found in the article by Israëls and Schatzman which Crews cites (and, if Crews's account is correct, also in the work of Esterson under review). In each case, it seems, the authors take Freud's descriptions of his unpublished work and theory of 1897 as intended accounts of the material in his papers of 1896, and so assume that Freud was somehow deeply engaged in the incoherent project of misrepresenting published work about hypothesized seduction by governesses (or nursemaids) and others as a theory about the role of fathers. Hence, of course, they find Freud's work on this topic highly suspicious, and full of the most astonishing confusions and contradictions. But as Crews's paragraph illustrates, it remains to be seen how many of these alleged confusions, contradictions, etc., are Freud's, and how many are due to misinterpretation on the part of these scholars themselves.

In this connection it is worth noting in particular that the letters to Fliess tend to show that, so far from involving fakery, Freud's practice over this period was in accord with the very methodological canons which Crews cites via the reference to Grünbaum in his first footnote. Thus we saw above that the letters show Freud using Mill's methods to test the hypothesis of suggestion, they also show Freud finding improvement in his patients with the confirmation of his theories in a way reminiscent of what Grünbaum calls Freud's "tally argument."

This can be seen clearly in the case of the patient E, whose symptoms Freud used to illustrate his developing theory on February 19, 1899. On December 21, 1899, Freud reports that this analysis has got to a deep unconscious scene in which "all the puzzles converge" and which is "everything at the same time—sexual, innocent, natural and the rest." As a result "the fellow is doing outrageously well," so that Freud can look forward to the conclusion of this analysis as a "happy prospect." In describing this analysis too Freud apparently speaks of what is unconscious scenes, but by now he is using the term to cover what may be fantasies, as in the paragraph about Eckstein quoted above. Then on April 6, 1900, Freud writes that

> E at last concluded his career as a patient by coming to my house to dinner. His riddle is almost completely solved; he is in excellent shape, his personality entirely changed. . . . I shall keep an eye on the man. Since he had to suffer through all my technical and theoretical errors, I actually think that a future case could be solved in half the time. May the Lord now send this next one. L. G. is doing very well. There is no longer any chance of failure.

Plainly this last statement was unduly optimistic, but the sequence of which it is a part provides a clear and detailed illustration of the way in which Freud's reasoning at this time linked truth with health. When Freud was able to frame a good analytic explanation relating the patient's symptoms to an unconscious scene recovered in analysis, this was correlated with improvement in the patient's condition. Since the best explanation of the improvement was that it was due to the recovery and understanding of the scene, the improvement was also a datum which tended to confirm the accuracy of the explanation. This mode of inference also seems to have played a significant role in the transition from the theory of paternal seduction to that of the Oedipus complex, for Freud evidently began to obtain what he regarded as satisfactory therapeutic results only while working with the latter. (See also the apparent success reported on May 16, 1900.) There are various ways in which this kind of inference might be characterized, but on any account it should be regarded as reasonable. ✳

HERBERT S. PEYSER, M.D., practices psychiatry in New York City. He writes:

Frederick Crews's article on "The Unknown Freud" deserves some discussion by a clinician working in the field. In this regard it is particularly fortunate that in addition to being a practicing clinical psychiatrist I am a member of a psychoanalytic study group, the Rapaport-Klein Group, that numbers among its members such people as those referred to and whose criticisms of psychoanalysis and Freud are quoted by Professor Crews: the philosopher Adolf Grünbaum, the historian Frank Sulloway, and the psychoanalyst/psychologist Robert Holt.

Over the years our group, including such critical people as Professor Crews has quoted, has repeatedly discussed these same issues, questioning the matter of proof, the validity and usefulness of Freud's hypotheses, the question of the scientific nature of the enterprise, and so forth. Indeed, many of us would agree with many of the points made in the article, perhaps most of them, certainly those made early in the article, the first page or so.

But as the article goes on an intemperate note enters into the argument, an angry and ad hominem note. A certain cast to the criticism develops that significantly alters the arguments of others. For example: Adolf Grünbaum, while demonstrating that Freud's methods of proof are not adequate for a truly scientific discipline, does not give up the idea of such proof being possible. He even points out ways to do it. He believes it can be done and should be done, as he has stated in his books. You would not know that from Professor Crews's article.

The angry note is interesting and, lacking any further information, I cannot account for it. But I know of a similarly angry note in an analogous situation. In my younger days it was the note found in the bitter criticisms of Marxism by former adherents, once devoted, now disillusioned and feeling betrayed. I cannot say that this is the origin of Professor Crews's point of view but the situation as it appears in a number of cases is similar. Two brilliant men, Marx and Freud, extremely ambitious, even messianic, are not content with merely valuable first order contributions of great importance but must organize a grand, unified synthesis, a universal, all embracing Weltanschauung, explaining everything. They then wrap it in the mantle of science but without the experimental probative factors and the rigorous self-denying quality that true science requires.

Their syntheses are applied and are found often not useful and at times even harmful. In the case of Marx this is self-evident. In the case of Freud psychoanalysis has not been found to be particularly useful in the treatment of the major disorders such as schizophrenia, major affective disorders, addiction, obsessive-compulsive disorder, etc.; indeed, this was noted by Freud himself as regards the former conditions. Furthermore, there were the tendencies of many psychoanalysts to blame others, usually the parents (as in the case of the erroneous concept of the "schizophrenogenic mother") and to minimize the factors of child abuse and molestation; all this was unfair and incorrect and led to much improperly imposed suffering, although certainly on a lesser scale than Marx's.

The grand theory in both instances collapsed. One could see multiple competing theories and schools arise in the case of psychoanalysis: classical, ego psychology, object relations, self psychology, Kleinian, systems theory, information theory, etc. These approaches saw things differently; their interventions, in timing and content, were different; and there was no way to prove one and eliminate the others. This has led some toward a radical hermeneutic position that in essence takes all theories as equally true and does not conceive of psychoanalysis as a science with utility and accountability. The picture tends toward, if not chaos, then at least disorder.

Marxism is in no better position, but what must be remembered is that the first order contributions have been taken up, worked over, and metabolized into the contiguous major disciplines in both instances: economics, sociology, and history in the case of Marx; psychiatry, psychology, and sociology in the case of Freud. In psychiatry such clinical concepts as unconscious mental activity, the role of early development and the part the past plays in the present, the phenomenon of transference, all are a part of everyday clinical practice even if they are difficult to pin down in a rigorous scientific way; they are nevertheless empirically invaluable to patients and therapists alike.

For example, a young woman who had done well in treatment returns, about to be married. She is very upset because, so she states, her mother does not like her fiance, and so she is holding off the wedding. I do not understand for I was never aware that her mother's opinion had such an influence on this somewhat strong-willed woman. We go on for a while without any increase in understanding of the matter or change in the situation until she tells me a dream involving her being in a shower, then emerging from the shower, followed by a snake coming through the bathroom wall, and finally her awaking with great anxiety. Based upon my understanding of Freud's hypotheses I suggest an ambivalence toward the phallus in particular and toward men in general: that aspect/representation of the matter which is clean and good (the shower) is seen positively but is bland, and that aspect/representation which is "wicked," even "evil" perhaps (the snake), is seen negatively but is highly emotional. I have developed an idea in my mind about this but I do not intrude. I say no more, asking her what she can contribute to our understanding of this.

She says nothing about this subject, speaks about something else, and the session ends. Subsequently she calls to cancel the treatment but returns a month or so later to tell me that there was something she was fully conscious of but guilty about and had not wanted to tell me. In fact she had planned not to until she heard my discussion of the dream and knew that I had guessed her secret. She appreciated my tact and now she had the courage to tell me. The ambivalence that I noted had been carried out in the real world for there was another man, a married man, a secret and "wicked" affair that was most exciting as compared to the bland relationship with the good, clean fiance. Guilty, unable to tell me, she was relieved that I had discovered it in the dream and that it had finally come out in the open. Now we were able to work on it and help resolve it so that she could become "unstuck" and proceed with her life.

In this both my patient and I are indebted to Freud. It is just a small example, an everyday story in practice. It was most useful despite the very serious problem that Freud's psychoanalysis, now almost a century old, has had in establishing itself as a true science and as an accountable technique in terms of cost and benefit in a sorely pressed health care system. But "gray are all theories and green the golden tree of life," and we are left, when all is said and done, with the usefulness of such formulations in everyday clinical experience, for which we are grateful to Freud, with all his warts. ✳

DAVID D. OLDS, M.D., is Associate Clinical Professor of Psychiatry at the Center for Psychoanalytic Training and Research at Columbia University, and he is in private practice in New York City. He writes:

The article by Frederick Crews reviewing "revisionist" books about Freud is an interesting one. It seems to have aroused the fear and rage of many psychoanalysts as well as current and former psychoanalytic patients. The review does indeed unleash a broadside against psychoanalysis as the author apparently imagines it is currently practiced. And because it describes some definitely "unscientific" aspects in the history of psychoanalysis, it implies that current practice is still wild, capricious, and self-serving on the part of analysts. It is common for commentators to attack what they think is psychoanalysis, but which is in fact the extremely shaky practices of early pioneers; it is like criticizing modern astrophysics by attacking Newtonian cosmology or by making ad hominem attacks on Isaac Newton.

What is most striking about the article is that it provides all the data for a really interesting conclusion; but, since it is devoted more to polemical detraction, it seems to miss the crucial point entirely.

When reading the article I thought of an acquaintance of mine, a skilled and well-trained surgeon practicing in a medically underserved area in northeastern Canada. At a time when he was the sole physician in a small hospital, he developed appendicitis and, since he was the only surgeon available, did the operation on himself. He had the help of competent nurses; but he injected the local anaesthesia, cut through his layers of skin and fascia, looked around inside with the aid of mirrors, probably nicked a few blood vessels that he shouldn't have, removed the inflamed appendix, and sutured himself up. The association is of course to Freud's self-analysis and his self-supervision in performing the first psychoanalyses ever performed. One can see right away that Freud's position was much more difficult even than that of the solo surgeon. If the surgeon had not done hundreds of appendectomies (a procedure then perfected over many years), if he was doing the first appendectomy, the first time anyone had ever cut into the abdomen of a live patient, and that patient were himself, then he would be approximating Freud's position.

Critics of psychoanalysis seldom see that it is a process of dealing with a wildly moving target from a slightly less wildly moving platform. The first person to do it was bound to make mistakes, as was the first person to do an appendectomy. The phenomenon of the erotic transference, in fact of any transference, took the early analysts by surprise. Freud's early collaborator, Josef Breuer, quit the field in the face of its awesome power. Freud, whose personality did include grandiosity, narcissism, self-delusion, and megalomania, had the imagination, creativity, and recklessness to push on, with no textbooks, maps, or guides. He and his first-generation disciples made some horrendous mistakes. There is no reason to idealize them as anything more than brilliant, dedicated, flawed human doctors. It may well be that Freud was some-what corrupted by the power that was thrust upon him, and which he no doubt enjoyed. But he did not sleep with his patients, nor found a lucrative ashram. His heart went mostly in a scientific direction, despite the peculiar nature of his instrument.

The nature of that instrument and the nature of psychoanalysis are both missed in the article. Freud had no supervision, no training analysis, other than his "self-analysis"—in his case an oxymoron. One has only to supervise beginning analysts, or in fact to be a beginning analyst oneself, to see the pitfalls beckoning the unwary. One quickly realizes the power of the analytic relationship to evoke the regressed neurotic aspects of both partners. The rigorous training analysis, and the intensive supervision—in most good institutes lasting five and more years—are for the purpose of organizing and using this power for the good of the patient, preventing it from causing some of the disasters the revisionists are fond of describing.

I do not wish to criticize the valuable work of the more fair-minded Freud scholars; in fact they do us a great service. Let's take a look at the old chestnut, "Is psychoanalysis scientific?" Usually we mean: Does it have hypotheses which can be proven or disproven empirically? Also we mean: Can we do outcome studies that show the benefit of psychoanalytic techniques? Without belaboring this argument, let us look at the time scale in which there is some empiricism at play. That is the historical time frame of one hundred years in which techniques have been tried and found wanting and improved upon. If such a trial and error method, which is common in the development of surgical techniques, is scientific, then the term applies here also. We have *learned* that giving financial advice to a patient, or sleeping with a patient, or lying to a patient, are *bad* techniques which interfere with the analytic process. We have learned, and this only in recent years, that the *countertransference*-generated urge to commit those errors can be used as valuable information. *When used properly*, countertransference has become a valuable lens rather than a destructive nuisance. Another thing we are in the process of learning is the difficulty of evaluating memories; the "false-memory" problem is a serious one. We are at least now sensitive to the danger of suggestibility, and we will have to develop the skills necessary to minimize the potential damage.

The point Professor Crews could have made is that, if we take a historical perspective, we can see that psychoanalysis has moved forward over the graves of bad ideas. In medicine, one remembers radiation therapy for acne, or DES, or Thalidomide. These lessons are not learned by all individuals; there are still unscrupulous and crazy therapists and physicians. But the majority of psychoanalysts attempt to make use of the wisdom learned over the years, and to improve on it. Ironically, we are indebted to Freud, and to the other founders, almost as much for their errors as for their successes. This is an aphorism appropriate in most progressive endeavors.  ✳

MARIAN TOLPIN, M.D., is a Training/Supervising Analyst at the Institute for Psychoanalysis in Chicago, and Clinical Professor of Psychiatry at Chicago Medical School. She writes:

Professor Crews's "The Unknown Freud" misleads readers who are not familiar with critical Freud studies in the psychoanalytic literature. For example, Crews cites Erik Erikson's 1962 "Reality and Actuality" only to imply that Erikson recommended Freud's treatment of Dora as a model for the treatment of adolescents and young adults. Nothing could be farther from the truth. In fact, in the paper cited Erikson began one of the most penetrating critiques of Freud and the Dora case yet written; and, making use of the case and Freud's failure to understand Dora and her needs, he began revolutionary advances that had a salutary effect on psychoanalysis and psychotherapy and paved the way for recent further advances.

Were Crews to divulge the thrust of Erikson's critique and his substantive clinical contribution he would have undermined his overriding imperative—to discredit all of Freud's work and to pronounce all of contemporary psychoanalysis worthless and/or destructive. Therefore, it is worth mentioning some specifics of Erikson's thinking about Dora and Freud. Erikson protested Freud's failure to recognize the import of the "traumatic sexual approaches" made to her by a man she expected to be trustworthy (p. 455); and he disputed Freud's assertions that the past and repressed childhood sexual wishes played a central role in Dora's disorder. Moreover, Erikson placed the traumatic sexual approaches to her in the wider causal nexus in which they belonged: the "pervading perfidy" with which Dora was treated by her parents and their friends (p. 459); and the family and culture that discouraged an intelligent young woman's use of her intellect and "did not [give her] a chance" for a future.

Thus Crews fails to even mention that Erikson refuted that Freud and father "know best" about women's place

(Dora, he said, was placed in the "role as an object of erotic barter," p. 456). In short, in what was to become his encompassing and influential theory of identity, Erikson staked out important "feminist" issues: "A vital identity fragment in [Dora's] young life . . . that of the woman intellectual" (p. 459) was nipped in the bud by a convergence of familial and cultural betrayal and lack of encouragement. The deepest significance of Dora's dream of a house on fire and her hope that her father would save her jewel box was neither sexual nor oedipal, as Freud insisted. Understood in the light of emerging identity theory, the dream contained the imperative unconscious need for help from Freud to save herself, her own female self, if you will, and her chances for a future (p. 461).

Crews omits additional insights of Erikson's that would also undermine his claim that he is revealing the Freud "unknown" to psychoanalysts. Erikson saw clearly that Freud was determined to prove "his kind of truth" (the theory of repressed sexuality); that the need to be right blinded him to Dora's psychological truth and led to the failure of her treatment; and this repetition of the failure by her adult world had lasting deleterious repercussions. Because of his understanding of transference (one of Freud's enduring discoveries) Erikson was able to take a step Freud could not take: he realized that Freud's failure was so important to Dora precisely because she turned to him with her ("transferred") needs and hopes for fidelity. From Freud, now, she wanted and expected "mutual verification" of her "actuality." The help she needed was a far cry from making unconscious sexual wishes conscious. Erikson's Dora needed help to get on with the interrupted tasks of her adolescence and young adult-hood: to find value in herself and salvage values to live by when her trust in herself and those most important to her was destroyed.

Intent on "proving his kind of truth," Crews fails to mention that psychoanalysis grows from scholarly Freud studies that do not have an axe to grind. For example, analysts know from Erikson, not from Freud, that many adolescents and young adults of our day are like Dora. They too suffer from what Erikson described as "malignant forms" of frustration of their basic needs for adults' fidelity; and when they cannot rely on parents, teachers, and others in their wider milieu, they too transfer their needs to therapists and expect understanding and responsiveness from them. Well trained therapists' understanding of their patients' quandary is an essential ingredient of their having another chance at a future. (Erikson was neither the first nor the last analyst to dispute Freud's contentions and to go on ahead of him. Crews fails to acknowledge past and present psychoanalytic work that does not support his thesis.)

In the final analysis, though, Crews is right in at least one respect. Freud's tendentious arguments to prove his point were extremely harmful to some of his patients and to the field he tried so hard to establish. Nevertheless psycho-analytic scholars continue to study Freud's theories and case histories as part of the ongoing effort to learn from Freud's frank histories and his mistakes, to widen knowledge about a still largely "unknown" psychological universe, to further clinical understanding and improve therapeutic efficacy. Perhaps Professor Crews can come to see that his selective omissions of analysts' critical studies, and what can be learned from them, are in the service of the tendentiousness of his argument, his insistence on his "truth" about psychoanalysis; and that, because these omissions mislead, they actually undermine his argument. If he cannot face this "truth" squarely, his "Unknown Freud" will remain as a classic case of the pot calling the kettle black. ✳

MORTIMER OSTOW, M.D., P.C., is a psychiatrist and psychoanalyst practicing in New York City, President of the Psychoanalytic Research and Development Fund, Attending Psychiatrist at Montefiore Medical Center, and Visiting Professor Emeritus in Pastoral Psychiatry at the Jewish Theological Seminary of America. He writes:

It should not be surprising if psychoanalysts felt impelled to respond to Crews's missile attack on their profession and its founder.

Perhaps one should start by stating the role of psychoanalysis in the current treatment of mental illness. In their extreme forms, two approaches may be described as follows. The first approach attempts to assess the patient's illness by an initial interview which is likely to include the use of a questionnaire, a so-called test "instrument," administered personally or even by computer. The results of this assessment lead the psychiatrist to a code number and diagnosis specified in the current *Diagnostic and Statistical Manual*. Armed with this information, the psychiatrist then turns to the three-volume handbook on *Treatments of Psychiatric*

*Disorders.*[1] There he will be told how to proceed. Such treatment is usually based primarily upon medication where that
is relevant, although other modalities are recommended too.
Fortunately this procedure often works out fairly well, especially when the disorder is a circumscribed episode of one of
the affective disorders, that is, disorders that lie on the
manic-depressive spectrum. It is the treatment preferred by
third-party payers and health maintenance organizations.

Other disorders do not lend themselves to such a
mechanical procedure. These include symptom neuroses and
personality disorders that impair the individual's ability to
enjoy a loving relation with another person, or to apply himself successfully to any vocation or to escape from a prevailing
self-defeating tendency. For these, various psychotherapies
are prescribed. Some psychotherapies address themselves to
specific symptoms rather than to the patient. They isolate
the prominent symptoms of the illness and attempt to sup-
press them by a kind of conditioning technique. The extraordinary rates of success advertised by the practitioners of such
methods are probably exaggerated, but there is no doubt that
the treatment does succeed in many instances.

However, for the treatment of other neuroses and the
personality disorders, a patient-oriented psychotherapy is
required. The patient learns about himself, his true desires,
and the conflicts that surround them, the salient themes in
his life, his major and continuing disabilities. He learns to

---

1. American Psychiatric Association, *Treatments of Psychiatric Disorders: A Task
Force Report of the American Psychiatric Association* (American Psychiatric
Association, 1989).

distinguish between difficulties created by external reality and internal fantasy. For such psychodynamic treatment, an understanding of the basic dynamic mechanisms recognized by Freud are essential: conflict, repression, transference, defense, sublimation, unconscious guilt, Oedipus complex, separation anxiety, the destructive effect of success, to name only a few. In fact, given the current situation in the treatment of mental illness in the United States, the transmission of the understanding of these dynamic mechanisms may be the primary legacy of psychoanalysis to American psychiatry and psychotherapy.

Professor Crews is right. Psychoanalysis has been experiencing a decline in the United States. However, one may question his understanding of its cause. As I have watched my practice change over recent years, I see a progressive loss of interest in psychoanalysis for two reasons. First, the drug treatments have created a climate of expectation of brief treatment. Second, patients have come to depend more and more on third-party—usually insurance company—payments. Insurance companies will not pay for any extended or intensive psychiatric care beyond the bare minimum, except in the case of the most generous policies. Among those segments of the population that can pay for treatment without external supplement, psychoanalysis remains desired. Elsewhere in the world, where economics are different, in Germany for example, and in many countries of South America, for example, psychoanalysis is flourishing.

Having acknowledged in his second sentence that some patients have found psychoanalysis helpful, Crews then feels free to devote the rest of the extended essay to its shortcomings and those of Freud. What are the facts? Establishing the efficacy of any kind of psychotherapy is difficult because personality and individual mental illness, constitutional disposition and temperament, resilience and motivation all differ greatly from one patient to another and it's difficult to assess these before treatment has started. Moreover it should be obvious that psychoanalysts differ in ability and experience among each other.

In 1979, I reviewed the outcome of thirty-seven former patients, all of my patients who had had at least a minimal amount of psychoanalytic treatment.[2] Five of these (14 percent) exhibited dramatic improvement, that is, improvement so striking that friends or relations who hadn't known that the patients were being treated commented on the distinct change. Nine others (almost 25 percent) were considered by themselves and their families to have improved impressively, as demonstrated by important changes in their ability to function in the several areas of life in which they had previously functioned badly. So these two categories together constituted about 40 percent of the group. Sixteen patients could be said to have achieved limited improvement. They functioned better in one or more areas of life but still far from optimally. In general, these patients and their families were pleased with the outcome but I was less pleased. Seven patients (19 percent) showed no improvement at all. I should add that in almost half of the sample I had used medication along with analysis. However, the changes that I

---

2. "The Outlook for Psychoanalysis," *Bulletin of the New York Academy of Medicine*, Vol. 59, No. 5, pp. 451–463.

looked for in evaluating the treatment were not the simple changes of mood that drugs produce, but rather alterations in personality function. The distribution of degrees of improvement among patients who had no medication did not differ from those who had medication. Considering the nature of the illness, the duration, and in many cases the constitutional basis, these findings are not at all discouraging. I should imagine that a more recent cohort would do even better.

The reader will note that Crews criticizes only those reports of Freud's work that were published before 1905, that is, reports of his very earliest psychoanalytic experience, when the discipline was being developed. Crews's comments did not apply to Freud's later work nor to psychoanalysis as it is practiced now.

Much has been made in recent years of Freud's seduction theory versus his subsequent theory that reports of early seduction are fantasy. The perceptive reader who is not looking for polemic would infer that in some instances actual seduction did take place, while in other instances the seduction took place in fantasy only, and in still others, innocent encounters were interpreted as seduction. In most instances, unless there is outside corroboration, it is difficult or impossible to distinguish among these possibilities. There is no conspiracy here either against children or their parents.

With respect to Freud's status as a scientist, Crews neglects to inform his readers that before his psychoanalytic work began, Freud had written and published well over 100 papers and monographs on neuroanatomy, neuroembryology, and clinical neurology. At least two of his major monographs,

*On Aphasia* and *On Cerebral Palsy*, are still considered both authoritative and valid statements.

I shall have nothing to say to Professor Crews's reports of Freud's personal behavior. We don't ordinarily evaluate a discipline by the ethics of its founders but if one thought it necessary to judge Freud's conduct, it would have been helpful if Professor Crews had made a serious effort to distinguish between established fact on the one hand and gossip, rumor, and speculation on the other. Sigmund Freud never claimed publicly that his personal behavior was exemplary, but those who knew him well thought that it was. The Pentateuch demonstrates that the founders of religious monotheism were not above reproach in their personal behavior, but we do not reject monotheistic religion on that account. ✳

LESTER LUBORSKY, PH.D., is Professor of Psychology in Psychiatry in the School of Medicine of the University of Pennsylvania. He has written six books and numerous papers on research in psychotherapy. He writes:

Frederick Crews, who wrote the review for you "The Unknown Freud," is clearly a man who reads and writes a lot about psychoanalysis, but there is no evidence that he has knowledge of studies on the comparison of the efficacy of psychoanalysis with other forms of psychotherapy. I have done the studies. I thought the readers would be interested in knowing the facts about the relative efficacy of different forms of psychotherapy including psychoanalysis, because he raised the issue. He says, for example, in his first paragraph in which he reviewed four books about different facts of psychoanalytic history, "in the aggregate psychoanalysis has proved to be an indifferently successful and vastly inefficient method of removing neurotic symptoms."

It is fashionable to make such statements, but in fact Crews should know the facts. His conclusions should have been: (1) There are no adequate studies comparing psychoanalysis with other forms of psychotherapy so there is no proof that it is better or it is worse. (2) It is probably at least as good as other forms of psychotherapy. The evidence for this is that for all treatment comparisons involving different forms of psychotherapy the overwhelming trend is for nonsignificant differences in benefits received from the different forms of psychotherapy, including psychodynamically oriented psychotherapy (which is a shorter form of psychoanalytic psychotherapy). (3) The evidence is overwhelming, in fact, that these different forms of psychotherapy produce very meaningful benefits for the majority of patients.

For Professor Crews and for the interested audience, which I know is very large, I will cite just a few reviews of comparative psychotherapy studies:

L. Luborsky, L. Diguer, E. Luborsky, B. Singer, and D. Dickter, "The efficacy of dynamic psychotherapies. Is it true that everyone has won so all shall have prizes?" in N. Miller et al., *Handbook of Dynamic Psychotherapy Research and Practice* (Basic Books, 1993).

L. Luborsky, N. Miller, J. Barber, and J. Docherty, "Where we are and what is next in dynamic therapy research and practice," in N. Miller et al., *Handbook of Dynamic Psychotherapy Research and Practice* (Basic Books, 1993).

L. Luborsky, B. Singer, and Lise Luborsky, "Comparative studies of psychotherapies: Is it true that 'Everyone has won and all must have prizes?'" *Archives of General Psychiatry*, 32 (1975), pp. 995–1008.

M. Smith, G. Glass, and T. Miller, *The Benefits of Psychotherapy* (Johns Hopkins University Press, 1980).

I will be glad to send some of these reprints to Professor Crews or any of the readers who write me for them. ✱

HAROLD P. BLUM, M.D., is the Executive Director of the Sigmund Freud Archives. BERNARD L. PACELLA, M.D., is the Secretary-Treasurer of the Sigmund Freud Archives and Past President of the American Psychoanalytic Association. They write:

It was very surprising and disappointing that such a distinguished periodical as *The New York Review of Books* would publish an article containing gross misunderstandings and scurrilous comments against Freud and psychoanalysis by Professor Frederick Crews. Readers of the *Review* should expect sober and scholarly appraisal rather than what appears to be a series of emotionally charged statements which deal more with misperceptions and misconceptions than scientific, objective evaluation. It appears that Freud cannot be allowed human frailty, any errors, or lack of present-day knowledge. Even his critics are criticized for not being critical enough. The enduring discoveries of his revolutionary genius are cavalierly dismissed with superficial consideration and supercilious contempt.

At this time, Freud's initial propositions, first findings, and landmark case reports are no longer vital for the validation of psychoanalytic formulation. Further, as psychoanalysis became popularized, many concepts were distorted and bowdlerized, a tendency which can be discerned in the Crews article.

Freud is part of our culture, our way of comprehending personality development and disorder. All rational psychotherapy is based upon psychoanalytic principles. Psychoanalysis provides a fundamental mode of exploring and understanding art and literature, biography and history, etc. Concepts of repression, regression, denial, projection, and "Freudian slip" have become part of our language. The vulgar idiom "jerk off" conveys thinly disguised castration anxiety. Lady Macbeth washes her hands because of underlying guilt, not because her hands are literally dirty. Shakespeare intuited ego defenses and can be invoked in "methinks Dr. Crews doth protest too much."

Dr. Crews implied that The Sigmund Freud Archives has concealed documents to protect Freud's reputation. This is contrary to the fact that The Sigmund Freud Archives' policy has been to derestrict and release Freud correspondence as quickly as legally and ethically possible. Professor Crews cites a document restricted to 2102 when he could have ascertained that this document was already derestricted by The Sigmund Freud Archives. The Archives are now largely derestricted and much of the new Freud documents have become available through The Sigmund Freud Archives.

Finally, the encompassing explanatory reach of psychoanalytic theory and the immense value of psychoanalytic therapy stand on their own merits having endured the test of time and continuing challenge. Psychoanalysis has developed independent of the person, personality, and personal life of its creator. But Freud could have, in the final analysis, ironically observed, "they may attack my theories by day, but they dream of them at night."  ✳

FREDERICK CREWS replies:
1. It does appear that, as the psychoanalyst David Olds reports above, "The Unknown Freud" has caused widespread "fear and rage" within the Freudian community. The result is a deluge of mail such as *The New York Review* has rarely seen. The letters above constitute only the most civil and temperate of countless protests mailed in by offended Freudians, most of them practicing psychoanalysts.

Those unpublished complaints deserve at least a passing mention here. In the rhetorical tradition perfected by Freud himself, they tend to concentrate not on the substance of my argument but on my allegedly defective personality, the main sign of which is precisely my incapacity to render a "balanced"—i.e., predominantly appreciative—assessment of Freud and his brainchild. The letters thus beg the question of whether, as I argue, Freud's scientific reputation has been grossly inflated, first through his own promotional efforts and later by self-interested disciples.

The unpublished letters also converge in calling my essay ad hominem, as several of the published letters do as well. I deny the charge. An ad hominem argument is one that ducks substantive issues by vilifying the person or kind of person who takes the position opposite to one's own. But though the main emphasis of "The Unknown Freud" is biographical, it begins by summarizing the objective grounds for deciding that the "clinical validation" of psychoanalytic ideas is hopelessly circular and that Freud's theories of personality and neurosis are woolly, strained, and unsupported. And it directs curious readers to sources that establish those judgments in a strictly evidence-based manner.[1] My essay makes it clear that I object to Freud's doctrine not because Freud himself displayed certain weaknesses of judgment and character but because his theoretical and therapeutic pretensions have been weighed and found to be hollow.

Although I can hardly expect psychoanalysts to be grateful for my restraint, moreover, I actually steered clear of their founder's least stable side—his lethal cocaine evangelism, his

---

1. To repeat, those sources are Adolf Grünbaum's *The Foundations of Psychoanalysis: A Philosophical Critique* (University of California Press, 1984) and Malcolm Macmillan's *Freud Evaluated: The Completed Arc* (North–Holland, 1991). Less technically inclined readers, I pointed out, can survey the case against Freudian psychoanalysis in Allen Esterson's briefer *Seductive Mirage: An Exploration of the Work of Sigmund Freud* (Open Court, 1993). For an elaboration and extension of Grünbaum's argument, see also his new *Validation in the Clinical Theory of Psychoanalysis: A Study in the Philosophy of Psychoanalysis* (International Universities Press, 1993).

phobias and psychosomatic fainting spells, his bizarre super-
stitions, his belief in the magic power of telephone and hotel
room numbers, his affinity for ESP, his gnostic ideas about the
primal horde and its Lamarckian effect on modern psyches,
his paranoid streak, and what even his hagiographer Ernest
Jones called his "twilight condition of mind" at the time of his
famous self-analysis.[2] My essay, however, eschews speculation
about the ways in which specific delusions on Freud's part may
have found their way into psychoanalytic theory.

Before answering the pro-Freudian letters that appear
above, let me refresh readers' memories by recapitulating the
claims of my essay:

—that Freud's uniquely psychoanalytic ideas have received no appreciable corroboration, and much discourage-
ment, from independent sources;

—that his method of reaching causal conclusions, even
in the idealized form described in his public writings, could
not have reliably yielded those conclusions by any imaginable
path of inference;

—that his actual method was far worse, namely, turning
hunches, borrowed notions, and corollaries of his other beliefs
into certainties and then depicting those "findings" as the
inescapable results of clinical experience;

—that his idea of corroboration was the fallacious one of
heaping up consilient-looking exercises of his interpretative
style, without regard for rival lines of possible explanation;

---

2. Ernest Jones, *The Life and Work of Sigmund Freud*, 3 volumes (Basic Books,
1953–1957), Vol. 1, p. 306. Jones discusses all of the traits I am mentioning
here.

—that his perceptions and diagnoses invariably served his self-interest, always shifting according to the propagandistic or polemical needs of the moment;

—that his therapeutic successes, supposedly the chief warrant that his psychological theory was correct, appear to have been nonexistent, and that he lied about them brazenly and often;

—that his rules of interpretation were so open-ended as to permit him to twist any presented feature to a predetermined emphasis;

—that he brushed aside as trivial the main threat to the integrity of psychoanalytic knowledge, namely, the contaminating effect of the therapist's suggestion;

—that, as a result, he failed to maintain even a minimal demarcation between his own obsessions and those of his patients;

—that the "stories" figuring crucially in the official version of his transit from the seduction theory to psychoanalysis proper were his own inventions, misascribed at first to his patients' early histories and soon after, more extravagantly, to their early fantasies—thus foisting off *his* "seduction" error on the contents of *their* minds when they were toddlers;

—that, consequently, there never was a need to import notions such as repression and the infantile-sexual basis of neurosis to account for what Freud "found" in the patients whom he now chose to regard in a psychoanalytic light;

—that the coercive tactics by which he attempted to win his patients' agreement to his own theory-driven surmises about their infantile histories rendered him the chief begetter of our contemporary "false memory syndrome";

—that, with his approval, his movement conducted itself less like a scientific-medical enterprise than like a polit-buro bent upon snuffing out deviationism; and

—that the "science" he invented was, and remains, a pseudoscience, in that it relies on unexamined dogma, lacks any safeguards against the drawing of arbitrary inferences, and insulates itself in several ways from the normal give-and-take of scientific debate.

Remarkably few of the letters above, written by eight American psychoanalysts and one British academic of a known Freudian persuasion, address any of these points in specific detail. Indeed, a number of the letters don't just leave my theses unchallenged but grant that they may be substantially correct. Curiously, however, such concessions leave the writers' general loyalty to Freudianism undiminished. Whereas the orthodox psychoanalysts in the group appear to be "massively into denial," the more liberal ones would like to embrace just enough criticism of Freud to distance themselves from his errors—thus skirting the awkward fact that their method of making "advances in insight" remains exactly as subjective as his own.

2. It is, for the most part, the liberal, modernizing analysts who are represented in the letters above. As a result, one sees there only traces of the misty-eyed Freudolatry that used to characterize psychoanalytic discourse—traces, for example, such as Dr. Olds's likening of Freud's muddled self-analysis to a heroic self-appendectomy,[3] or Dr. Ostow's tribute to the

---

3. I have discussed the incoherence and absurdity of Freud's self-analysis in *Skeptical Engagements* (Oxford University Press, 1986), pp. 60–62.

humble Freud's "exemplary" personal behavior.[4] Nevertheless, some of these writers do claim that I have misrepresented Freud in important respects. Let us see if their charges hold up.

Dr. Jean Schimek was the first psychoanalyst to have squarely faced Freud's conflicting accounts of his seduction theory.[5] Now, understandably, Schimek prefers to renounce any credit for having inspired "The Unknown Freud." Since he neglects to show where my "Freud bashing" was factually incorrect, however, his letter serves no purpose other than self-exculpation within the notoriously unforgiving Freudian community.

Nevertheless, I am glad for the opportunity to commend Schimek's pioneering article and to point out the very modest extent to which my essay went beyond it. Briefly,

---

4. According to Ostow, Freud never told us what a good person he was. On the contrary, his pervasive account of himself as a self-sacrificing man of science has proved to be his most enduring creation. As David Olds says above, Freud's personality included "grandiosity, narcissism, self-delusion, and megalomania." It is now widely acknowledged that he was also manipulative and vindictive, even to the extent of plotting the successful plagiarism of his former best friend's unpublished ideas and of driving a severely depressed ex-protégé (Viktor Tausk) to suicide by coldly ordering his analyst to abandon him. Yet this veteran of the world's only self-analysis possessed no insight whatever into the darker side of his nature. As he wrote to James Putnam in 1915, "I believe that when it comes to a sense of justice and consideration for others, to the dislike of making others suffer or taking advantage of them, I can measure myself with the best people I have known. I have never done anything mean or malicious.... If only more of [an urge towards the ideal] could be found in other human beings!" *Letters of Sigmund Freud*, selected and edited by Ernst L. Jones (Dover, 1992), p. 308.
5. Jean G. Schimek, "Fact and Fantasy in the Seduction Theory: A Historical Review," *Journal of the American Psychoanalytic Association*, Vol. 35 (1987), pp. 937–965.

Schimek establishes the untruthfulness of Freud's later statements about what his seduction patients "told" him about their molestations in early childhood, and he then asks "why, in 1896, Freud presented his data in an ambiguous and inconsistent fashion, and why he saw them as much clearer and stronger ('almost all of my women patients told me...') once they had become evidence for universal oedipal fantasies rather than proof of the past misdeeds of some individual fathers" (Schimek, p. 961). My essay supplies the answer that is already implicit in this delicately posed question: Freud misrepresented what his hysterics had "told" him because it suited his later theoretical interests to do so.

3. It is too bad that James Hopkins couldn't have studied Schimek's article before writing his own letter, which does at least get down to specifics. Those details just don't lead to the conclusions he thinks they do. It is Schimek, not Hopkins, who clearly recognizes Freud's contradictions over "seduction" and who understands the nonclinical basis on which "the father" came to dominate the last phase of Freud's prepsychoanalytic thought. I will draw on Schimek's findings in the following response to Hopkins.

The core of Hopkins's letter is his allegation that, by overlooking the evolution of Freud's seduction theory in the last year of its existence, 1897, I have created a false discrepancy between Freud's early and late accounts of that theory, thus unjustly impugning his integrity. Specifically, says Hopkins, Freud did, in his private letters to Fliess, blame fathers for the molestations he believed his hysterical patients to have undergone—and so he was being strictly truthful when he later characterized his abandoned theory in the same terms.

Hopkins's letter goes awry on several points that will require explanation, but it is also wrong in a global way that can be stated at once. My brief against Freud in the seduction matter was a double one. First, Freud later pretended that nearly all of his female hysterics had *directly told him* about early childhood molestations which in fact were sheer inventions of his own; and second, he eventually maintained that those patients had *named their fathers* as the culprits. If, as his three relevant papers of 1896 abundantly show, Freud conjectured the infantile scenes that his patients never did succeed in remembering, then his later versions of the story, including the one that incriminates fathers, are manifestly false. No conclusions drawn from the Freud–Fliess Letters could challenge this assertion, which pertains to inconsistencies in Freud's published writings. Hopkins's laboriously reasoned indictment is thus much ado about nothing.

Hopkins would have us believe that Freud in all of his later statements was merely recalling the final, never published, phase of his séduction theory, in which "the father" indeed served as the evil protagonist. How odd, then, that fathers aren't even mentioned in Freud's first retrospective comments about the theory in 1914, when he began making self-serving misstatements about the authorship of the infantile scenes. Indeed, it took Freud until 1925, in his *Autobiographical Study*, to assert that most of his women patients in the 1890s had explicitly blamed their fathers. When he repeated that claim more strongly in 1933, in his *New Introductory Lectures*, his reason for doing so was made transparently clear by a following sentence: "It was only later that I was able to recognize in this phantasy of being seduced by the father the expression of the typical Oedipus complex in women" (SE, 22:120).[6]

A further aim on Hopkins's part is to show, through several examples, that Freud's hysterics did offer him uncoerced reports of sexual abuse, in direct contradiction of my claim that the scenes were invented. In making this argument, however, Hopkins reveals that he has misunderstood the seduction theory in all of its variations. As Schimek explains, Freud's theory anticipated the retrieval of sexual material from two stages of a hysteric's life: a molestation between the ages of two and five and a disturbing incident after the onset of puberty. The latter could be anything from "the stroking of the hand or the hearing of a mildly obscene joke" (Schimek, p. 941) to a fully incestuous relationship. The inevitability that some recollection on a patient's part would fall into such a vast category rendered this aspect of his interrogations relatively uninteresting to Freud, *even when adolescent incest was involved.* If the seduction theory was not to topple, he would have to go further and show that the Ur-traumas from ages two to five had actually occurred.[7] And those same "scenes" were to become

---

6. As Peter Swales has pointed out to me, the very fact that we refer to a "seduction theory" about the rape of small children attests to Freud's success in the airbrushing of history. Once Freud had adopted his notion (actually borrowed from Fliess) of infantile sexuality and had endowed all children with a wish to "seduce" a parent, it became useful for him to claim that his patients had symmetrically (mis)remembered their own "seductions." I will keep to Freud's retrospective nomenclature here, but students of his thought would do well to change the name of the seduction theory to the "molestation theory."

7. "If the first-discovered scene is unsatisfactory, we tell our patient that this experience explains nothing, but that behind it there must be hidden a more significant, earlier, experience" (SE, 3:195–196).

no less indispensable to psychoanalysis itself, which came into being as an attempt to account for them as repressed oedipal fantasy. But since the scenes existed only in Freud's head, the only thing that required explaining was his own fanaticism.

Hopkins's error will become clearer if we look at one of the cases he cites, that of a patient who consciously recollected that her father had lasciviously fondled her between the ages of eight and twelve. Hopkins believes that such narratives gave Freud just the key information he was seeking. Freud, however, saw the matter very differently, and his account to Fliess, on April 28, 1897, of his two initial sessions with this patient displays the prodding and coaching that Hopkins is at such pains to deny.

The patient was a young woman who had become insomniac after seeing her brother hauled off to an insane asylum. Characteristically brushing aside that palpable trauma, Freud told her that "[i]n my analyses the guilty people are close relatives, father or brother." Apparently without coercion, the woman then revealed her molestation by her father in her pre-adolescent years. Here again lay a likely source of mental disturbance in the present. For Freud's purposes, however, such direct reporting of actual abuse beyond age five was little more than a challenge to his powers as a psychic detective. "Of course," he relates to Fliess, "*when I told her that similar and worse things must have happened in her earliest childhood, she could not find it incredible*" (Freud–Fliess Letters, p. 238; italics added).

Did Freud in the "seduction" period, as Hopkins proposes, make serious attempts to guard against the effects of his own suggestion? Readers can judge for themselves by studying both the letter just quoted and the "*Habemus papam!*" letter of January 3, 1897, that Hopkins also attempts to enlist in his behalf. There Freud tells Fliess that he has solved the case of a patient (a cousin of Fliess's) who must have been molested by her father:

> When I thrust the explanation at her, she was at first won over; then she committed the folly of questioning the old man himself, who at the very first intimation exclaimed indignantly, "Are you implying that I was the one?" and swore a holy oath to his innocence.
>
> She is now in the throes of the most vehement resistance, claims to believe him, but attests to her identification with him by having become dishonest and swearing false oaths. (Freud–Fliess Letters, pp. 220–221)

As I indicated in my essay, Freud believed that even the tortures inflicted by witch interrogators yielded uncontaminated psychic data—a position to which he still adhered after founding psychoanalysis.[8] Not surprisingly, then, he expended as much ingenuity on the uncontrolled and egregiously leading pursuit of infantile "primal scenes" and repressed fantasies as he had previously devoted to infantile incest. This is not the

---

8. "Why," Freud asked Fliess, "are [the accused witches'] confessions under torture so like the communications made by my patients in psychic treatment?" (p. 224). Freud's answer was that the "witches" were fantasizing in a manner that was true in every detail to the experience of their repressed infantile molestations. Much later, he broached the subject of witch trials again with his psychoanalytic colleagues, telling them: "We find unmistakably infantile elements in those fantasies that were not created by torture but merely squeezed out by it." See *Minutes of the Vienna Psychoanalytic Society*, Vol. 2, 1908–1910, edited by Herman Nunberg and Ernest Federn (International Universities Press, 1967), p. 123.

Freud described in Hopkins's letter, but so much the worse for Hopkins's ability to read the record discerningly.[9]

4. The psychoanalysts represented above share a belief, widely held among the uninformed public, that Freud, though fallible, bequeathed us a precious store of permanently valid discoveries and concepts. Their inventory includes the unconscious, infantile sexuality, dream symbolism, repression, regression, projection, sublimation, denial, transference, countertransference, "Freudian slips," and of course the centerpiece of it all, the universal Oedipus complex. These notions are thrown

---

9. Hopkins stumbles in other respects as well. It is pointless to argue, as he tries to do, that Freud's "father etiology," which was soon transmuted into the Oedipus complex, rested solidly on his clinical cases. Everyone knows that it came directly from his self-analysis. Schimek, referring to the very cases cited by Hopkins, observes that "It is hard to tell what was presented by the patients as memories or as dreams and hallucinations; it is also difficult to separate Freud's suggestions and interpretations from the patients' direct and spontaneous statements. Furthermore, two out of the three cases refer to later periods of childhood, and in one instance the father is only indirectly incriminated" (p. 952).

Similarly, when Hopkins justifies Freud's shift to an oedipal etiology by citing its superior therapeutic results, he is whistling in the dark. According to the Freud–Fliess Letters, many of Freud's hysterics had forsaken his services by 1897. Does Hopkins think that Freud got back in touch with them, broke the news that they were all suffering from Oedipus complexes, and thereby relieved them of their symptoms? And where do we learn about the critical mass of new patients who did so much better from the outset? Freud was eager, as Hopkins inadvertently documents, to draw hasty correlations between symptom abatement and interpretation. He knew, however, that his finished cases were nothing to boast about.

Hopkins's whole letter manifests a desire to take what Freud thought he was doing (being inductive à la John Stuart Mill, correlating hypotheses with therapeutic outcomes, etc.) as sufficient evidence of his actual procedures, which were aprioristic and peremptory in the extreme. From Freud's point of view as a rhetorician, Hopkins would seem to constitute his ideally gullible reader.

back at me as if only ingratitude had kept me from paying due obeisance to them. Astonishingly, most of the writers seem unaware that their conceptual stock-in-trade is even controversial, much less that it lacks corroboration that can be taken seriously outside the precincts of the Freudian village.

How can this be? The answer is that these analysts, like their colleagues around the world, fail to grasp what is required of an adequate scientific explanation. With Freud, they believe that the instancing of a causal hypothesis—showing that it "works" in "covering" the phenomenon in question—suffices to prove its worth. The mere fact that generations of Freudians have been able to organize their data according to Freudian categories strikes them as settling the matter.[10] They thus inhabit a kind of scientific preschool in which no one divulges the grown-up secret that successful causal explanation must be *differential*, establishing the *superiority* of a given hypothesis to all of its extant rivals.

Whenever that standard has been applied, Freudian notions have failed to pass muster. Nor should we be surprised, since the entire psychoanalytic system was assembled deductively as an elaboration of Freud's infantile-sexual etiology of neurosis, about which even the analysts themselves now feel distinctly queasy. Every Freudian idea, it turns out, suffers

---

10. I make no exception here for "responsible" Freudians like Dr. Peyser, who appears to agree that "Freud's methods of proof are not adequate for a truly scientific discipline." Amid its ecumenical gestures, Peyser's letter glibly refers to Freud's "empirically invaluable" findings and "first order contributions of great importance." This is to say that Peyser's homage to scientific prudence, like his attempt to portray my friends Adolf Grünbaum and Frank Sulloway as admirers of psychoanalysis, is nothing more than a gambit.

from several of the following deadly flaws: *vagueness* (no deter-
minate consequences can be predicted by its use), *excessiveness*
(the explained phenomena can be accounted for more satis-
factorily by more plausible suppositions), *logical dependency on
other dubious notions*, and *superfluousness* (the explained phenomena are themselves illusory products of the theory).

Take, for example, the concept of transference, regarded
by virtually all modern analysts as the most axiomatic of
Freudian theoretical entities. Transference as Freud understood it is the patient's reliving of infantile cravings and disap-
pointments through an unconscious casting of the therapist as
a substitute parent. It is thus an artifact of the Oedipus complex, itself a colossal overgeneralization of Freud's hunches
about the origin of his own hysterical tendency.[11] And since
transference can be either "positive" or "negative" without our
possessing any guidelines for knowing which kind to expect
next, no behavioral consequences flow from it, and it is therefore at once irrefutable and operationally devoid of meaning.

The usefulness of transference to Freud, however, was
considerable. Like its constituent defense mechanism of "resistance," transference explained why Freud's patients failed to
recall the "memories" he proffered them and why they acquired
"no sense of conviction of the correctness of the construction

---

11. For the misgivings of analysts themselves about the Oedipus complex, see
Macmillan, *Freud Evaluated*, pp. 489–491. Anthropological objections are
summarized by Bruce Bower, "Oedipus Wrecked," *Science News*, Vol. 140
(October 19, 1991), pp. 248–250. And for a powerful challenge to the concept
from an informed evolutionary perspective, see Martin Daly and Margo Wilson,
"Is Parent-Offspring Conflict Sex-Linked? Freudian and Darwinian Models,"
*Journal of Personality*, Vol. 58 (March 1990), pp. 163–189.

that [had] been communicated" to them (SE, 18:18). In short, transference could be invoked to spare Freud from recognizing that he might be wrong.

The concept first acquired prominence, in fact, when "Dora" refused to accept Freud's thesis that she was in love with the adulterous pedophile and chambermaid seducer "Herr K," whose advances to his friend's daughter Freud deemed "neither tactless nor offensive" (SE, 7:38n). Instead of asking himself whether Dora might not be a better judge of her own amorous feelings than he was, Freud decided that her love for Herr K—ultimately derived, as he explained to her, from her desire to commit sex acts with her father—had now blossomed into love of Freud himself. Thus when Dora dreamed of smoke, Freud concluded that she was really pining unconsciously for a kiss from his own cigar-scented lips (SE, 7:74). And when Dora reasonably decided that nothing could be gained from continuing to consult such a physician, Freud once again laid all the blame on the tumultuous effects of transference (SE, 7:118-19).[12]

Needless to say, liberal contemporary analysts feel that they have purged transference of its wild-card hermeneutic function and its narrowly oedipal basis. In Dr. Marian Tolpin's

---

12. As David Olds mentions above, transference also supposedly accounted for the famous passion of "Anna O" for the alarmed Josef Breuer, who, Freud told us, fled in consternation from Anna and her hysterical pregnancy. Olds could profit from reading Henri Ellenberger's investigation of that pre-psychoanalytic event, which never actually occurred; it was a malicious fiction invented by Freud to discredit his former mentor and benefactor and to advertise his own superior courage. See Ellenberger, "The Story of 'Anna O': A Critical Review with New Data," *Journal of the History of the Behavioral Sciences*, Vol. 8 (1972), pp. 267–279.

letter above, for example, little remains of the concept but a Cheshire cat smile—a bland hope on the part of patients that their "basic needs for adults' fidelity" will be better met by therapists than they were by parents. I do not begrudge the liberals this retreat from Freud's sexual house of horrors into Mr. Rogers's neighborhood. But I must point out that their revised understanding of transference becomes less objectionable precisely to the degree that it sheds its uniquely psychoanalytic character.

Meanwhile, the concept inevitably remains entangled in the therapeutically questionable practice of fostering a "transference neurosis," or childish overinvolvement with the analyst, which will then take years to "work through." As Dr. Olds frankly points out above, another likely outcome is that "the regressed neurotic aspects of both partners" will bring about "disasters." By fetishizing *emotional* distortions on both sides, moreover, the whole transference-countertransference rigmarole deflects attention from the *cognitive* dubiety of psychoanalytic formulations in general and of the analyst's surmises in particular. All in all, then, this pivotal notion has proved itself to be not only scientifically vacuous but also considerably worse than useless as a guide to the rational addressing of patients' initial complaints.

A similar critique could be made of every other Freudian heirloom prized by my correspondents. We have already seen, for instance, that Freud's own favorite idea, repression, arose to meet a wholly imaginary need. When Freud conceded the absence of the early sexual events posited by his seduction theory, the concept of repression was elevated into an article of sheer faith in undetectable subterranean transactions, without even a hypothetical link to the recoverable misfortunes of children. In full-blown psychoanalytic theory, repression serves as a pseudo-explanation of a pseudo-phenomenon, the personality-forming renunciation by children of their primary desire to do away with one parent and copulate with the other. Well-designed experimental studies have not produced a shred of evidence for the existence of such a mechanism.[13]

The concept of repression has nonetheless survived and prospered, thanks to a conjunction of several factors: the analytic fraternity's century-long cover-up of Freud's bungling in the birth hour of psychoanalysis; Freud's public relations success in enlisting repression to "explain" dreams, jokes, and errors;[14] the enticingness of the concept as a means of facilely negating manifest appearances; and a failure, by both analysts and the lay public, to appreciate the difference between isolated traumatic amnesia (a real but unusual occurrence) and Freudian repression, which entails all the epistemic liabilities of the Oedipus complex, the castration complex, and a demonstrably erroneous idea of the way human memories are typically made unavailable to consciousness.

This last point deserves emphasis because of its bearing on the urgent question of the moment, false memory syn-

---

13. For gaining an appreciation of the difference between Freudian and scientific standards of research design, there is still no better source than Hans J. Eysenck and Glenn D. Wilson, *The Experimental Study of Freudian Theories* (Methuen, 1973).
14. It was *The Psychopathology of Everyday Life* (1901) that chiefly caught the fancy of Freud's lay admirers, who continue to believe that "Freudian slips" neatly demonstrate the truth of psychoanalysis. It has been shown, however, not only that Freud's theory of parapraxes is conceptually dubious but that the book announcing it contains not a single satisfactory illustration of that theory. See Sebastiano Timpanaro, *The Freudian Slip: Psychoanalysis and Textual Criticism* (New Left Books, 1976).

drome. As Richard Ofshe and Ethan Watters have shown, unscrupulous or incompetent therapists who induce patients to "recall" fictitious molestations with hallucinatory vividness are employing a souped-up but still recognizably Freudian idea of repression.[15] They share with Freud the discredited belief that all experience, even from earliest infancy, is photographically stored and retained without normal degradation over time. Like Freud, they deem that *only repression* can account for the inaccessibility of a given memory at a given moment. Again, they subscribe to his groundless tenet that repression can block the memory not just of a sudden shocking assault but also of whole years' worth of psychically unacceptable events. And most significantly, they also share his conviction that a patient's disorientation and distress when confronted with alarming suggestions about his childhood must constitute a partial lifting of repression—that is, a delayed activation of the affect that could not be felt at the time.

Similarly, prosecutors who browbeat innocent persons into confessing to satanistic sexual crimes are reaping the legacy of Freud's utter refusal to make allowance for the contaminating effect of suggestion. In his own words,

> We must not be led astray by initial denials. If we keep firmly to what we have inferred, we shall in the end conquer every resistance by emphasizing the unshakeable nature of our convictions.... Moreover, the idea that one might, by one's insistence, cause a patient who is

15. Ofshe and Watters, "Making Monsters," *Society*, Vol. 30 (March/April 1993), pp. 4–16.

psychically normal to accuse himself falsely of sexual misdemeanours—such an idea may safely be disregarded as an imaginary danger (SE, 3:269).[16]

5. The psychoanalysts represented above are most exercised of all by my apparent imputation that their guild has made no intellectual or behavioral improvement since Freud's day. But this is to misconstrue my argument. The outlandishness of Freud's beliefs and practices virtually guaranteed that any sane, honest, and compassionate successor would make fewer incredible assertions and achieve better clinical results than he and the members of his doctrinaire and unethical circle did. If, as Dr. Olds tells us, analysts have learned through "trial and error" the imprudence of seducing their patients, I will not deny that this is a step in the right direction. And I, too, like Dr. Tolpin, find Erik Erikson's avuncular wisdom more congenial than Freud's relentless biologism. That Erikson has proved to be a better therapist and moral counselor than Freud strikes me as the safest bet in the world.[17]

---

16. This is Freud in quaint pursuit of his own pet "misdemeanor," masturbation. Modern analysts, of course, do not share his Victorian prejudice in this regard. Nor have they taken much interest in incest as a literal tragic event. [*Later*: But see pp. 15–29 above.] Yet by continuing to turn their backs on the critical problem of experimenter effects, and by "normalizing" the relatively rare and physiologically based phenomenon of traumatic amnesia, they are not without their own share of responsibility for our national epidemic of false memory accusations. In this connection, see Paul R. McHugh, "Psychotherapy Awry," *The American Scholar*, Vol. 63 (Winter 1994), pp. 17–30.

17. Dr. Tolpin wishes that I had written a friendly essay about Erikson instead of a harsh one about Freud. In my *Skeptical Engagements* she can find a whole chapter that correlates Erikson's sweetening of Freudian dogma with his protean

Still, there is a problem here. Neither Erikson's postulates nor those of any other neo-Freudian can be regarded as bearing the slightest *scientific* (as opposed to moral-ideological) weight. All of the defining traits of pseudoscience that I listed in note 24 of my essay apply equally to Freud's work and to that of his improvers. For, although each of Freud's ideas has been challenged from within his own tradition, that tradition itself remains one of deplorable conceptual sloppiness and circularity.

To my knowledge, for example, no modern analyst has renounced the cardinal Freudian investigative tool of "free association," which is inherently incapable of yielding knowledge about the determinants of dreams and symptoms.[18] None has even started to make due allowance for the leading and indoctrinating effects of the therapy itself. None, again, has revised the theory so as to endow it with clear predictive implications —a step whose absence means that any number of schismatic Freudian sects can proliferate without appeal to a factual basis for adjudicating between them. And none has removed the ultimate joker from the Freudian deck—the principle that an analyst is entitled, in Freud's words, to "handle unconscious ideas,

---

adaptability to shifting currents of American ideology.

Tolpin also makes much of my dereliction in implying that Erikson "recommended Freud's treatment of Dora as a model for the treatment of adolescents and young adults." I implied no such thing. Erikson, I said, *reported* that the Dora case was still (in 1962) being touted in psychoanalytic training as "the classical analysis of the structure and genesis of hysteria." My statement revealed nothing of Erikson's own views about hysteria, much less about the unmentioned treatment of adolescents.

18. On this point, see Macmillan's *Freud Evaluated*, Chapter 15—a devastating critique of the entire psychoanalytic means of gathering and interpreting data.

unconscious trains of thought, and unconscious impulses as though they were no less valid and unimpeachable psychological data than conscious ones" (SE, 7:113). As Malcolm Macmillan puts it,

> We are never told that the so-called discoveries are dependent upon methods of inquiry and interpretation so defective that even practitioners trained in their use are unable to reach vaguely congruent conclusions about such things as the interpretation of a dream or a symptom[,] let alone the basic clinical characteristics of infantile or perverse sexuality or the reconstruction of the early stages of an individual's development or... the functions that make up a given structure.[19]

On this basis, moreover, I must qualify my praise of modern analysts for doing better than Freud in their therapeutic work. They want us to believe that the improvements they have achieved were made possible in part by a scientific honing of their concepts over time. It is true, certainly, that merely by refraining from reliance on such backward ideas as inevitable female masochism and the fateful consequences of

19. Macmillan, *Freud Evaluated*, p. 505. This last point applies forcefully to Erikson, whose humanistic pronouncements have been grafted onto a schematized, fanciful extension of Freud's empirically unanchored theory of psychosexual stages. Note, too, that Erikson's reading of Dora's dreams, like dozens of other mutually incompatible efforts, offers no basic challenge to the open-season license of Freudian dream interpretation but merely exercises that license, as Dr. Tolpin puts it, "in the light of emerging identity theory." This is a game that any number may play, but to no purpose other than the exemplification of predetermined lessons.

masturbation, any contemporary therapist would have a head start over Freud. But because the liberalized versions of psycho-analysis continue to use amorphous uncharacterized terms and to make untested claims, the relationship between psycho-analytic dogma and therapeutic effects remains as imprecise and prayerful as ever.

In this connection, much can be learned from Dr. Peyser's story of his female patient who returned to treatment because of anxiety about her impending marriage—an anxiety caused, Peyser later learned, by her involvement with a second and more alluring man. She was of course "fully conscious" of this problem when she consulted Peyser, but because of indirections that are built into psychoanalytic technique, the topic didn't come up, and the doctor's fees, we can safely assume, kept mounting. ("We go on for a while without any increase in understanding of the matter or change in the situation. . . . ") After again suspending the treatment for a month, however, the patient returned to announce that an astute prior dream interpretation on Peyser's part had enabled her to tell him about her dilemma at last. (He had already guessed, but, good Freudian clinician that he is, he hadn't wanted to intrude.) And then comes the less than cathartic denouement: "Now we were able to work on [her secret] and help resolve it so that she could become 'unstuck' and proceed with her life" — but in which direction and with what success we are not told.

This narrative really seems to illustrate the way psycho-analysis itself can become an extra burden for a client. One gets the impression that merely keeping the therapeutic rela-tionship going had become a goal for both parties and that a fear of displeasing her analyst was needlessly costing this woman a good deal of time and money. Would she not have done better to discuss her problem with a few sympathetic friends? And can Peyser be sure that it was really his dream interpretation, and not some other development in the woman's life, that allowed his sessions with her to resume?

And then there is the question of whether Peyser had "correctly" decoded his patient's snake-in-the-shower dream. That someone who, at the time, was keeping two lovers busy suffered from "ambivalence towards the phallus" appears far from self-evident. It may be, of course, that Peyser and his patient were using dreams and their glossing as an Aesopian language for the discreet trading of hints; as the psychoanalyst Judd Marmor observed long ago, patients in various styles of psychotherapy learn to edit their dream reports in ways that suit the theoretical expectations of their doctors. What must be firmly rejected, however, is Peyser's implication that the unique correctness of Freudian ideas allowed him to reach an outcome (whatever it was!) that couldn't have been attained in any number of less roundabout ways.

For all the advanced company he keeps in "the Rapaport–Klein Group," Dr. Peyser is still enmired in the primitive *post hoc, ergo propter hoc* style of thought that pervades psycho-analytic discourse. As independent students of therapeutic outcomes understand, it is not enough to observe that, after a lapse of months or years, some favorable change occurred in a patient's attitude or mood. The question must always be whether factors specific to the therapist's mode of treatment — and not factors shared by all treatments or factors originating outside the treatment — brought about the good result. The same problem bedevils Dr. Ostow's letter, which reports on a follow-up of thirty-seven of his former patients. It is sad enough that, even though Ostow had employed "medication along with analysis," a full 62 percent of those patients had improved very little or not at all. But more pathetic still is Ostow's total unawareness that, thanks to his failure to control for nonpsychoanalytic effects, his survey lacks any validity.

6. There is, however, one letter above from a correspondent who has spent a lifetime doing just what I am recommending here, the comparative study of Freudian and non-Freudian therapeutic outcomes. Lester Luborsky believes that I need to undertake a crash course of reading on the topic. But Luborsky goes badly wrong in several assertions, the least important of which is his claim that I am unfamiliar with his writings. As early as 1980, I was not only citing his work but also disputing the unwarranted partisan conclusions that he even now persists in drawing from it.

In his letter, Luborsky asserts that all psychotherapies (that is, "talking cures") may be about equally effective and that I am therefore out of line in calling psychoanalysis "indifferently successful" and "vastly inefficient." This only shows that Luborsky has yet to learn what the words "indifferently" and "inefficient" mean. As I wrote in 1980, "if one therapy worked about as well as another, only people with severely impaired reasoning, or with motives other than a wish to be speedily cured, would choose the one that is most disruptive of their budgets and work schedules."[20]

Luborsky is on record as believing that Freudian analysts

---

20. *Skeptical Engagements*, p. 21.

are in possession, not of a counterintuitive and embattled system of decoding, but of "a unique store of clinical wisdom."[21] He recognizes, however, that psychoanalysis has had to retreat from the claim of superior curative power that Freud cited as the cardinal proof of his theory's correctness. Long ago, therefore, Luborsky adopted a more furtive strategy, that of making psychoanalysis look as inconspicuous as possible within a modestly cheerful assessment of all psychotherapies. This, once again, is the purpose of his present letter.

But Luborsky has fared poorly even in this low-profile endeavor. Consider, for example, the book by Glass et al. mentioned in the remedial reading list he has prepared for my edification. Glass himself later acknowledged that his 1980 study failed to cover a single "outcome evaluation of orthodox Freudian psychoanalysis."[22] Moreover, the criterion of therapeutic effectiveness employed by both Glass et al. and Luborsky —namely, better results than no treatment at all—has been rejected as too lax by a number of independent researchers, who cogently maintain that placebo treatment, not an absence of treatment, ought to serve as the baseline of comparison. And according to authors who have specifically reanalyzed and disputed the work of Glass et al., "there is no evidence that the benefits of psychotherapy are greater than those of placebo

21. Lester Luborsky and Donald P. Spence, "Quantitative Research on Psychoanalytic Therapy," in *Handbook of Psychotherapy and Behavior Change: An Empirical Analysis*, second edition, edited by Sol L. Garfield and Allen E. Bergin (Wiley, 1978), p. 360.
22. Gene V. Glass and Reinhold M. Kliegl, "An Apology for Research Integration in the Study of Psychotherapy," *Journal of Consulting and Clinical Psychology*, Vol. 51 (1983), p. 40.

treatment."[23] Thus Luborsky's attempt, in his letter, to tuck psychoanalytic treatment beneath the skirts of short-term "dynamically oriented [i.e., Freudian] psychotherapy" is as futile as it is shabby, given the failure *even of such brief therapy* to show significantly better results than hand-holding control treatments.

The real import of Luborsky's work, as he himself elsewhere admits, is that psychotherapies succeed (when they do) thanks to factors that they all share—that is, placebo factors.[24] Thus, *contra* Freud, occasional happy outcomes of Freudian therapy are incapable of vouching either for the truth of psychoanalytic notions about the mind or for the posited mechanism of psychoanalytic cure. No doubt it is motivationally useful for each of the myriad extant psychotherapies to offer its clients some structure of belief—whether it be about undoing infantile repression, contacting the inner child, surrendering to the collective unconscious, or reliving previous incarnations. But as Luborsky understands, such notions are window dressing for the more mundane and mildly effective process of renting a solicitous helper.

Once this point sinks in, psychoanalytic patients may well question why they should be spending years reconstructing early memories, fantasies, and feelings which, even if they should happen to be genuine, will prove therapeutically inert.

---

23. Leslie Prioleau, Martha Murdock, and Nathan Brody, "An Analysis of Psychotherapy versus Placebo Studies," *Behavioral and Brain Sciences*, Vol. 6 (1983), p. 275.

24. "The most potent explanatory factor [for the apparent equivalence of outcomes] is that different forms of psychotherapy have major common elements—a helping relationship with a therapist is present in all of them, along with other related, nonspecific effects such as suggestion and abreaction" (Luborsky et al., 1975, p. 1006).

And if some patients still won't care, the devisers of their medical benefits surely will.

7. I reserve for last the haughty letter composed jointly by Drs. Harold P. Blum and Bernard L. Pacella, the executive director of the Sigmund Freud Archives and president of the American Psychoanalytic Association, respectively. These eminences charge me with many "gross misunderstandings" but are able to name only one, my failure to realize that a certain letter in the Archives originally restricted until the year 2102 is now available for viewing. No such date, however, appears in my essay. I suppose that Blum and Pacella must be referring to an actual letter that they know to have been originally destined for release in 2102. Perhaps they can tell us which letter it is, how recently it was declassified, and how it first came to be salted away for an intended age.

I raise these questions because, insofar as the Blum–Pacella letter attempts to deny that "the Sigmund Freud Archives has concealed documents to protect Freud's reputation," it whitewashes a sordid history that Blum knows only too intimately. Blum was appointed to replace Kurt Eissler when the latter's reign of Stalinesque censorship, which began with the founding of the archives in the early 1950s, was exposed to worldwide ridicule by Janet Malcolm in the 1980s. It was that mortifying episode, not any long-standing policy, that eventually induced the Archives' trustees to begin counteracting Eissler's mischief by giving Blum a different mandate. And even so, the current "Restricted Section" catalog, as of December 1993, still includes whole sets of documents that are supposed to remain inaccessible until such dates as 2020, 2050, 2053, 2056, 2057, and 2113.

132

What Blum more particularly fails to disclose is that the Eissler regime has cast a sinister afterglow over his own contrary efforts. Eissler remains the executor of all documents donated by Anna Freud in the wake of the Jeffrey Masson brouhaha that Malcolm so entertainingly related, and he has continued to guard those documents against possible defilers of Freud's shrine. When Eissler ruled the Archives, moreover, he solicited gifts of documents for the Library of Congress but "redonated" them in the name of the Archives, thus affording himself the right to impose absurdly long periods of sequestration.[25] It is a pity that Blum feels he must put such shameful conduct under the rug in the interest of closing Freudian ranks against the "scurrilous" Crews.

But Blum also has some explaining of his own to do. On October 8, 1989, he told an interviewer:

> We recently released letters that were considered highly sensitive and that everyone was waiting to see, namely, the Freud–Anna Freud and the Freud–Minna Bernays correspondence. There have been wild speculations about Freud's having had an affair with Minna. That correspondence is available now to all, and they can draw their own conclusions. But no one has yet inferred from anything in the letters that there is any evidence of any impropriety.[26]

---

25. Eissler did, however, grant *echt* Freudians occasional selective access to some restricted papers. Such a policy can have had no other purpose than to perpetuate the Freud legend.

26. William Jeffrey, "A Conversation with Harold Blum," *The American Psychoanalyst*, Vol. 24, No. 3 (Fall 1990), p. 16.

The documents characterized here include the same Freud–Minna letters of 1893–1910 that Peter Gay declared missing when, having been told that they were ready for examination, he applied to see them in 1989. In fact, however, the letters were neither missing nor accessible. Rather, they were under restriction, and they still are. If Dr. Blum himself has lost track of them, he can find them (I am told) in Container Z3, whose contents are banned from view until the year 2000. Is it believable that Blum was unaware of that fact when he said the opposite in 1989?[27]

The Blum–Pacella letter is also noteworthy for the speed with which it performs an agile two-step that is attempted in some of the other letters as well: praising "the enduring discoveries of [Freud's] revolutionary genius" and assuring us that present-day psychoanalysis has left those same treasures safely behind where they will cause no further harm. Freud's propositions, say Blum and Pacella, "are no longer vital for the validation of psychoanalytic formulation." Well, what is the new basis of such validation? Quite simply, there is none at all that could impress an independent observer.

I have claimed above that psychoanalysts cannot seem to grasp the rudiments of scientific explanation. As if to illustrate the point, Drs. Blum and Pacella remind us that "Lady Macbeth washes her hands because of underlying guilt, not because her hands are literally dirty." The logic here is that since both Shakespeare and Freud touched on the same

---

27. Even the available Freud–Minna letters are not altogether unrestricted. Scholars who apply to examine them are given photocopies in which the names of Freud's patients have been deleted, thus causing needless uncertainty about identities which can hardly be considered sensitive after the lapse of a century or so.

phenomenon, guilt, Freud's structure of postulates about guilt is thereby validated. Yes, in just the way that the undeniable existence of stars demonstrates the propositions of astrology.

And then there is the sublimely fatuous clincher: "The vulgar idiom 'jerk off' conveys thinly disguised castration anxiety." Nowhere could one find a more perfect instance of Freudian question begging and dogmatic intellectual slumber. I would like to instruct the president of the American Psychoanalytic Association that something other than a penis comes off as a result of masturbation and that still another castration threat, Ockham's razor, could be usefully employed here. But will he even understand my criticism? Writing in these pages nearly twenty years ago, Peter Medawar called doctrinaire psychoanalytic theory "the most stupendous intellectual confidence trick of the twentieth century."[28] He could have added that like many another such instrument of deception, its first and most enduring dupes are its own practitioners.


JAMES L. RICE, Professor of Russian and Comparative Literatures at the University of Oregon, is the author of *Dostoevsky and the Healing Art* and *Freud's Russia: National Identity in the Evolution of Psychoanalysis.* He writes:

Frederick Crews includes an amiable critique of my book, *Freud's Russia*, in his essay on "The Unknown Freud." I would like to clarify some of the points raised. Freud's many

---

28. P. B. Medawar, "Victims of Psychiatry," *The New York Review*, January 23, 1975, p. 17.

kin now known to have resided in the Russian Empire were not in Lithuania, but chiefly in Odessa, where his mother spent part of her childhood. It was the paternal line that Freud traced to Lithuania, whence they began to emigrate in the eighteenth century. Some unknown relatives, I conjecture, must have remained behind, eventually to endure the worst official Russian anti-Semitism. In any case, family roots on both sides made Russian history and politics personally significant to Freud.

I would not characterize Freud, after 1917, as a "disillusioned revolutionary." He scoffed at the grandiose Bolshevik schemes as early as 1919, before the "Russian experiment" had even begun. Skepticism and irony toward political and religious authority were always hallmarks of his character. On the other hand, he never became a misanthrope, with malice toward the species. He had hope, even in the mid-Thirties, that the Jews would some day thrive under more enlightened conditions. And he believed that nutrition, pharmacology, and radical organic therapies could in time displace the imperfect art of psychoanalysis, to some degree.

Freud's ill-will toward Dostoevsky, such as it was, I do not describe as "gratuitous." The underlying factor, I believe, was Dostoevsky's late anti-Semitism, which had become known in the West in Freud's circle, though it was not well documented. On the other hand, Freud profoundly admired Dostoevsky's "great intellect" deployed against religious faith ("The Grand Inquisitor"). This indicates the essential rapport between them, and in turn raises the question of Freud's own Jewish identity, which had great strength on social and personal levels, but none in terms of conventional faith. These are some of the essential elements in Freud's labored "psycho-analysis" of Dostoevsky, but of course not the whole story.

I have no bone to pick with Freud for the lapses in his art. A number of drugs now used for depressive patients like Freud's may cause sudden suicide with no prior tendency. There is no evidence, I think, that Freud's psychoanalytic sessions caused fatalities. He made mistakes, but his therapy was a pioneering theory in an age with no medical options. Real suffering drove patients to seek his help. My own interest in Freud has less to do with his clinical methods than with the design and humor of his world view, and with his idiosyncratic constitution, recently summed up by a Harvard psychiatrist as "crafty and inventive" (George E. Vaillant, *The Wisdom of the Ego*). ✳

FREDERICK CREWS replies:
In denying that Freud was a "disillusioned revolutionary," James L. Rice makes it appear that I regard Freud as having once been an ardent fellow traveler of Bolshevism. Not at all. That phrase of mine appears in a paragraph that has nothing to do with the Russian Revolution. What I do say, later, is that although Freud "feared Russian extremism as strongly as he was drawn to it," he initially *looked to* the Soviet assault on the old order for a political equivalent of his own *scientific* revolutionism. It is Rice himself, in *Freud's Russia*, who writes of Freud's "revolutionary idealism, which lasted (with growing reservations) into the early years of the Stalin era" (p. 12). Again, Rice detects "some measure of optimism about 'the Russian experiment' on Freud's part, at the outset of Lenin's

137

rule" (p. 166). And he quotes Freud himself, in a 1930 letter to Arnold Zweig, to the effect that "any such hope [of human improvement in Russia] that I may have cherished has disappeared in this decade of Soviet rule" (p. 166).

I am sorry if I saddled Rice with my personal sense of Freud's lurking nihilism. *Freud's Russia* does show that Freud was drawn toward what he and others perceived as a "Russian" strain of nihilism, but more in the sense of a passion for destruction than of exasperation with the defective human race. Although there is plenty of evidence for this latter apprehension of Freud, Rice's disavowal of it should be noted.

Rice needn't have insisted, however, that he takes a more sanguine view of Freud's accomplishments than I do. I made the same point myself, referring to his and other authors' "mixed feelings about Freud's stature and the legitimacy of psychoanalytic claims." Rice uncovers the fanciful character of Freud's analyses in every examined instance, but, like many another humanist, he shrinks from facing the wholesale unfoundedness of psychoanalysis as a hermeneutic system. For Rice, Freud is still a great if eccentric discoverer whose *Interpretation of Dreams*, for example, deserves praise for its "insight into the structure and function of dreams" (p. 60)—even though Rice's own unraveling of the Wolf Man's dream specimen would seem to point in the opposite direction. My own view is that people who write confidently about "the structure and function of dreams" should first learn something about controlled research on the topic, which seriously undermines Freud's claims.

Rice wants us to remember that Freud felt empathy as well as dislike for Dostoevsky. Just how deeply Freud respected the novelist, however, seems more open to question than Rice acknowledges. Dostoevsky endowed some of his major characters with a high degree of conscious psychological reflection, thus anticipating some features of Freud's doctrine but suspending them, as Freud could not, in sophisticated fictive uncertainty and irony. Such a figure must have struck Freud above all as a rival who deserved the treatment he always reserved for his adversaries: reduction to a helpless example of his own pet notions about unconscious infantile compulsion.

Rice also feels compelled to point out that Freud's interventions never caused fatalities. Had I said that psychoanalysis is lethal? And is Rice really so complacent as to approve a therapy on the grounds that its patients remain alive? (Compare, above, the admission by the psychoanalysts Herbert Peyser and Marian Tolpin that Freud's errors "led to much improperly imposed suffering" and "were extremely harmful to some of his patients.") In contrasting Freud's method to perilous drug therapy, moreover, Rice shows an unawareness that Freud administered cocaine and morphine to his early hysterics, at once endangering their health and compromising any inferences he might otherwise have been able to draw about the efficacy of his "talking cure" alone.

ROBERT R. HOLT is Professor Emeritus of Psychology at New York University and the former director of the Research Center for Mental Health. He is the author of *Freud Reappraised.* He writes:

In answering the objectors to his "The Unknown Freud," Frederick Crews wrote: "To my knowledge, no modern analyst has renounced the cardinal Freudian investigative tool of 'free association,' which is inherently incapable of yielding knowledge about the determinants of dreams and symptoms." Not to my knowledge, either, and for good reason: because the alleged inherent incapability has not been demonstrated. Instead of attempting to do that, Crews simply refers us to Macmillan's *Freud Evaluated*, Chapter 15, which he calls "a devastating critique."

The burden of that chapter is easily summarized. Macmillan reaches the radical conclusion that there "can not be any guidelines to how these data [those of the free association method] should be interpreted" (p. 549) because "the absence of a second script prevents any rules from ever being formulated" (p. 564). That is, taking as inherent to the psychoanalytic method Freud's notion that for every manifest dream, there exists a latent dream the text (script) of which can be discovered, Macmillan makes the quite plausible argument that we have no way of ever directly accessing latent dreams. If that were the only possible way of devising guidelines for analyzing psychoanalytic data, then the conclusion—the inherent incapability of which Crews speaks—would indeed follow. But it is not, and hence Macmillan's case collapses.

About fifty years ago, when I was learning the art of diagnostic psychological testing,[1] I was confronted with the task of reaching valid conclusions about the persons studied in personality research and about psychiatric patients on the basis of their free verbal responses to such projective techniques as the Rorschach ink blots and the pictures of the Thematic Apperception Test (TAT). The problem with the resulting data was that they were much more like free associations than like the results of administering intelligence tests or personality questionnaires. My mentors, Henry A. Murray and David Rapaport, were at that time fully aware of the pitfalls of psychoanalytic interpretation, which make analysts disagree with one another to an alarming extent, and had discovered a way out. I have since tried to detail it and to show its basic similarity to scientific method.[2]

The starting point is the realization that neither free association, the TAT, or the Rorschach is a test—the sort of attempt to measure a specific aspect of personality or ability that we mean by that term. Hence, there is no single criterion, no independent measure of the same construct against which we can check the instrument we wish to validate. Instead, free association (and the projective techniques inspired by it) are sources of data, like interviewing or direct observation of

---

1. See D. Rapaport, M. M. Gill, and R. Schafer, *Diagnostic Psychological Testing*, originally published in 1945 and later revised by me (International Universities Press, 1968); and Henry A. Murray et al., *Thematic Apperception Test* (Harvard University Press, 1943).
2. R. R. Holt, *Assessing Personality* (Harcourt Brace Jovanovich, 1971); R. R. Holt, *Methods in Clinical Psychology: Assessment, Prediction and Research*, 2 volumes (Plenum, 1978).

behavior. Neither Crews nor Macmillan seems to have grasped this basic fact. But how should you work with such data? You can do so casually, irresponsibly, or in earnest ignorance of ways to do it with any control over manifold sources of error, as most psychoanalysts do. Or you can record your data objectively and analyze them in disciplined ways.

For that, you have to be clear on the difference between getting insights and checking them.[3] Alas, not only the practitioners of psychoanalysis but many of their critics seem unaware that every science has two phases, which make quite different cognitive demands: first you have to get hunches, insights, or hypotheses; and then you have to test them. In the former, creative phase, there are and can be no complete rules; but that is true in all sciences. Kekule got the hypothesis of the ring structure at the heart of organic molecules in a dreamlike reverie, but he realized that it was only a bright idea until it was checked against independent data. Not so easy, for at the time there did not exist the chemical equivalent of a "second script"—a direct method of seeing the carbon ring. So he had to draw inferences about what would happen in various chemical experiments if his surmise was correct or if other possible structures existed, and then check them out.

To work scientifically with psychoanalytic data, you have to make inferences from them (interpret them) and then *attempt to refute those inferences* by confronting them

---

3. Hans Reichenbach distinguished these phases as the context of discovery vs. the context of justification, e.g., in *The Rise of Scientific Philosophy* (University of California Press, 1951), p. 231; and Karl R. Popper used the terms conjectures vs. refutations, e.g., in *Conjectures and Refutations: The Growth of Scientific Knowledge* (Basic Books, 1962).

with additional, independent information. That is a great deal easier for clinical psychologists, who have at their disposal data from a variety of techniques of gathering relevant information, than it is for practicing psychoanalysts. It has been difficult for the latter to take seriously their plight: treating patients exposes them to extraordinarily rich data, but the nature of the situation restricts them to forming hypotheses for others to verify or refute. Moreover, scientific work on free associations requires that they be objectively recorded. Hence, Hartvig Dahl has for decades been attempting to persuade other psychoanalysts to join in assembling a library of tape-recorded psychoanalyses.[4] With the complete transcript in hand, one can get consensual judgments on the degree to which any particular segment of data are contaminated by suggestion. All that Grünbaum has done—*pace* Crews—is to make a strong a priori case that psychoanalytic data are thus contaminated; he has not proved that any particular set of free associations are useless as the basis of a given type of inference.[5] All scientific data are subject to contamination; that doesn't make science impossible, only difficult. Scientific methodology is the study of ways to reach useful and asymptotically valid conclusions on the basis of fallible data gathered by fallible human beings.

---

4. See, for examples, Hartvig Dahl, "A Quantitative Study of Psychoanalysis," *Psychoanalysis and Contemporary Science*, Vol. 1 (1972), pp. 237–257; and Dahl, Horst Kächele, and Helmut Thomä, editors, *Psychoanalytic Process Strategies* (Springer–Verlag, 1988).
5. See my critique of Grünbaum: "Some Reflections on Testing Psychoanalytic Hypotheses," *Behavioral and Brain Sciences*, Vol. 9 (1986), pp. 242–244.

Many critics of psychoanalysis (Crews and Macmillan are not the only ones) make the understandable error of believing that it is intrinsically impossible to do disciplined, responsible scientific work with free verbal data on aspects of psychoanalytic theory. Having devoted most of my career to learning how to do it and, with the aid of my colleagues at New York University's Research Center for Mental Health, carrying out a good deal of such research, I can testify that it is not easy, quick, or inexpensive; it is no longer fashionable or easy to fund; and the undertaking cannot be recommended to a young scientist eager to get ahead in an academic career —the payoff in publishable findings is too slow. Hence, the future of psychoanalysis as a science is hardly rosy; but neither is it merely a dream of self-deluded people.  ✳

MORRIS EAGLE, PH.D., is a professor at the Derner Institute of Advanced Psychological Studies, Adelphi University, President-Elect of the Division of Psychoanalysis, American Psychological Association, and the author of *Recent Developments in Psychoanalysis: A Critical Evaluation.* He writes:

There is one issue that, I believe, is the most substantively central one in evaluating psychoanalytic theory or any other theory that is not adequately addressed in Crews's original essay, in the letters responding to that essay, or in Crews's reply to these letters. That issue is the heuristic value of psychoanalytic theory.

In presenting his indictment of psychoanalysis as a pseudoscience, Crews appears to assume that psychoanalytic theory belongs to the psychoanalytic establishment and that its parochial practices are decisive for determining the status of the theory. But psychoanalytic theory belongs to the intellectual and scientific community and, as I will show, has had a significant heuristic impact on that community. He also assumes—and is able to do so because broadsides substitute for careful argumentation—that psychoanalysis is a monolithic entity. It is not. It consists of a somewhat heterogeneous body of propositions, formulations, assumptions, and hypotheses, some of which are foundational assumptions, some of which are indeed relatively immune to refutation, and some of which are eminently testable. For example, Freud's claim that the major part of mental life goes on outside of conscious awareness could be seen as a foundational assumption which, by the way, is shared by most contemporary cognitive scientists. Freud's ideas about life and death instincts can serve as a good example of a proposition relatively immune to empirical test. And as a final example, some of Freud's propositions regarding repression and the wish-fulfillment theory of dreams seem eminently testable. (It seems clear that sufficient evidence has accumulated to lead one to conclude that the claim that unconscious wishes represent an invariant component of dreams has been falsified.) But in order to make these distinctions, Crews would have to be more knowledgeable about and more interested in the details of psychoanalytic propositions than in other matters with which he is preoccupied.

A critical consideration in assessing the status of any theory is its heuristic value in generating research and further theory-building. This issue, far more important than any of the other matters taken up in his essay, Crews totally ignores. Let me provide merely one example: During the last number of years, an exciting and important body of research on "repressive style" and its correlates has appeared in scientific psychology journals and books.[1] This work indicates that people who are characterized as employing a repressive style are more likely to show, among other things, higher physiological arousal (including higher blood pressure and cardiac rates) during stress, are more susceptible to certain physical illnesses (e.g., hypertension), and show poorer immune responses. Most important in the present context, this work is clearly and explicitly generated by Freud's concept of repression. Furthermore, the research thus generated is likely to feed back and further operationalize and modify both the concept of repression and the hypotheses surrounding it. Crews does not appear to be aware of this kind of work. It certainly does not enter into his evaluation of psychoanalytic theory.

There may be and undoubtedly are other aspects of Freudian theory that have not been heuristic and, indeed, may be misleading and harmful. The task, then, for the intellectual and scientific community is to identify and either modify or reject these features of the theory. But such efforts are characterized by careful, discriminating, and detailed appraisals rather than wholesale condemnation or wholesale loyalties.

---

1. See P. J. David, "Repression and the Inaccessibility of Emotional Memories," in *Repression and Dissociation*, edited by J. L. Singer (University of Chicago Press, 1990), pp. 387–403; also G. E. Schwartz, "Psychobiology of Repression and Health: A Systems Approach," Singer, *Repression and Dissociation*, pp. 405–434; and D. A. Weinberger, "The Construct Validity of the Repressive Coping Style," Singer, *Repression and Dissociation*, pp. 337–386.

I would submit that in any serious evaluation of the status of psychoanalytic theory, the kind of heuristic impact I have briefly described is of far greater import and significance than the personal and admittedly juicier tidbits emphasized by Crews.  ✳

ALLEN ESTERSON graduated in physics from University College, London, in 1958 and has lectured in mathematics and physics. He is now an independent Freud researcher and is the author of *Seductive Mirage: An Exploration of the Work of Sigmund Freud*. He writes:

I would like to correct some misconceptions which occur in J. Schimek's response to Frederick Crews's article "The Unknown Freud." Schimek's findings contained in his 1987 paper "Fact and Fantasy in the Seduction Theory" were not "taken out of context and misused" in my book *Seductive Mirage*; nor did I "conclude from [his] arguments that Freud made up all the sexual material he got from his patients." I wrote the first draft of my account of the infantile seduction theory episode in 1984; as I state explicitly in my book, the chapter in question was written completely independently of Schimek's research. Hence I neither misused nor drew any conclusions from his paper, the existence of which I was unaware of until December 1988; the writings from which I drew conclusions were Freud's own. Schimek is also mistaken in supposing that it was on the basis of the seduction theory episode that I drew the conclusion that Freud made up all the sexual material he got from his patients. (I would prefer to say that, though he certainly resorted to invention on occasion, he inferred most of that material on grossly inadequate grounds and misleadingly presented it as his "findings of analytic research.") As my book demonstrates, the evidence for the dubious nature of almost all of Freud's supposed sexual findings can be found throughout his work.

In regard to the seduction theory episode, it is a pity that James Hopkins, like Schimek, did not take the trouble to actually read my chapter on the subject before making assumptions about its contents. Had he done so he would have found (p. 20) that it contains an implicit refutation of his claim that when Freud later wrote of his female patients reporting paternal seductions in the context of his "error" he was referring not to his self-proclaimed "source of the Nile" discovery put forward publicly in the seduction theory papers of 1896, but to an unpublished transitional notion he adopted privately a little later. As Crews writes, this latter notion was no more than a speculative theory for which Freud determinedly sought analytic corroboration. Hopkins expresses skepticism about the "alleged" contradictions and anomalies to which several scholars have now directed attention, implying that for the most part they result from misinterpretations of Freud's words. The anomalies are too numerous to cite here, but one example (the one Hopkins attempts to deal with) is the discrepancy between the original claim of the uncovering by analytic inference, in every one of his current cases (mostly women), of infantile sexual molestation by a variety of carefully listed and grouped assailants (but no fathers), and the belated (post-1924) claim that "almost all" of his female patients around that same period *reported* paternal childhood seductions. (The notion that the discrepancy can be accounted for by discretion on Freud's part is totally incompatible with the facts and is disposed of in my book [pp. 20–21]. It can also be seen that Hopkins's purported explanation would have been inadequate even had it not had an erroneous basis.) Then there is the curious fact that it was only for the period during which he held to the seduction theory that Freud claimed to have received such numerous reports from his female patients. Again, one wonders why Hopkins apparently is untroubled by Freud's claiming one hundred percent success (in uncovering repressed infantile sexual traumas) in 1896, an achievement unheard of in the annals of psychiatry in regard to the confirmation of any theory—and made even more remarkable by the fact that it was a theory he was to abandon within a short time!

It can scarcely be a coincidence that it was at precisely the time (1924–25) that Freud turned his mind to the detailed development of his theories of female sexuality that the phony story of reports from his early female patients of paternal seductions was first published, thereby underwriting the Oedipal theory. A corresponding only apparent coincidence occurs in relation to the belated (1925) psychoanalytic discovery that the first attachment of infant girls is to the mother (SE, 19:251). In his second paper on female sexuality (1931) Freud suddenly announced the "very common" occurrence of (analytically reconstructed) phantasies of maternal seductions in regard to his female patients (SE, 21:232). Within a short time the story had become that his female patients "regularly accuse" their mothers of seducing

149

them (SE, 21:238). The parallels with the seduction theory discrepancy discussed above are too obvious to labor the point, but they indicate that, far from that discrepancy being innocuous, as Schimek would have us believe, it is an early example of the fact (repeatedly demonstrated in my book) that Freud's reporting of his clinical experiences is not to be trusted.

May I conclude with a suggestion (proposed by Arthur Koestler in a rather different context) for those who, while not being zealots, still remain under the spell of Freud. They should be sentenced to a year's hard reading. Crews has supplied the initial booklist; in particular, anyone who has not read Macmillan's comprehensive critique *Freud Evaluated* has scarcely begun to take the measure of current scholarly criticism of the Freudian enterprise. And there is the promise of more volumes to come from two other scholars, Han Israëls in Holland and, in Sweden, Max Scharnberg, who has already published two volumes of his projected opus *The Non-Authentic Nature of Freud's Observations* (Acta Universitatis Upsaliensis, Uppsala Studies in Education, Uppsala, Sweden). ✳

FREDERICK CREWS replies:
In their long-standing concern to discriminate between the wheat and chaff in psychoanalytic theory, Robert R. Holt and Morris Eagle represent the highest standard of empirical responsibility to which the Freudian tradition can lay claim. It is telling, then, that neither of them appears capable of even addressing, much less confuting, the specific charges against

psychoanalysis levied in my essay and in my subsequent response to critics.

The issue dodged in Holt's letter is whether, as I claimed, free association is "inherently incapable of yielding knowledge about the *determinants* of dreams and symptoms" (italics added). Is there, even in principle, any trustworthy path of inference from a patient's verbal associations to the causes of a given dream or symptom? My contention, cited but then ignored by Holt, is that you can't get there from here. Let us review three well-established reasons why this is so.

In the first place, "free" associations aren't free at all, since they have been amply shown to lack the imperviousness to suggestibility that Freud rashly ascribed to them. Freudian therapists and patients come to share a causal outlook predetermining the kinds of factors that both parties will consider significant, and both the patient's verbal productions and the therapist's thematically pointed selection among them cannot escape being influenced by that bias. As Morris Eagle himself once put it, "suggestion and compliance, however subtle and complex, are critical factors in generating these supposedly confirming data," and thus "each therapist, whatever his or her theoretical persuasion, can reach the verdict that they constitute confirmations."[1]

Second, a patient's free associations point at best to current preoccupations that may or may not have begun before the dream or symptom that is to be explained. Even an

---

1. Morris N. Eagle, "The Epistemological Status of Recent Developments in Psychoanalytic Theory," in *Physics, Philosophy and Psychoanalysis: Essays in Honor of Adolf Grünbaum*, edited by R.S. Cohen and L. Laudan (D. Reidel, 1983), p. 39.

enduring preoccupation is by no means necessarily a pathogen. Only by invoking Freud's purported "logic of the unconscious" could one maintain the contrary, but that logic is precisely what stands in question here. Unfortunately, Freud "discovered" it by fiat and defended it, as his followers still do, merely by applying it interpretatively and treating the resultant speculations as corroborative findings. To my knowledge, the vast theoretical literature of psychoanalysis contains not a single cogent effort to show how a mere *theme* in a patient's contemporary mind can be certified as an early *determinant* of that patient's neurotic disposition.

And third, even if associations did point to potential causal factors, psychoanalysts would still face the obstacle of trying to decide which ones actually governed a particular dream or symptom. Freud himself acknowledged that some factors must be "suppressed by others because they are too weak, and they therefore do not affect the final result" (SE, 18:168). Moreover, Freud conceded, at the time of analysis there is no way of knowing which factor is dominant: "We only say at the end that those which succeeded must have been the stronger" (SE, 18:168). Thus psychoanalysts guess blindly at causes but later seek reassurance from the fact that a long concatenation of such hunches has yielded a self-consistent view of the patient's case. Yet if the method of drawing causal inferences from free associations is wild in each individual occurrence, it must also be wild in the aggregate.

These circumstances help to explain why psychoanalysts, as Holt reports, "disagree with one another to an alarming extent." Quite simply, they are winging it from start to finish. This is not just my judgment but, if one reads carefully,

Holt's as well. Freudian practitioners, he tells us, habitually neglect the crucial difference between forming hypotheses and adequately testing them, and the "hardly rosy" future of psychoanalysis as a science should be consigned to hands other than theirs.

Holt's proposed rescue operation, such as it is, entails the extraction of taped free associations as data that can be assessed (presumably by investigators of a Freudian bent, since no one else would be interested) for the degree to which those data are contaminated by suggestion. Two questions about this scheme immediately spring to mind. First, how could psychoanalytically trained researchers be expected to mark the limits of suggestion in any given case when, as critics have decisively shown, the whole process of analyst-patient interaction is steeped in indoctrinating effects? And second, how much impact could such studies have on what Holt calls the "earnest ignorance" of analysts in their daily therapeutic work?

I am afraid that Holt's invoking of methodological commonplaces from Hans Reichenbach and Karl Popper serves no purpose beyond a cosmetic "scientizing" one. More to the point is Popper's judgment of psychoanalysis as it is actually conducted: "those 'clinical observations' which analysts naively believe confirm their theory cannot do this any more than the daily confirmations which astrologers find in their practice."[2] Though Holt does not say so explicitly, it is apparent that he agrees with Popper in this regard.

---

2. Karl R. Popper, *Conjectures and Refutations: The Growth of Scientific Knowledge*, second edition (Basic Books, 1965), pp. 37–38.

Morris Eagle's letter can be answered more briefly, for it rests on a manifestly untenable premise. This is that "heuristic value," or stimulation to further insight, ought to be weighed more heavily than intrinsic plausibility in the scrutinizing of propositions about the mind. When, I wonder, did Eagle arrive at this quixotic means of safeguarding his favorite notions? I find no trace of it in any of his previous writings— including the most recent—that evaluate points of psychological doctrine.[3] Quite typical, for example, is a paper of 1983 where he denounces certain post-Freudian claims that "are either incoherent or without any evidential support."[4] According to his revised outlook, Eagle should instead have scolded people who fail to look beyond such narrow considerations as coherence and supporting evidence.

Psychoanalysis has indeed borne many heuristic consequences, but most of them have proved, to borrow Eagle's words, "misleading and harmful." Moreover, repression— Eagle's one example of a heuristically fruitful psychoanalytic idea—has been involved in every pernicious instance that could be named, from the supposed causes of homosexuality and female irrationality through false memory syndrome. One may doubt whether the alleged conceptual breakthrough of

3. See, e.g., Eagle's "Critical Notice: A. Grünbaum's 'The Foundations of Psychoanalysis: A Philosophical Critique,'" *Philosophy of Science*, Vol. 53 (1986), pp. 65–88; "Theoretical and Clinical Shifts in Psychoanalysis," *American Journal of Orthopsychiatry*, Vol. 57, pp. 175–185; *Recent Developments in Psychoanalysis: A Critical Evaluation* (Harvard University Press, 1987); and "The Dynamics of Theory Change in Psychoanalysis," in J. Earman et al., *Philosophical Problems of the Internal and External Worlds: Essays on the Philosophy of Adolf Grünbaum* (University of Pittsburgh Press, 1993), pp. 373–408.
4. Eagle, "Epistemological Status," p. 49.

"repressive style" is adequate recompense for all the inconvenience, anguish, and confusion wrought by Freud's theory of repression. And even if it were, repression would still have to stand or fall on its own empirical merits, not on its having contributed an adjective to the name of a cluster of behaviors. As Eagle well knows, but now chooses to forget, the identifying of an authentic psychological "style" does not thereby validate any given explanation of how that style gets developmentally formed.

Finally, Eagle is mistaken in saying that I overlook the heterogeneity of psychoanalytic propositions. They are so heterogeneous, I have argued, as to constitute a self-condemning jumble of dubious and incompatible claims. I am concerned to explore the laxity of method that makes such chaos inevitable. So, too, is Allen Esterson, whose *Seductive Mirage* can be recommended to all readers who have sensed that Freud's "scientific greatness" is now ripe for thoroughgoing reappraisal.

# THE REVENGE OF THE REPRESSED

PART ONE

## I.

Throughout the past decade or so, a shock wave has been sweeping across North American psychotherapy, and in the process causing major repercussions within our families, courts, and hospitals. A single diagnosis for miscellaneous complaints —that of unconsciously repressed sexual abuse in childhood — has grown in this brief span from virtual nonexistence to epidemic frequency. As Mark Pendergrast shows in his recently published *Victims of Memory*, if we put together the number of licensed American psychotherapists (roughly 255,000) with survey results about their beliefs and practices, it appears that well over 50,000 of them are now willing to help their clients realize that they must have endured early molestation.[1] Those professionals have been joined by countless untrained operators

---

1. Pendergrast, *Victims of Memory: Incest Accusations and Shattered Lives* (Upper Access, 1995), pp. 357–358.

who use the yellow pages and flea market ads to solicit "incest work." It is hard to form even a rough idea of the number of persuaded clients, because most of them take no publicly recorded action against the accused, but a conservative guess would be a million persons since 1988 alone (see Pendergrast, p. 358). The number *affected* is of course vastly higher, since, as all parties acknowledge, virtually every case sows dissension and sorrow throughout a family.

When one explanation for mental distress rockets to prominence so quickly, we ought to ask whether we are looking at a medical breakthrough or a fad. However, the choice between those alternatives is not always simple. As its main proponents insist, "recovered memory" is by now not just a diagnosis but a formidable sociopolitical movement. In the words of one of that movement's founders, the Harvard psychiatrist Judith Lewis Herman,

> The study of trauma in sexual and domestic life becomes legitimate only in a context that challenges the subordination of women and children. Advances in the field occur only when they are supported by a political movement powerful enough to legitimate an alliance between investigators and patients and to counteract the ordinary social processes of silencing and denial.

The larger movement in question is, of course, women's liberation, including what Herman calls "a collective feminist project of reinventing the basic concepts of normal development and abnormal psychology . . ."[2]

---

2. Herman, *Trauma and Recovery* (Basic Books, 1992), pp. 9, ix.

However uneasy one may feel about an ideologically driven "reinvention" of scientific notions, it is possible that the feminist critique of received psychological lore is substantially right. Feminists were certainly warranted, in the 1970s and 1980s, in declaring that the sexual abuse of children was being scandalously underreported. If they now go on to claim that untold millions of victims, mostly female, have *forgotten* what was done to them, their claim cannot be discredited by the mere fact that it sprang from an activist commitment. Obviously, it needs to be assessed on independent grounds.

Yet such grounds are hard to come by. How can one count authentic cases of repressed memory when the very concept of repression stands in doubt? And what, for that matter, do the champions of recovered memory mean by repression? It is fruitless to press them very hard on this point, since most of them show an impatience with or outright ignorance of conceptual subtleties. Thus in the movement's most influential document, *The Courage to Heal*, first published in 1988, Ellen Bass and Laura Davis proclaim that "none of what is presented here is based on psychological theories."[3] Instead, Bass and Davis appeal directly to "the experiences of survivors"—who, however, may or may not *be* survivors of abuse, depending on whether they have actually learned the previously repressed truth or succumbed to therapeutically induced delusion.

Although it is no secret that the idea of repression

3. Bass and Davis, *The Courage to Heal: A Guide for Women Survivors of Child Sexual Abuse* (1988; third edition, Harper Perennial, 1994), p. 18.

derives from Sigmund Freud, few of the movement's practitioners have actually studied his texts. Consequently, they are unrestrained by certain ambiguities and outright contradictions implicit in the Freudian theory of repression.[4] Freud's uncertainty, for example, whether *events* or *fantasies* make up the typical content of the repressed gets resolved in favor of events; as Herman puts it in the opening sentence of *Trauma and Recovery*, "the ordinary response to atrocities is to banish them from consciousness." Again, whereas Freud confusingly treated repression as both a conscious and an unconscious mechanism, his activist successors think of it as strictly unconscious—so much so, indeed, that they can routinely regard a young incest victim as leading two parallel but wholly independent lives, one in the warm daylight of normal family affection and the other in continually repressed horror. And while Freud only occasionally portrayed the dissolving of repression as yielding undisguised, accurate information about a patient's early past, contemporary "retrievers" entertain no doubts on the point; with the right coaxing, their patients can allegedly reproduce the exact details of their long-repressed traumas.

---

4. On this point, see Matthew H. Erdelyi, "Repression, Reconstruction, and Defense: History and Integration of the Psychoanalytic and Experimental Frameworks," in *Repression and Dissociation: Implications for Personality Theory, Psychopathology, and Health*, edited by Jerome L. Singer (University of Chicago Press, 1990), pp. 1–32. Remarkably, Erdelyi welcomes Freud's unclarity as providing a sound basis for integrating the "dynamic" with the cognitive unconscious. The idea is that since Freud didn't really know what he meant by repression, we are free to bring the concept into alignment with current research while still thinking of ourselves as Freudians.

By today, recovered memory has enlisted the enthusiasm of many psychotherapists who lack the explicit feminist agenda of Herman, Bass and Davis, and other advocates whose views we will examine later. But all parties do share the core tenet of repression—namely, that the mind can shield itself from ugly experiences, thoughts, or feelings by relegating them to a special "timeless" region where they indefinitely retain a symptom-producing virulence. Clinical experience, the therapists agree, has proven the cogency of this tenet in numberless successfully resolved cases.

But has it, really? When arbitrary assumptions leak into "clinical experience," confirming results can be pumped out as easily as bilge water. That is why research psychologists would insist that the concept of repression be required to pass tests in which variables are controlled and rival explanations for the gathered data are weighed. Yet while psychoanalytic loyalists have repeatedly attempted to conduct just such experiments, their positive results have at best shown a compatibility with repression, not a demonstration of its existence. As David S. Holmes recently concluded after reviewing a sixty-year history of such efforts, "there is no controlled laboratory evidence supporting the concept of repression."[5]

Of course, repression cannot be experimentally disproved, either. Since the concept entails no agreed-upon behavioral markers, we are free to posit its operation whenever we please—just as we are free to invoke orgone energy or

---

5. David S. Holmes, "The Evidence for Repression: An Examination of Sixty Years of Research," in Singer, *Repression and Dissociation*, pp. 85–102; the quotation is from p. 96.

chakras or the life force. Indeed, as Elizabeth Loftus and Katherine Ketcham remark in their lively new book, *The Myth of Repressed Memory*, belief in repression has the same standing as belief in God.[6] The idea may be true, but it is consistent with too many eventualities to be falsifiable — that is, amenable to scientific assessment.

It *is* possible, however, to mount experimental challenges to corollary tenets that are crucial to recovered memory therapy. That is just what Loftus, a highly regarded researcher and a professor of psychology at the University of Washington, has done in her own experimental work—and that is also why she has been pilloried by the recovered memory movement as an enemy of incest survivors. *The Myth of Repressed Memory* recounts some of that vilification and tries to head off more of it by taking a conciliatory tone wherever possible. But there is simply nothing to negotiate over. The burden of Loftus's argument is that memory does not function in anything like the way that writers such as Bass and Davis presuppose.

Thus, Loftus offers no encouragement to the retrievers' notion that "videotaped" records of events are stored in a special part of the brain and then suddenly yielded up to near-perfect recall. Empirical science, she reports, has established that memory is inherently sketchy, reconstructive, and unlocalizable. Whether pleasant or unpleasant, it decays drastically over time, though less so if the experience in question gets periodically "rehearsed" —just the opposite of what

---

6. Loftus and Ketcham, *The Myth of Repressed Memory: False Memories and Allegations of Sexual Abuse* (St. Martin's, 1994), p. 64.

the retrievers' theory would predict. Furthermore, memory is easily corrupted, if not with an experimenter's deliberate intervention or a therapist's unwitting one, then with a normal "retrospective bias" that accommodates one's sense of the past to one's present values. Flashbacks to an early age, then, are highly unreliable sources of information about any event. All in all, Loftus finds no basis for thinking that repression, as opposed to a gradual avoidance and atrophy of painful recollections, has figured in a single molestation case to date.

Once we have recognized that a memory can disappear because of factors other than repression, even the best anecdotal evidence for that mechanism loses its punch. Consider, for example, the closely watched case of Ross Cheit, a Brown University professor who has recently proved beyond question that his suddenly recalled 1968 molestation by a music camp administrator was real.[7] But had that abuse been repressed in the first place? In a phone conversation with me on September 7, 1994, Cheit declared that while he takes no position on the existence of repression, he is inclined to doubt that he abruptly and completely consigned his experience to oblivion. What Cheit does fervently believe is that this *forgotten* ordeal, and not any others that he may have remembered or some further unspecified factor, is responsible for anguish that he experienced many years later as an adult. But that belief is only a

---

7. *Later:* A full and sympathetic account of Cheit's experience, based on interviews with him, can be found in Mike Stanton's two-part article, "Bearing Witness: A Man's Recovery of His Sexual Abuse as a Child," *Providence Journal–Bulletin*, May 7 and 9, 1995, pp. 1A and following. See also Miriam Horn, "Memories Lost and Found," *U.S. News & World Report*, November 29, 1993, pp. 52–63.

supposition. The possibility—indeed, the likelihood—that Cheit lost track of the incident at issue through an ordinary process of atrophy renders the example of his restored memory useless as a proof of repression.[8]

Useless, that is, from the standpoint of logic. For another purpose, that of inducing popular belief in the theory of repression, anecdotes can be powerfully effective. The very idea of repression and its unraveling is an embryonic romance about a hidden mystery, an arduous journey, and a gratifyingly neat denouement that can ascribe our otherwise drab shortcomings and pains to deep necessity. When that romance is fleshed out by a gifted storyteller who also bears impressive credentials as an expert on the mind, most readers in our culture will be disinclined to put up intellectual resistance.

One such narrator, of course, was Freud, whose shifting views about the content of the repressed will prove pivotal to an understanding of the recovered memory movement's intellectual ancestry. But Freud's stories purportedly explaining tics, obsessions, and inhibitions among the turn-of-the-century Austrian bourgeoisie are beginning to seem not just remote but eccentric. Not so the case histories recounted by the memory retrievers' most distinguished and fluent ally, Lenore Terr,

---

8. *Later:* This paragraph has been rewritten to exclude an error pointed out to me by Professor Cheit. Originally, I had speculated that perhaps "the adult Cheit *refocused* his faded but unrepressed experiences after he had read a book about pedophilia (as he did) and became morally exercised about it." At the urging of his psychotherapist, Cheit did read that book, Mic Hunter's *Abused Boys: Neglected Victims of Sexual Abuse* (Lexington Books, 1990). But since the reading occurred *after* Cheit's memory had returned, my speculation was off the mark.

who is not only a practicing therapist but also a professor of psychiatry at the University of California at San Francisco. Terr's deftly written book, *Unchained Memories: True Stories of Traumatic Memories, Lost and Found,*[9] has already been welcomed both by the Book of the Month Club and by reviewers who perceived it as a balanced and learned brief for repression.

The publication of *Unchained Memories* has been especially cheering to recovered memory advocates because Terr is not afraid to challenge their *bête noire*, Elizabeth Loftus. "[P]sychological experiments on university students," Terr writes, taking dead aim at Loftus's work,

> do not duplicate in any way the clinician's observations. What comes from the memory lab does not apply well to the perceptions, storage, and retrieval of such things as childhood murders, rapes, or kidnappings. Trauma sets up new rules for memory. (Terr, pp. 51–52)

From Loftus's vantage, of course, such a passage begs the question of how these new rules are to be validated without succumbing to the notorious circularity of "clinical experience." Isn't Terr simply handing herself a conceptual blank check? Nevertheless, she scores a strong rhetorical point with her animadversion against hothouse science. If Terr is right about the special character of real-world trauma, we may have to fall back on sheer stories after all.

---

9. Basic Books, 1994.

# 2.

Among Terr's own stories, none carries more weight than the George Franklin/Eileen Lipsker case, which occupies the first two chapters of her book. The case, in which Terr herself served as an expert witness "to explain," as she says, "'repression' and 'the return of the repressed'" (Terr, p. 30), came to national attention in 1989 with newspaper and television reports of Eileen Franklin Lipsker's long-buried but amazingly lucid recollection of the way her father, in her terrified presence in 1969, had raped her eight-year-old best friend in the back of his Volkswagen bus and then shattered the girl's skull with a rock and covered the body on a wooded hillside south of San Francisco. In Terr's rendering, this story has about it a ring of unanswerable truth, backed up by the soberest of corroborators, a jury in a murder trial.

But Terr's account is not the only one available. It was preceded by Harry N. MacLean's scrupulous book-length retelling of the murder story, *Once Upon a Time*, and now it has been scrutinized by MacLean himself, by Elizabeth Loftus and Katherine Ketcham in *The Myth of Repressed Memory*, and by Richard Ofshe, professor of sociology at the University of California, Berkeley, and Ethan Watters in their even more trenchant book, *Making Monsters*.[10] In view of their findings, the Franklin matter may come to serve as a very different object lesson from the one that Terr intended. If so, a man's

---

10. See MacLean's *Once Upon a Time: A True Story of Memory, Murder, and the Law* (HarperCollins, 1993), and Ofshe and Watters, *Making Monsters: False Memories, Psychotherapy, and Sexual Hysteria* (Scribners, 1994). See also MacLean's critique of Terr in the September 1994 *False Memory Syndrome Foundation Newsletter* (Philadelphia, PA).

freedom hangs in the balance —not a good man, surely, but a man who may have been wrongly convicted.

During the 1990 murder trial in Redwood City, California, it turned out that no concrete evidence implicated Franklin in Susan Nason's death. On the contrary, Franklin's junked van from 1969, located and microscopically studied by police investigators, bore no trace of the twenty-year-old crime (Terr, p. 23). Until a recollection on the part of Eileen's vindictive sister Janice was conveniently revised under therapy, Franklin had a solid alibi for his whereabouts at the time of the abduction (Ofshe and Watters, p. 259). The jury, however, determined with little difficulty that Eileen Lipsker's recovered memory too closely matched the known facts of the unsolved murder to be considered specious. As a result, Franklin is now serving a life sentence in state prison, and the theory of recovered memory has acquired an imposing trophy.[11]

Lenore Terr appears to have assumed from the outset that Franklin was guilty as charged, and she was eager to make herself useful to the prosecution. Awkwardly, however, her research interest in actual cases of repressed memory was quite new (see Terr, p. 30; Ofshe and Watters, p. 264); it seems to have postdated the writing of her 1990 book, *Too Scared to Cry*, which contains no index entry for "repression" and which reports on cases of continuously remembered rather than

---

11. *Later:* On April 3, 1995, U.S. District Judge D. Lowell Jensen reversed George Franklin's conviction, citing several improprieties in the trial and noting that the reliability of recovered memories such as Eileen Lipsker's has not been scientifically established. On June 19, 1995, Judge Jensen set Franklin's bail at $1 million, thus ensuring that he will remain imprisoned while awaiting a retrial.

forgotten trauma.[12] Terr's expertise on sudden recall, more-over, dated from her first interview with Eileen Lipsker her-self—and was then swelled by a flood of highly dubious anec-dotes about other women's therapeutically prompted visions of incest. But Terr is a thoroughly trained Freudian, and as such she felt qualified, after all, to offer the Franklin jury what she calls "an education" in the reality of repressed memory and its retrieval (Terr, p. 40). Coordinating strategy with the pros-ecutor and tailoring her testimony, as she now relates (pp. 38–40), to the job of rendering Eileen Lipsker a wholly cred-ible witness, Terr exceeded the expectations of her temporary employers.

Of course, Terr testified, an expert such as herself can verify the authenticity of a recovered memory through careful interpretation of the subject's symptoms. In some cases, she continued, the expert can even reliably infer the nature of an *unknown* trauma. Indeed, she herself had recently done exactly that, deducing from Stephen King's novels and films the cer-tain knowledge that in his childhood King had watched a playmate die under the wheels of a railroad train.

As Terr now recounts, she mentioned that feat of detec-tion in order to create a helpful analogy in the jurors' minds.[13] She hoped they would see that, like Stephen King in his violence-ridden fiction, Eileen Franklin, for five years after the

---

12. Terr, *Too Scared to Cry: Psychic Trauma in Childhood* (Basic Books, 1992).
13. Whether Terr had actually detected anything is open to doubt. The upset-ting death of King's boyhood friend was already familiar to her from King's autobiography—where, however, King reports that, so far as he knows, he did not witness the accident in question. Thus Terr's courtroom example of trustworthy clinical reasoning—proceeding from obsessive themes in King's

murder, had symptomatically acted out the awful scene that she had observed but almost immediately repressed. According to prosecutors, between the ages of nine and fourteen Eileen had continually pulled out all the hair from one segment of her crown, leaving what Terr calls "a big, bleeding bald spot" (Terr, p. 35). That spot uncannily corresponded to the part of Susan Nason's head that had allegedly been smashed by George Franklin. Eileen, then, had apparently turned herself into a living hieroglyph of a crime that Terr could have inferred all by herself, simply by translating the language of Eileen's symptomatic behavior into its mnemonic source within her repressed unconscious.

In an ordinary trial, caught up in claims and counter-claims about the purport of submitted evidence, the mesmerizing quality of Terr's self-depiction as a Freudian Sherlock Holmes could scarcely have assumed much importance. But this was no ordinary trial. Factually impoverished, it came down to little more than a twelve-person referendum on the photographic return of the repressed. According to the later word of several jurors, and to Terr's great present satisfaction, her testimony was decisive in obtaining George Franklin's conviction.

What most impressed both Terr and the jury about Eileen Lipsker's recovered memory was its extraordinary vividness and precision. The brands of beer and cigarettes consumed

---

eventual artistic productions to a "repressed" fact about one early day in his life—actually dealt with a *still uncorroborated* detail superadded to a story in the public domain. Insofar, then, as the Franklin trial hinged on Terr's testimony about Stephen King, it appears that one no-evidence case was decided on the basis of another.

by George Franklin at the murder scene; Susan Nason's raising her right hand to ward off the fatal blow; the glint of the sun in her clear blue eyes as George brought the rock down on her head; "a crushed, stoneless, silver child's ring" (Terr, p. 4) on the now lifeless hand—all of these details and more were as fresh to Eileen in 1989, Terr says, as they had allegedly been twenty years before. How, then, could they not be authentic and conclusively damning?

One answer to that question was provided at the trial by none other than Elizabeth Loftus herself, an expert witness on the other side. Tests on thousands of subjects have shown conclusively, Loftus told the court, not only that memory always fades with the passage of time but that it readily incorporates "post-event information" (whether true or false) that becomes indistinguishable from the actual event (Loftus and Ketcham, p. 62). Those two facts together suggest that the sharpness of Eileen Lipsker's "memory" must have been caused by recent images—and, as we will see, there was no shortage of such potential contaminants at hand.[14]

With coaching from Terr, however, the prosecution was ready to remove the sting from Loftus's reported findings. Did any of her experiments, she was asked in cross-examination, deal with memories that were two decades old? Wasn't it the case that her experimentally induced distortions of memory

14. Eileen Lipsker's problems with memory are echoed by Terr's own in her capacity as storyteller. Eileen never testified about seeing what Terr calls "white socks and white child-size underwear" in the rape scene, but only something white. And Terr, bent upon condemning George Franklin as a rapist, has lately supplied the useful "fact," which is false, that semen was found in the dead Susan Nason's vagina (MacLean, *FMS Newsletter*).

affected only some details and not loss of the brute fact that an event had occurred? And had she ever studied a repressed memory? No, she hadn't, for two excellent reasons: she wasn't sure that such memories exist, and even if they do, she couldn't imagine how one could get at them for controlled study.

Regrettably, however, this answer occurred to Loftus after she had left the stand. What she replied instead was that post-event information would probably corrupt a repressed memory in just the way that it assuredly corrupts a non-repressed one. The concept of repression was thus left unchallenged, and the befuddled jury had no recourse but to side with the rival expert witness—the one who boasted intimacy with the dark and subtle workings of the unconscious.

But Lenore Terr first needed to tiptoe across a theoretical minefield of her own. Her studies of children who had lived through the notorious Chowchilla bus kidnapping and the *Challenger* explosion had shown unambiguously that such experiences do not get repressed. Why, then, should the jury believe that Eileen Lipsker had repressed her harrowing ordeal? Just in time for the trial, but too late for prior publication, Terr came up with a face-saving theory.[15] True, she granted, one-time trauma victims always remember the event; but victims of multiple trauma like Eileen Lipsker, whose father had been a bullying drunk and a sexual abuser of two of his other daughters, turn repression into a daily routine. By the time of the murder, according to Terr, Eileen had become an old hand at stuffing bad memories into the mental freezer.

---

15. See Terr, "Childhood Traumas: An Outline and Overview," *American Journal of Psychiatry*, Vol. 148 (1991), pp. 10–20.

Terr's brainstorm was remarkable in several respects. For one thing, it overlooked the fact, later acknowledged in *Unchained Memories*, that Eileen had always remembered her father's violence around the house (Terr, p. 11). Second, it contradicted universal human experience of protracted duress. Has anyone past the age of, say, six who has survived racial persecution, a famine, a bombing campaign, or a brutal enemy occupation ever forgotten that it occurred? Terr had evidently confused the normal fading of *individual instances* of repeated, patterned mistreatment with willed unawareness of that mistreatment. And third, Terr was refusing to grant any distinction in memorability between George Franklin's usual brutality and the witnessed rape and murder of Eileen's best girlhood friend.

Beyond the already mentioned dubieties in Terr's version of the Franklin case lie a good number of others emphasized by MacLean, Loftus and Ketcham, and Ofshe and Watters, and more briefly by Mark Pendergrast in his *Victims of Memory* as well. The cardinal point is that Eileen Lipsker's certainty that she had attended the murder of Susan Nason did not overwhelm her in a single unprompted flash on what Terr calls "a quiet winter afternoon in 1989" (Terr, p. 3). That was the least plausible of five distinct stories that Lipsker kept changing to forestall objections. As the trial record shows, Lipsker, whom Terr characterizes as having known "nothing at all" about repression (Terr, pp. 3–4), had already been consulting two therapists who were helping her probe her childhood "memories" and her conscious, long-standing suspicions about the murder. Both practitioners employed the theory of repression and had discussed it with her. Moreover, Eileen was aided in producing increasingly bizarre visions of George Franklin committing another murder—this one not just unsolved but completely unknown to police or anyone else—with herself as a witness (MacLean, *Once Upon a Time*, pp. 244–247) and of his raping or otherwise sexually abusing her, sometimes in the presence of oblivious family members, from the ages of three through fourteen. She even came to believe that George had physically assisted her godfather in raping her. Incredibly, though, none of these barbarities had left a glint of long-term memory in her conscious mind.[16]

Terr omits any mention of George's second "murder" committed in Eileen's presence, but she does cite the equally implausible memories of witnessed incest scenes. In doing so, however, she offers no clue that all this knowledge emanated from a regimen of therapeutic dowsing and that some of it *preceded* the original murder flashback. This latter fact is important because Eileen's newly formed belief that she had spent her childhood being molested provided her with an extra motive for wanting to see George imprisoned. Terr as author is no more interested in dwelling on such motives than the prosecution was. She uses Eileen's sexual "memories" only

---

16. Indeed, as Terr reports, so unaware was Eileen that her subsequently divorced father had been raping her that she went off to live with him for a while at age fourteen, right after the alleged eleven years of violation had ended (Terr, p. 36). Later, the two of them drove across the country together to Florida, employing the back of the VW van, the supposed site of Susan Nason's rape, as their joint sleeping quarters. For Eileen's nineteenth birthday celebration, she took a similar trip with George to Ensenada in the same vehicle. How strange that "the repressed" produced no symptoms or qualms to warn her against taking those risks with the rapist-murderer!

in the partisan and highly effective way that they were used in the trial, to establish that a beast like George was just the sort of person who could have raped Susan Nason and then bludgeoned her to death.

The fact that memory therapy lay at the very heart of the Franklin case was manifested in little-noted testimony from one of Eileen's therapists, Kirk Barrett. According to Barrett, as Ofshe and Watters report,

> Eileen's memories "developed" over the course of the therapy sessions and often during the encounter itself. With the relaxation exercises and the free-association techniques, these memories often became more detailed during their hour-and-a-half meetings....
>
> Barrett remembers that from June [1989], when she initially visualized the first element of what was to become the crime scene, through July, Eileen worked both in and out of the sessions trying to sort out the meaning of her feelings, visualizations, and memories. He assured Eileen at the time that it "wasn't important... whether her visualizations were real or not," and that they could "sort that out later." In and out of therapy the details slowly cohered into a narrative. One day she came in and reported to Barrett that she had seen a flash image of someone hitting Susan with a rock — *but that she couldn't make out who the person was.* According to Barrett it was several sessions later, in a highly emotional moment, that Eileen revealed that she was finally able to see the face of the man who killed [Susan]. It was her father's. (Ofshe and Watters, p. 257)

Eileen Lipsker originally told her brother that the murder scene had revealed itself to her *in hypnosis* during her therapy. Later, she told a sister that she had *dreamed* the crucial knowledge—an equally suggestive fact, since recovered memory therapy often employs either hypnosis or dream analysis or both. Lenore Terr wants us to regard these statements as forgivable "lies" and to put our trust in the more enchanting image of Eileen's single flashback to the murder scene. It makes a good deal more sense to suppose that Eileen only belatedly learned that evidence from hypnosis had recently been deemed inadmissible in California courts (MacLean, *Once Upon a Time*, pp. 156–157).

Kirk Barrett's neglected testimony does exculpate Eileen Lipsker in one respect: she had sincerely come to believe that her father was the murderer. Once committed to having him put away, however, she allowed her "memories" to evolve as expediency required, picking up new details and dropping others as newspaper reports disclosed the content of old police records. As Ofshe and Watters remark, virtually the only correct details in her original report were "that Susan had been killed with a rock and that her ring had been crushed—facts that she had told Barrett she had known all her life."[17]

---

17. Ofshe and Watters, p. 258. Intriguingly, one of the tiny errors that survived in Eileen's testimony, having to do with a confusion between two rings on Susan Nason's hands, corresponded exactly to a mistake made in a newspaper story in 1969. That could only mean that Eileen's "memories" were tainted by misinformation that she had either heard or, more probably, read in old clippings or on microfilm. Quixotically, however, the judge ruled all journalism from the murder period inadmissible—as if the only possible question to settle were whether Eileen was revealing the sheer truth or telling lies, instead perhaps of unknowingly

There remains, however, the one striking detail that captivated both the jurors and, I am sure, the early readers of Terr's book: the bleeding bald spot that was said to have marred Eileen Franklin's pate for five straight years after the murder. Quite simply, it turns out to be a figment of Eileen's adult imagination. As Ofshe and Watters discovered, more than forty photographs of her in the relevant period—potential exhibits that the prosecution wrongly withheld from the defense—show no trace of missing hair. Eileen's mother, Leah, who has changed her mind about George's guilt after finding the narrative in *Unchained Memories* so erroneous, has told Ofshe and Watters that she couldn't have failed to notice any such disfiguration if it had occurred even once. An older and a younger sister have also refuted this claim. If, as Terr believes, every symptom tells a story, in this instance the story is a fairy tale.

Once understood in its true lineaments, the Franklin/Lipsker matter turns out to be highly typical of other recovered memory cases. There is, in the first place, the eerily dreamlike quality of the "memories" themselves, whose floating perspective, blow-up details, and motivational anomalies point to the contribution of fantasy.[18] There is the therapist's

---

recycling second-hand lore. Such bits of truth and error were available to her at all times, thanks to the fact that within her family George Franklin had always been considered a suspect in the Nason murder.

18. As for anomalies, why did George Franklin take his daughter along to watch the rape and murder of her dearest friend? How could he not have expected to be found out? Why would he then make Eileen witness another killing? Why did no one in a crowded living room notice George inserting his finger in Eileen's vagina? Etc.

reckless encouragement of the client to indulge her visions and worry "later" —usually never—whether or not they are true, along with his "supportive" absence of concern to check the emerging allegations against available knowledge. There is the interpretation of the "survivor's" moral frailties as further evidence that she is a "trauma victim."[19] There is also, we can infer, the therapist's false promise that excavation of the repressed past will lead to psychic mending instead of to the actual, nearly inevitable, result—disorientation, panic, vengefulness, and the severing of family ties. And there is the flouting or overlooking of what is scientifically known about memory, leaving the field free for dubious theories exfoliating from the original dogma of repression.

One remaining feature of the Lipsker case turns out to be reproduced in nearly every controversy over therapeutically assisted recall. The Franklin jury members, like many people who must weigh the credibility of "survivors," felt that they had to accept Eileen's story because she stood to gain nothing and lose everything by accusing her own father of murder. Of course, that was an oversimplification; Eileen felt that the pedophile George was a threat to her own child, and besides,

---

19. As Loftus and Ketcham say, "With that diagnosis all the quirks and idiosyncrasies of Eileen Franklin's personality could be explained away. Yes, she lied about being hypnotized... but that's understandable because she is a trauma victim. Yes, she used drugs and was arrested for prostitution... but her behavior makes sense given that she is a trauma victim. Yes, she repressed the memory for twenty years... but that's a defensive reaction common to trauma victims. Anything the defense might say in an attempt to undermine Eileen's credibility as a witness could be turned around and presented as an ongoing symptom..." (pp. 61–62).

as many observers perceived, she had a distinct taste for fame.[20] In a deeper sense, however, the jury was right: Eileen had opened a Pandora's box of bitterness and recrimination that will probably trouble her for the rest of her life. Nevertheless, the cardinal point about all this self-destructiveness went completely unnoticed. Eileen Lipsker did not *decide* to send her mind into a tailspin after making rational calculations about the opposing claims of justice and filial loyalty; she was progressively *encouraged* to do so by therapists who believed that full psychic health must wait upon a vomiting up of the repressed past.

Disastrously missed at the trial, this cardinal fact slipped away once again on a subsequent Faith Daniels talk show where, for the first time, Eileen Lipsker and Elizabeth Loftus sat down together. "Why would you want to suffer if you didn't have to?" asked one member of the audience who, like nearly all the others, believed Eileen's story and considered Loftus a heartless crank. "Why would you want to put yourself through it? There's no logic behind it" (Loftus and Ketcham, p. 71). As Loftus now tells us in her book, she smiled stoically as the audience continued to berate her and rally to Lipsker's cause. And then the program was over.

Reading about this episode, one experiences an extreme frustration. Couldn't Loftus have pointed out that other

---

20. Lipsker quickly become a heroine in psychotherapeutic circles, appeared on *Sixty Minutes*, collaborated on an as-told-to book, and found herself flatteringly portrayed by Shelley Long in a made-for-TV movie about the case. Her book and movie contracts, negotiated by a Hollywood entertainment lawyer, were signed before the case had gone to trial.

parties besides Eileen had "put her through it"? That, however, was four years ago, when no one yet had an explanatory handle on the burgeoning plague that still besieges us. Now at last, thanks to the inquiries of Loftus and others, it is starting to make an eerie kind of sense.

## 3.

The Franklin/Lipsker case, so attractive to Lenore Terr as Exhibit A of validated repression, actually shows how a "memory" originating in conscious hunches and resentments can be crystallized by protracted therapeutic *suggestion*, or the subliminal contagion of ideas between a dominant and a subordinate party. That is what we regularly find when missing elements of recovered memory stories are filled in; where repression was, there shall suggestion be. Indeed, someone who reviews many such cases will eventually realize that the salient question isn't whether or not a bona fide instance of repression can be found, but rather whether there are any limits at all to the malleability of the human mind. Therapists, it seems, are helpful but not strictly necessary to the production of wildly fantastic memories. Given a facilitating belief structure, the compliant subject can use the merest hints as triggers to delusion.

To illustrate this fact, there is nothing quite like the sequence of events recounted in Lawrence Wright's *Remembering Satan*, a short but gripping and brilliantly constructed book that began as a pair of articles in *The New Yorker* in May 1993.[21] Wright tells of Paul Ingram, an Olympia,

---

21. Alfred A. Knopf, 1994.

Washington, sheriff's deputy, a born-again Christian, and the chair of his county Republican committee, who was eventually thought to have raped both of his daughters as well as one of his sons innumerable times, to have passed the daughters around sexually as poker nights at home turned into gang rapes, to have hideously tortured the girls and forced them and his wife to have sex with goats and dogs, and to have murdered and cannibalized many babies at huge gatherings of his Satanic cult—where, be it noted, long gowns, pitchforks, and "Viking hats" were de rigueur. The still greater novelty, however, is that Ingram, though he initially remembered none of those atrocities, succeeded in visualizing most of them through the exercise of prayerful introspection. Indeed, he labored so hard to admit to new crimes that his tale-spinning daughters sometimes fell behind his pace.

All this would be hilarious Thurberesque Americana if it were not also inexpressibly sad. Whereas the Franklin household, when Eileen Lipsker went public with her vision, no longer contained a married couple or any children, in the Ingram case a devout family of seven was shattered for good. Moreover, Ingram, who is now serving a twenty-year term in prison after having confessed to six counts of child molestation, came close to being joined there by others who were caught in a widening net of lunacy—and at least two of them, who were in fact jailed briefly and then kept under house arrest for five months each, will never recover their reputations. Even those men had to think long and hard about whether they might have unknowingly lived double lives; and Ingram's wife, Sandy, did conclude that she must have been a secret Satanist. She has moved away now and lives under a different name, as does the only one of her five children who hasn't fled Olympia.

What is most arresting about the Ingram calamity is how little suggestion—indeed, how little *auto*-suggestion—was required to set it in motion and then to keep it hurtling toward its climax. Ericka Ingram had a history of making unsubstantiated sexual charges prior to her "realization" at age twenty-two that her father had been raping her. That insight did not occur during therapy but at a Christian retreat in August 1988 at which a visiting charismatic healer told Ericka the news, relayed to her by the Holy Spirit, that she had been molested as a child. Ericka immediately accepted the diagnosis—and, six years later, she apparently still does.[22]

Similarly, during the second day of his questioning Paul Ingram easily allowed himself to be led into a trance, resulting in his confession to all of the crimes with which he was eventually charged after prosecutors had deleted the witches' sabbath material, which could have raised awkward questions in jurors' minds if the case had come to trial. Ingram's prolific later admissions were facilitated not only by prayer but by "relaxation techniques," one of which he had picked up from a magazine. And two of his sons also developed a knack of instantly becoming "dissociated" in order to provide inquisitors with the required lurid reminiscences.

---

22. At the sentencing, Ericka was instrumental in seeing that her father receive the stiffest allowable punishment, and afterward, like Eileen Lipsker, she advanced her cause on the tabloid talk shows. Today, I gather, she is still concerned with denouncing a coven of Satanists within the Olympia police department.

This is not to say that the Ingram family generated hallucinations entirely under its own steam. To begin with, Paul Ingram's police colleagues exerted unscrupulous (though hardly unusual) pressure on him, extending the second interrogation over a mind-buckling eight-hour period and using his piety as a wedge to confession. They lied to him about what others had revealed and assured him that if he would only begin by admitting his guilt, the relevant memories would come flooding back.[23] By that second day, furthermore, Paul was being advised by a Tacoma psychologist whose recent practice had included Satanic abuse cases, and who later helped Paul's son Chad to conclude that his remembered childhood dreams were proof of molestation. An assistant pastor in the Church of Living Water also helped both Paul and his wife to sustain the cleansing flow of visions. During five months of interrogation, no fewer than five psychologists and counselors kept the heat on Paul, preventing him from ever stepping back to test whether the grimmer yet more tentative of his two memory systems—his "horror movie," as he called it—was anchored to actual events.

When all this pressure has been duly weighed, however, the fact remains that the Ingram case displays a breathtaking

23. The Olympia police authorities never conducted an investigation in the usual meaning of that term. "Believe the children" was their tacit motto from the word go. To this day they haven't realized the unfairness of collecting a mountain of absurd and contradictory stories from patently unstable witnesses, lopping off the charges that would be most likely to arouse a jury's suspicions about the reliability of those sources, and using the remaining, equally unsubstantiated, charges to hustle a respected colleague off to prison. Nor, in Wright's words, did the detectives "ever consider the possibility that the source of the memories was the investigation itself" (Wright, p. 195).

readiness on the part of its major players to form lasting "memories" on very slight provocation. And this is important for grasping the explosive potentiality of recovered memory allegations. There was nothing exceptional about the Ingram family's prelapsarian makeup or the Olympia scene in general. Apparently, a community steeped in Biblical literalism on the one hand and *Geraldo* on the other needs only a triggering mechanism to set off a long chain reaction of paranoia.[24] Yet such a community epitomizes a good portion of North America. The potential for mass havoc from "memory"-based accusations is thus no smaller today than it was in the seventeenth century. In fact, it is incomparably greater, thanks to the power of our sensation-seeking media to spread the illness instantaneously from one town or region to another.

As Lawrence Wright properly stresses, one further ingredient acts as a multiplier of trouble. Not surprisingly, it is a shared belief in the theory of repression. Only a few hours into his first grilling, Paul Ingram was ready to state, "I did violate them and abuse them and probably for a long period of time. I've repressed it" (Wright, p. 8). His questioners, of course, held the same view, which took on firmer contours as more psychologists were called in; before long, the official version was that Paul had repressed each of his myriad offenses just as soon as he had finished committing it. A county under-sheriff (himself falsely accused of Satanism, but still an enthusiastic

---

24. One month before Paul Ingram was summoned to police headquarters for his first grilling, the Ingram family sat down to watch Geraldo Rivera's prime-time special, *Devil Worship: Exposing Satan's Underground.* The previous day's program, which they may or may not have seen, was called *Satanic Breeders: Babies for Sacrifice.*

believer in its reality) became so enamored of this notion that he started moonlighting as a counselor to survivor groups and writing theoretical papers about the effects of repression.[25] One can only second Lawrence Wright's conclusion: "[w]hatever the value of repression as a scientific concept or a therapeutic tool, unquestioning belief in it has become as dangerous as the belief in witches" (Wright, pp. 199–200).

Some secular-minded readers may feel that the Ingram case, in view of its fundamentalist soil and its resultant exotic blossom of Satanism, is too outlandish to tell us much about the prudent and responsible search for incest memories. Yet the more one learns about the scare over "Satanic ritual abuse," the more porous its boundary with the larger recovered memory movement appears to be. According to surveys taken by the False Memory Syndrome Foundation, at least 15 percent of all memory retrievers come to recall Satanic torture in childhood—this despite a lack of evidence to support the existence of any sadistic devil-worshiping cults in North America or anywhere else.[26] The fact is that "memories" of baby barbecues and the like are usually evoked through the same techniques of psychic exploration commended by pres-

25. Ingram himself learned, pathetically, how to talk the self-pitying lingo of the recovered memory movement. "I have also been a victim since I was five years old," he told an interrogator, "and I learned very early that the easiest way to handle this was to hide it in unconscious memory . . . " (Wright, p. 173)
26. For a reliable account of the way that the mania over "Satanic ritual abuse" has blended with the recovered memory movement, see Jeffrey S. Victor, *Satanic Panic: The Creation of a Contemporary Legend* (Open Court, 1993). For the FBI's inability to locate any such abuse, see Kenneth V. Lanning, "Satanic, Occult, Ritualistic Crime: A Law Enforcement Perspective," *The Police Chief,* October 1989, pp. 62–83.

tigious academics such as Judith Herman and Lenore Terr. Indeed, as she testified at the Franklin trial, Terr herself has treated "victims" who thought they recalled having been forced to watch ritual human sacrifices.

Until the recovered memory movement got properly launched in the later 1980s, most Satanism charges were brought against child-care workers who were thought to have molested their little clients for the devil's sake. In such prosecutions, which continue today, a vengeful or mentally unhinged adult typically launches the accusations, which are immediately believed by police and social workers. These authorities then disconcert the toddlers with rectal and vaginal prodding, with invitations to act out naughtiness on "anatomically correct" dolls with bloated genitals, and, of course, with leading questions that persist until the child reverses an initial denial that anything happened and begins weaving the kind of tale that appears to be demanded. As many studies have shown, small children can be readily induced to believe that they have experienced just about any fictitious occurrence. In this respect, however, they do not stand fundamentally apart from their elders. The only real difference is that the grown-ups, in order to become as gullible as three-year-olds, must first subscribe to a theory such as that of demonic possession or its scientific counterpart, Freudian repression. They then become putty in the hands of their would-be helpers.

As it happens, the most impressive controlled illustration of this fact to date came directly from the Paul Ingram case, after the prosecutors—not the defense!—had invited the social psychologist Richard Ofshe to Olympia as an expert on cults and mind control. Perhaps, they thought, Ofshe could cast some light into the murky Satanic corner of the affair. But Ofshe, immediately struck by the conditional quality of Ingram's confessions and by their suggestion that a scene was taking place in the mind's eye ("I would've," "I must have," "I see it," etc.), decided to test Ingram's suggestibility by proposing a false memory for him to accept or reject.

"I was talking to one of your sons and one of your daughters . . . , " Ofshe told Ingram. "It was about a time when you made them have sex with each other while you watched." This was one charge that had not been levied and would never be, but one day later, Paul proudly submitted a new written confession:

> . . . I ask or tell Paul Jr. & Ericka to come upstairs. . . .
> I tell Ericka to knell [sic] and to caress Paul's genitals.
> When erect I tell her to put the penis into her mouth
> and to orally stimulate him. . . . I may have told the
> children that they needed to learn the sex acts and how
> to do them right. . . . I may have anal sex with Paul, not
> real clear. . . . Someone may have told me to do this
> with the kids. This is a feeling I have.

When Ofshe then informed Ingram that this memory was specious, Ingram refused to believe him. "It's just as real to me as anything else," he protested (Wright, pp. 144–146).

When, months later, Ofshe phoned Ingram in jail and begged him not to plead guilty, Ingram wavered but declined. Apart from consideration for the daughters who had so egregiously betrayed him, he cited the likelihood that he was still repressing material that would make the whole case clear. Protected at last from the ministrations of his "counselors," he did change his mind shortly thereafter, but his guilty plea had already been accepted by the court, and two subsequent appeals have failed.

The criminal cases we have examined suffice to show that the "return of the repressed," however bland its uses within the amorphous aims of Freudian therapy, can turn noxious when it is considered by police, prosecutors, jurors, and even accused malefactors to be a source of unimpeachable truth. In the light of the actual recovered memory *movement*, however, the Franklin and Ingram examples can be seen to lack a baleful but typical ingredient. So far as we know, neither Eileen Lipsker nor Ericka Ingram (not to mention Paul Ingram himself) was systematically recruited by self-help books to believe that certain despicable deeds must have been committed and then wholly repressed.

Just such solicitation—we can think of it as suggestion-at-a-distance—has by now been brought to bear on myriad vulnerable people, mostly women, by advocates in search of ideological and/or financial gain. The result has been a widespread tragedy that is still unfolding before our incredulous eyes. To lay bare not just its nature but also its causes, both proximate and remote, is a socially urgent task. With the help of several excellent new critical works, we will explore that ground in the concluding portion of this essay.

*November 17, 1994*

PART TWO

I.

Throughout the American 1980s and beyond, the interrogation of small children for their memories of recent sexual abuse played a role in many a criminal case against accused molesters who had not, in fact, done anything wrong. The social and financial costs have been enormous. To take only the most famous example, staff members of the McMartin Preschool in Manhattan Beach, California, who were accused of every imaginable horror associated with devil worship, had to endure the longest (almost seven years) and most expensive ($15 million) trial in American history before the case collapsed from the weight of its accumulated absurdities. In other instances, draconian sentences are being served and plea bargains are still being coerced in the face of transparently clear signs that the charges are bogus. Even today, our criminal justice system is just beginning to erect safeguards against the error that makes such outrages possible: the assumption that children are still reliable witnesses after exposure to their parents' and inquisitors' not-so-subtle hints that certain kinds of revelations are expected of them.

Not even that much progress, however, is being made with respect to curbing parallel travesties involving the therapeutically manufactured memories of adults who decide that they must have been molested in their own childhood. On the contrary: by extending their statutes of limitation to allow for thirty years and more of nonrecollection, our states have been codifying a pseudoscientific notion of repressed-yet-vividly-retrieved memory that can cause not merely injustice but enormous grief and havoc. Obviously, the impetus for such legislative backwardness is not coming from reputable psychological research—which, as we have seen, offers no support to the concept of repression even in its mildest form. The momentum comes rather from a combination of broad popular belief and a relatively narrow but intense crusading fervor.

Since 1988, the most successful communicators of both the belief and the fervor have been Ellen Bass and Laura Davis, through their "recovery manual" *The Courage to Heal.* A teacher of creative writing and her student, Bass and Davis were radical feminists who lacked any background in psychology. Their knowledge base consisted of stories they had heard from women who clearly remembered that they had been sexually abused in childhood but who had been rebuffed by uncaring therapists and family members. Noting the high numbers of such cases reported within women's collectives, and further noting that other women in such groups eventually produced incest "memories" of their own, Bass and Davis soon decided that repressed abuse must be even more pervasive than remembered abuse. The more likely explanation of the late-blooming cases—namely, that the dynamics of the group encouraged false memory formation by making victimhood into a test of authentic belonging—has yet to dawn on these collaborators.

Precisely because their minds were unclouded by research findings, Bass and Davis uncannily reflected the ideological spirit of their moment and milieu. As Mark Pendergrast relates in *Victims of Memory*, the mounting (and very legitimate) concern about the underreported incidence of real child molestation formed only one corner of the picture. Bass and Davis also spoke to a public mood of impatient moral absolutism; an obsession with the themes, popularized by John Bradshaw and others, of codependency, the "dysfunctional family," and the "inner child"; a widespread susceptibility to occult beliefs; the rise of "lookism" and other manifestations of hypersensitivity to the violation of personal space; and the angry conviction in some quarters that all men are rapists at heart. While Andrea Dworkin and Susan Brownmiller were hypothesizing that American fathers regularly rape their daughters in order to teach them what it means to be inferior, Bass and Davis set about to succor the tens of millions of victims who must have repressed that ordeal.

No single book, of course, can make a social movement. Although *The Courage to Heal* had already sold over three quarters of a million copies before its recent third edition appeared, and although its spinoff volumes constitute a small industry in their own right, Bass and Davis have been joined by a considerable number of other writers who share their slant.[1] Moreover, the recovered memory business quickly outgrew the motives of its founders. By now, as the books by Pendergrast and by Richard Ofshe and Ethan Watters show, it has evolved into a highly lucrative enterprise not just of therapy and publishing but also of counseling, workshop hosting, custody litigation, criminal prosecution, forced hospitalization, and insurance and "victim compensation" claims.

Bass and Davis's movement, it must be plainly understood, is not primarily addressed to people who always knew about their sexual victimization. Its main intended audience is women who aren't at all sure that they were molested, and its purpose is to convince them of that fact and embolden them to act upon it. As for genuine victims, the comfort they are proffered may look attractive at first, but it is of debatable long-term value. *The Courage to Heal* and its fellow manuals are not about surmounting one's tragic girlhood but about keeping the psychic wounds open, refusing forgiveness or reconciliation, and joining the permanently embittered corps of "survivors."

In the eyes of the movement's leaders, as many as half of all American women are veterans of childhood sexual abuse (Blume, p. xiv). If so, the logic seems to run, you can hardly fail to unearth a victim wherever you look and by however desultory a means of detection. But a revealing game with

---

1. Other key movement documents include Renee Fredrickson, *Repressed Memories: A Journey to Recovery from Sexual Abuse* (Fireside/Parkside, 1992); E. Sue Blume, *Secret Survivors: Uncovering Incest and Its Aftereffects in Women* (Wiley, 1990); and Patricia Love, *The Emotional Incest Syndrome: What To Do When a Parent's Love Rules Your Life* (Bantam, 1990).

definitions is being played here. For writers like Bass and Davis, Renee Fredrickson, and E. Sue Blume, sexual molestation occurs whenever the victim thinks—or later comes to believe that she must have thought—that an inappropriate kind of contact is occurring. Blume, indeed, denies that physical touching need be involved at all. "Incest," she explains, "can occur through words, sounds, or even exposure of the child to sights or acts that are sexual but do not involve her" (Blume, p. 5). And still another movement writer denounces what she calls "emotional incest," which can be committed by parents who "appear loving and devoted," "spend a great deal of time with their children and lavish them with praise and material gifts," but do so merely "as an unconscious ploy to satisfy their own unmet needs" (Love, p. 1).

From the standpoint of public health, what's most disturbing here is a likely growth in the number of "false positives"—women who were never molested but who are enticed into believing that they were. The mavens of recovered memory concern themselves almost entirely with means of *reinforcing* incest suspicions, not with means of checking them against solid evidence pro or con. Their advice to friends and counselors of a woman who has been led to suspect early molestation is generally the same: never cast doubt on those suspicions. So, too, she herself is urged to stifle all doubts. In Renee Fredrickson's words, "You may be convinced that your disbelief is a rational questioning of the reality versus unreality of your memories, but it is partially a misguided attempt to repress the memories again" (p. 161).

It is little wonder, then, that Bass and Davis, through the first two editions of *The Courage to Heal*, had yet to encounter a single woman who "suspected she might have been abused, explored it, and determined that she wasn't."[2] Now, in a third edition that is beginning to sound nervous about "the backlash" in general and pending damage suits in particular, it is admitted that some therapists "have pushed clients to acknowledge abuse... that did not occur" (p. 485). But even those few bad apples, in Bass and Davis's still erroneous judgment, cannot "create new memories in their clients" (p. 508); and the women who change their minds after leaving therapy "represent only a tiny fraction of the millions of actual survivors..." (p. 509).

The "false positives" problem has been exacerbated by the checklists of telltale symptoms that adorn the movement's self-help manuals and advice columns. Smarting from criticism of their earlier checklists, Bass and Davis adopt a warier posture now; nevertheless, they still leave the implication that if you "feel different from other people" (p. 39), incest is a likely cause. E. Sue Blume tells you that you were probably molested if you speak too softly, or wear too many clothes, or have "no awareness at all" of having been violated (pp. xviii–xxi). If you have checked the questionnaire items "I neglect my teeth" or "There are certain things I seem to have a strange affection or attraction for," Renee Fredrickson knows why (p. 49). And according to the ubiquitous John Bradshaw, a victim can be spotted either by her sexual promiscuity or, as the case may be, by her lack of interest in sex.[3] These are all

2. Bass and Davis, *The Courage to Heal*, second edition (HarperPerennial, 1992), p. 347.

sterling examples of what experimentally minded psychologists dryly call a "confirmatory bias."[4]

Once she is drawn into memory therapy, a client will find her suspicions of abuse verified by one or more techniques of investigation that are, in Fredrickson's words, "as unlimited as human creativity" (p. 141). With or without the therapist's direct assurance that the patient's symptoms are "consistent with abuse," repression can supposedly be dislodged through "feelings work," "body work," "dream work," "imagistic work," "trance work," and "group work"; through the production of journals and pictures that are sure to yield symbols of violation; through the cultivation of flashbacks, which are always deemed to reveal the truth of a past situation rather than compliance with current expectations; through administration of the tongue-loosening "truth serum" sodium amytal; and, of course, through hypnosis, including its deep-end forms of "age regression" and even "past life regression."[5] The considerable body of technical literature showing that none of these methods reliably leads to uncontaminated memories is simply ignored.

---

3. John Bradshaw, "Incest: When You Wonder If It Happened to You," *Lear's*, August 1992, pp. 43–44.

4. Controlled research indicates that there is nothing easy about identifying incest victims from their symptoms. See, e.g., Thomas M. Horner et al., "The Biases of Child Sexual Abuse Experts: Believing Is Seeing," *Bulletin of the American Academy of Psychiatry Law*, Vol. 21 (1993), pp. 281–292. Horner found that forty-eight experts, all examining the same material, could reach no significant agreement as to whether a child had been molested by her father.

5. See Loftus and Ketcham, *The Myth of Repressed Memory*, pp. 167–169, 162–164, 158–160, 156–158, 24, 169–171, 160–162, and Pendergrast, *Victims of Memory*, pp. 118, 122–123, 108ff.

The recovered memory movement's feminist affinity should not lead anyone to suppose that its incitement to militant victimhood serves the best interests of women. It is precisely women who make up most of the movement's casualties. Once a patient is invited to believe that her inner child was suffocated at an early age, she may well put the major blame on her mother; that is just what we see in a significant minority of cases. Estrangement between sisters—one converted to hellishly revised memories of their years together, the other refusing to go along—is also a regular aftermath of therapy. But above all, the chief sufferer usually turns out to be the female patient herself.

Self-help manuals preach the doctrine of "abreaction," whereby a patient must painfully relive each repressed memory if she is to stand a chance of freeing herself from it. The experience is guaranteed to be rough. In Lenore Terr's version of this truth, "Clinicians find that once repression lifts, individuals become far more symptomatic. They become anxious, depressed, sometimes suicidal, and far more fearful of items suggestive of their traumas."[6] Bass and Davis agree. "Don't hurt or try to kill yourself...," they feel compelled to advise. "Sit tight and ride out the storm" (p. 75). For many women, however, the storm doesn't end, or else it ends all too abruptly with suicide. And even in the best of cases, a "survivor" is coached to reject the happiest actual memories of her

---

6. Terr, *Unchained Memories*, p. 52. Renee Fredrickson goes a step farther, remarking that patients may not notice *any symptoms at all* "until they are immersed in the process of dealing with their memories" *(Repressed Memories*, p. 36). Then the torment begins.

childhood as being inconsistent with the stark truth of molestation. The result is a lasting sacrifice of resilience, security of identity, humor, capacity to show affection, and connection to the people who have cared most steadily about this woman's happiness.

## 2.

Although much of this woe is irreparable, there is no need for fatalism about its indefinite extension to new cases. On the contrary: the tide is already being turned. The current books that are hastening this shift of opinion follow upon influential exposés by such courageous journalists as Michael Morris, Debbie Nathan, Stephanie Salter, the late Darrell Sifford, and Bill Taylor, along with trenchant warnings by academics like Carol Tavris, Paul McHugh, and Robyn Dawes. And a number of other book-length critiques are just now arriving on the scene.[7] Above all, steady progress in public enlightenment has been forged, over the past two and a half years, by the False Memory Syndrome Foundation, most of whose members are themselves slandered relatives of "survivors."

---

7. See Michael D. Yapko, *Suggestions of Abuse: True and False Memories of Childhood Sexual Trauma* (Simon and Schuster, 1994); Hollida Wakefield and Ralph Underwager, *Return of the Furies: An Investigation into Recovered Memory Therapy* (Open Court, 1994); Claudette Wassil-Grimm, *Diagnosis for Disaster: The Devastating Truth about False Memory Syndrome and Its Impact on Accusers and Families* (Overlook, 1995); and Charles R. Kelley and Eric C. Kelley, *Now I Remember: Recovered Memories of Sexual Abuse* (K/R Publications, 1994). Other important recent books include Eleanor Goldstein and Kevin Farmer, *Confabulations* (SIRS Books, 1992) and *True Stories of False Memories* (SIRS Books, 1993).

All three of the most convincing new books on false memory—those by Elizabeth Loftus and Katherine Ketcham, Richard Ofshe and Ethan Watters, and Mark Pendergrast—address the full tragedy and folly of the recovered memory movement. All are astute, scientifically informed, and compassionate toward the movement's casualties; all contain wrenching accounts of sudden accusation and insult, alienation, family grief, false imprisonment, and death without reconciliation. Any of these overlapping works would serve a reader well as a survey, analysis, and call to corrective action. But the most unflinching and broadest-ranging studies appear to be Ofshe and Watters's *Making Monsters* and Pendergrast's *Victims of Memory*.

As befits a coauthor (Ofshe) whose research specialty has been the tactics of exerting undue influence, *Making Monsters* is finely attuned to the thralldom that would-be healers impose upon their clients, whose mundane initial complaints are typically supplanted by anxiety, suggestibility, and a desperate dependency. What distinguishes this book is its focus on the resultant psychological transformation of patients. For Ofshe and Watters, the speciousness of the so-called memories is incidental to the real tragedy, a "brutalization and psychological torture" of people who get stripped of their actual early memories, infused with fanatical hatred of their parents, and disabled for normal coping in the world beyond the drifting lifeboat of survivorship (Ofshe and Watters, p. 7). The patients themselves become grotesque in the very act of "making monsters" out of the people who nurtured them.

Ofshe and Watters offer us the clearest account of how the very inefficacy of memory treatment—its indefinite postponing of an expected self-restoration—can lock the patient and therapist in an ever more macabre embrace. Thus:

> Therapists often find themselves forced to explain why, after the first series of recovered memories, the client's symptoms do not disappear as promised. The easiest answer is to presume that the abuse must have been more serious than originally thought, and that more repressed memories are hidden in the patient's unconscious. As the therapist pushes to find more hidden memories, the client, who is already trained in the process, often comes up with still more accounts of having been abused.... [Eventually,] the client's worst fears are forged into memories. What could be more psychologically damaging than being raped by one's father? Having to have his baby. What could be worse than having to give birth to your father's child? Having to kill the child. What could be worse than having to kill a baby? Having to eat the baby after you've killed it. What could be worse than all this? Having to do these things during ritualized worship of the Devil. (p. 177)

At such a juncture, readers may suppose, both parties to the "therapy" must surely awaken and realize that they have been taking a magic carpet ride. But for reasons that Ofshe and Watters supply, it doesn't happen. The therapist feels honor bound to avoid "revictimizing" the patient by expressing doubts, and the patient, precisely by virtue of having renounced the actual memories that used to moor her identity, has lost contact with reality and is desperate to retain the therapist's approval. The outcome is a potentially lethal *folie à deux*.[8]

*Making Monsters* is a book about iatrogenesis, or the molding of a patient's illness by the incompetent doctor's own ministrations. The authors carry this theme quite far, not just in explaining individual cases but also in challenging an entire disease entity linked to false memory cases, so-called multiple personality disorder (MPD). They are hardly the first parties to express misgivings about this staple of Hollywood, sensational TV, and the criminal courts, where "one of my other personalities did it" has become the murderer's last alibi. But Ofshe and Watters regard MPD as a pure product of suggestion. They see it as a behavioral pattern learned chiefly from hypnotherapists who tend, themselves, to be believers in Satanic possession and other forms of conspiratorial mind control, and who characteristically prod their patients not only to remember hideous ordeals but also to manifest the dissociated selves that must have been brought into being by flight from those ordeals. With MPD, Ofshe and Watters argue, we stand at the outer edge of medical

---

8. Ofshe and Watters rightly perceive the Satanic connection as "the Achilles' heel of the recovered memory movement" (p. 194). Radical feminists who prefer all-female "survivor families" to the nuclear family make strange bedfellows with abortion-hating fundamentalists, but the record speaks for itself. "None of us want to believe such stories," write Bass and Davis of the ridiculous tales about babies being forced to eat feces in Satan's honor, "but for the sake of the survivors we must" (Bass and Davis, p. 522). As *Making Monsters* shows, Bass and Davis's own carte-blanche approach to the authenticating of incest cases leaves them with no way of drawing a line between sane and crazy allegations made by their Christian counterparts from across the ideological tracks.

derangement, yet well within the methodological boundaries of the recovered memory movement.[9]

In their assault on MPD, Ofshe and Watters are joined, independently, by the investigative journalist Mark Pendergrast, whose *Victims of Memory* constitutes the most ambitious and comprehensive, as well as the most emotionally committed, of all the studies before us. Pendergrast's book stands out from the others in several respects. For one thing, it transcribes his numerous interviews with therapists, "survivors," "retractors," and accused "perpetrators," allowing the cruel unreason of the recovered memory movement to be voiced with a minimum of editorial mediation. Second, he is the author who delves most deeply into the movement's antecedents in witchcraft lore, mesmerism, early hypnotherapy, and the treatment of so-called hysteria—itself a faddish malady whose distribution was suspiciously well correlated with possession of the means to pay for treatment. Third, Pendergrast offers illuminating material about physiological states (sleep paralysis, panic attacks) that have traditionally been mistaken for "body memories" of one lurid kind or another. And it is Pendergrast who devotes the most effort to analyzing the contemporary Zeitgeist in which the recovery movement thrives.

Like Loftus and Ketcham and Ofshe and Watters, Pendergrast offers case histories that will wring the classic emotions of pity and terror from any unbiased reader. But here,

---

9. In recently redesignating MPD as "dissociative identity disorder," the American Psychiatric Association has started to back away from the syndrome's more lurid implications. So long as MPD promoters remain influential within the association, however, fundamental criticism such as Ofshe and Watters's is not to be expected.

too, there is a difference: the most affecting (though by no means the most drastic) of Pendergrast's stories is his own. He himself has lost his grown daughters to the recovered memory movement. Within therapy that featured the overcoming of repression, both of them came to believe that he did something awful—they won't say what—to one of them, and both have met his pleas for communication with the icy formalism inculcated by *The Courage to Heal*—a book, ironically, that Pendergrast bought and gave to one daughter when she first mentioned that uncrystallized sexual scenes were beginning to haunt her mind. Now both daughters have taken different last names, and in concluding his book with a poignant letter to them, Pendergrast further protects their identities by assigning them fictitious first names as well. Let us hope that they will read not just that letter but the whole of *Victims of Memory*, which, though it is hardly addressed to them alone, rests partly on the desperate premise that a 603-page dose of history, logic, and exhortation may be able to turn well-coached zealots back into the amiable young women Pendergrast once knew.

Finally, and understandably, *Victims of Memory* is distinguished by the urgency and specificity of its call to action. Among other recommendations, Pendergrast wants professional associations and licensing boards to stop waffling about repression and to insist that therapists acquaint themselves with what is actually known about memory. He wants reconsideration of laws that have created standing "abuse bureaucracies" and that have rashly extended statutes of limitation. He favors third-party suits for damages against therapists whose implanting of false accusations has destroyed families and livelihoods.[10] He wants the adoption of higher standards for expert testimony and for the evaluation of therapists' claims that they were mere bystanders to their patients' mnemonic feats. And most pressingly, he asks for a special judicial review of criminal convictions that have been based solely on the alleged retrieval of long-dormant memories or on the manipulated fantasies of small children.

Some people who have always remembered their own sexual victimization will regard the legal and legislative parts of this agenda as regressive, a signal to real molesters that they can exploit children with impunity. Such fears are understandable; pedophiles *will* undoubtedly try to portray any accuser as deluded by a trick of memory. But that only makes it more imperative that the air be cleared. Until our courts can learn to apply the same evidential criteria to abuse charges that they require for all others, they will remain enmired in phony cases that persecute the innocent and squander resources that are needed to address the real problem of child abuse. Meanwhile, simple justice demands that prison sentences resting on a combination of delusion and misinformation be overturned.

---

10. The prototype of such suits was brought by Gary Ramona of Petaluma, California, who won a $500,000 judgment in 1994 against a therapist, a psychiatrist, and a hospital for their role in bringing about his daughter Holly's "memory" that he had molested her. Sued by Holly, Ramona had countersued the other parties for compensation of the loss of his job, marriage, and reputation. (Lenore Terr, incidentally, put in her customary court appearance, offering an expert opinion that Holly Ramona's current aversion to pickles and bananas confirms her childhood trauma of forced oral sex.) The Ramona verdict will be appealed, but for now, at least, it constitutes the darkest cloud hanging over the recovered memory movement.

# 3.

Once the bizarre and sinister features of the recovered memory movement are widely known, sophisticated readers will not hesitate to distance themselves from it. But that very likelihood holds out another danger, that bobbing for repressed memories will be perceived simply as a ludicrous, dismissible aberration from a fundamentally sound psychotherapeutic tradition. If that view prevails, we will have learned little of lasting value from the recovered memory fiasco. It is essential to grasp that induced memory retrieval emerged from mainstream ideas about the psyche and that it bears a strong kinship with every other style of treatment that ties curative power to restoration of the patient's early past.

Despite their feminist affiliation, the champions of survivorship cheerfully acknowledge Sigmund Freud, the male chauvinist par excellence, as their chief intellectual and clinical forebear (see, e.g., Bass and Davis, pp. 479–480). They are quite justified in that opinion. Indeed, the ties between Freud's methods and theirs are more intricate and enveloping —and immeasurably more compromising to both parties— than they imagine. Precisely that kinship explains why other therapeutic descendants of Freudianism ought to be doing some soul-searching just now.

Needless to say, it is not classic psychoanalysis to which writers like Bass and Davis feel indebted. They have in mind the pre-psychoanalytic Freud, the one who supposedly took pity on his hysterical patients, found that they were all harboring memories of early abuse, "listened and understood and gave them permission to remember and speak of these terrible events,"[11] and cured them by unknotting their repression. Unfortunately (the story continues), he then suffered a failure of nerve; too many fathers were being identified as perpetrators, and patriarchy itself threatened to teeter on its throne. As a result, Freud withdrew into psychoanalysis, a doctrine that ascribes incestuous designs not to adult molesters but, grotesquely, to children themselves.

As I explained in "The Unknown Freud," this fable contains at least one nugget of truth: Freud had no empirical warrant for shifting to an oedipal perspective. The founding of his signature doctrine was indeed a retreat—one designed, however, not to shield guilty fathers but to keep in play his favorite concept of repression—"the cornerstone," as he would later say, "on which the whole structure of psychoanalysis rests" (SE, 14:16)—after its already announced therapeutic victories had failed to materialize. Freud finally had to cope with the disagreeable thought that his hysterics' "stories" of very early abuse had been peremptory inventions of his own. He did so, however, through a dumbfoundingly illogical, historically momentous expedient, ascribing to his patients' unconscious minds a repressed *desire for* the precocious couplings that he had hitherto urged them to remember having helplessly undergone. That is how psychoanalysis as we know it came into being.

Even people who accept this well-founded correction of the Freud legend may be slow to realize how high and dry it leaves the dogma of repression. Freud and Josef Breuer had first invoked repression in 1893 to cover miscellaneous symptom-

---

11. Jeffrey Moussaieff Masson, *The Assault on Truth: Freud's Suppression of the Seduction Theory* (Farrar, Straus and Giroux, 1984), p. 9.

producing "things which the patient wished to forget" (SE, 2:10); but Freud quickly became uncomfortable both with the random character of the offending thoughts and with his source of information about the repressed, namely, hypnosis. Then, with the seduction theory, he adapted the idea of repression to cover the failure of patients to remember molestations that he soon conceded to have been imaginary. Still later, it covered fantasies (and some events) whose existence could be known only by positing the action of repression itself. In none of these phases do we encounter raw behavioral data that an outsider would feel obliged to label "the repressed." Thus we really ought to redefine the repressed as follows: "inaccessible and possibly nonexistent psychic material to which the theorist or therapist is nevertheless determined to assign explanatory power." Exactly the same point applies to the repressed as it operates in the discourse of the recovered memory movement.

Among the many respects in which the memory retrievers' glorification of Freud's "seduction theory" misfires, the least noticed has to do with his alleged sympathy for incest sufferers. It is certainly true that after he became properly "Freudian" and cast children as the would-be seducers, he showed precious little pity for child sexual victims. Before 1897, for example, Freud could hardly have condemned the fourteen-year-old Dora as abnormal for spurning "an occasion for sexual excitement" proffered by her father's married friend (SE, 7: 28). Like Bass and Davis, however, the early Freud was less interested in comforting certified veterans of molestation than in rounding up converts to his all-purpose diagnosis. And the spirit of his interventions, as revealed in his papers and letters of the period, was not compassionate but monomaniacal. It is little wonder that Ofshe and Watters regard him as having "cut the very figure of a recovered memory therapist."[12]

Listen to Freud's own words:

> The work keeps on coming to a stop and they keep on maintaining that this time nothing has occurred to them. We must not believe what they say, we must always assume, and tell them, too, that they have kept something back.... We must insist on this, we must repeat the pressure and represent ourselves as infallible, till at last we are really told something.... There are cases, too, in which the patient tries to disown [the memory] even after its return. "Something has occurred to me now, but you obviously put it into my head."... In all such cases, I remain unshakably firm. I... explain to the patient that [these distinctions] are only forms of his resistance and pretexts raised by it against reproducing this particular memory, which we must recognize in spite of all this. (SE, 2:279–280)[13]

The patient's typical response to such hectoring was an agitation that Freud, like his counterparts a century later,

---

12. Ofshe and Watters, p. 293. Mark Pendergrast, too, understands the deep affinity between Freud's methods and those of our contemporary retrievers. The odd book out in this respect is Elizabeth Loftus and Katherine Ketcham's, which puts a maximum distance between memory therapy and what she calls Freud's "spare, elegant theories."
13. This passage is cited in a pertinent article by Russell A. Powell and Douglas P. Boer, "Did Freud Mislead Patients to Confabulate Memories of Abuse?" *Psychological Reports*, Vol. 74 (1994), pp. 1283–1298.

paraded as validation of his guesswork: "The behaviour of patients while they are reproducing these infantile experiences is in every respect incompatible with the assumption that the scenes are anything else than a reality which is being felt with distress and reproduced with the greatest reluctance" (SE, 3:204). Note as well how the psychoanalytic concept of resistance (the memory retrievers prefer to call it "denial") was already pulling its weight in the mid-1890s. When Renee Fredrickson now avers that the "existence of profound disbelief is an indication that memories are real" (Fredrickson, p. 171), she is manifesting loyalty to the sturdiest, as well as the most capricious, of Freudian traditions.

Critics of recovered memory have remarked on the movement's puritanical alarmism, whereby a mere touch or look gets invested with traumatic consequences that supposedly remain virulent for thirty years and more. In this respect, too, Freud anticipated the contemporary trend. So long as he cared at all about molestation as an etiological factor, he completely overlooked its real psychological effects, such as fear, moral confusion, and a diminished sense of selfhood. Instead, he dwelt on mechanical cause-and-effect relations between symptomatology and the premature stimulation of one body zone or another. And he regarded masturbation not only as a cause of indigestion, headaches, and lassitude but also as a sign of prior "seduction." The early Freud's truest contemporary heirs are those adults who see toddlers playing doctor and immediately phone the police.[14]

---

14. This is not a fanciful example. Last year Kenneth Bruce Perkins, a Texas

It was Freud, too, who pioneered the modern memory sleuths' technique of thematically matching a patient's symptom with a sexually symmetrical "memory." Before he decided that it made no difference whether a trauma was real or imaginary, Freud was tireless in his pursuit of such causal linkages. Lesions in the mouth were signs that a penis had been there first; dyspepsia or "worm irritation" must have stemmed from the insertion of a tongue or a finger in the former baby's anus; a paralysis of the lower limbs meant that the sufferer had been "required to stimulate the genitals of a grown-up woman with his foot"; and so forth.[15] Freud apparently arrived at such quack conclusions in the same way that his incest-happy legatees do, by taking the symptom as a puzzle to be jointly addressed with the patient and then solving it through direct probing, dream analysis, and the study of tactically selected verbal associations.[16]

---

grandfather, was convicted and sentenced to four concurrent thirty-year terms in prison after his daughter spotted her children engaging in sexual exploration and inferred that he must have been molesting one or more of them.

15. See, respectively, Freud–Fliess Letters, pp. 220, 223, and SE, 3:215.

16. It must be admitted, however, that no one has yet approached Freud's level of ingenuity in turning his own punning associations into knowledge about his patients' histories. See, e.g., the letter of 1899 in which he tells Fliess about a patient who "deflowers" women because he failed botany and who, as a teenager, once masturbated in a contorted position so that he could keep the Jungfrau in view (Freud–Fliess Letters, p. 346). As Robert Wilcocks remarks in a brilliant new book, "Surely *only Freud* (or perhaps Alfred Jarry?) could have imagined a 14-year-old boy masturbating with a view of that massive rugged rockpile, his adolescent ardor aroused to ejaculation by the provocative mountain *because its name means 'virgin.'*" See *Maelzel's Chess Player: Sigmund Freud and the Rhetoric of Deceit* (Rowman and Littlefield, 1994), p. 198.

The early Freud must also be awarded precedence for the cluster of ideas about memory that has landed so many of our fellow citizens in litigation and/or prison. I refer not just to repression but to the mind's ability to take snapshots of extremely early scenes and reproduce them in detail several decades later. When Lenore Terr, for example, uncritically accepts a man's "memory" from babyhood of his sadistic mother having totally submerged him in the bathtub as he was noticing "light gray walls all around me, a foul smell in the air" (Terr, p. 116), she may be defying what is known about brain development, but she is perfectly in key with Freud. Let one example, a letter from 1897, suffice:

> The early period before the age of one and one half years is becoming ever more significant. I am inclined to distinguish several periods even within it. Thus I was able to trace back, with certainty, a hysteria that developed in the context of a periodic mild depression to a seduction, which occurred for the first time at 11 months[,] and [I could] hear again the words that were exchanged between two adults at that time! It is as though it comes from a phonograph. (Freud–Fliess Letters, p. 226)

Given that Freud here accepts a "phonographic" memory of an adult conversation recorded when the patient was presumably still struggling to say "mama," this passage must rank among his most credulous ever. Yet the claim being made is scarcely more inane than any number of others from the same epoch.

Even the most adventuresome of modern memory enthusiasts, those who believe in Satan cults and who induce "past life regression" in their clients, had a predecessor of sorts in Freud. Though he didn't go in for reincarnation, Freud subscribed to the Lamarckian idea that memory traces from prehistory are passed along genetically ad infinitum, predisposing us to traumas analogous to those once endured by our hominid forebears and their progeny. Thus, in the same letter (cited in "The Unknown Freud") where he reported having "obtained a scene" from a patient who saw herself being forced to eat a morsel of her circumcised labium minor, he mused: "it is as though in the perversions, of which hysteria is the negative, we have before us a remnant of a primeval sexual cult, which once was—perhaps still is—a religion in the Semitic East . . . " (Freud–Fliess Letters, p. 227).

In theory, Freud could have come upon such prehistoric psychic material while exploring any given hysteric's repressed unconscious. That is presumably why he added, "I dream, therefore, of a primeval devil religion with rites that are carried on secretly, and understand the harsh therapy of the witches' judges" (p. 227). As I have previously shown, Freud, amazingly indifferent to the effects of suggestion, believed that the torture of accused witches elicited from them uncontaminated fantasies deriving from their own sexual molestation in childhood. Only the absence of a theological commitment, it seems, prevented him from stumbling over the final step and unearthing "Satanic ritual abuse."[17]

---

17. Or did it? Freud's muddled prose about his self-cannibalizing patient Emma Eckstein makes her look like an actual victim of such abuse. The "scene" in

# 4.

A Freudian's predictable way of handling all such embarrassments will be to say that they predated the birth of psychoanalysis. Yes, but most of them also persisted far beyond it. Long after 1897, Freud continued to badger his patients with ready-made hypotheses and to dismiss their objections as mere resistance; he still took their distress at his morbid insinuations as a further signal of his correctness; he still regarded symptoms as allegories of repressed mental contents; his Flintstones Lamarckism became more rather than less extravagant; and he never flagged in his quest to forge precise causal links between vividly reconstructed sexual events from infancy (either witnessed or personally endured) and adult mental disturbance.[18] Without the éclat of psychoanalysis, moreover, our memory gurus would never have been drawn to the molestation-minded Freud whom they now prefer. Nor, lacking his imprimatur, could they have bandied about notions of repression, abreaction, and unconscious symbolism without feeling a need to argue for their cogency.

A chasm does yawn, however, between the principles

---

question includes an apparently ritualistic drinking of blood from the girl's mutilated vaginal lip, which, Freud informs Fliess, "is even shorter today" (Freud–Fliess Letters, p. 227). That assertion may or may not have been true (just how could Freud have known?), but in either case it pertains to the realm of fact, not fantasy. The anatomical detail would seem to imply Freud's literal belief in his patient's devilish "scene." If, on the other hand, he was trying to correlate a false memory with a real disfiguration, his very sanity stands in doubt.

18. Indeed, as Frank J. Sulloway has pointed out, after the seduction fiasco Freud's "theory of the neuroses became, in significant part, a theory about infantile... masturbation." See *Freud, Biologist of the Mind: Beyond the Psychoanalytic Legend* (1979; revised edition, Harvard University Press, 1992), p. 185.

of the recovered memory movement and psychoanalysis in Freud's most familiar articulation of it. In contrast to Freud's own habit, the ideal Freudian therapist is supposed to be cool, nonjudgmental, and slow to reach closure about diagnoses and thematic connections. He is also asked to honor a number of methodological niceties that deter simplistic translations between any given sign and the event or wish that supposedly brought it into being.

There is, for instance, the concept of "screen memories" that are not to be taken at face value, and there are numerous posited defense mechanisms that supposedly warp dreams, symptoms, and errors into relatively obscure compromise formations. Although these refinements brought about an ominous problem of their own—in the full labyrinth of hermeneutic possibilities, how can we ever know which is the true path back to the supposedly originating scene?—they do militate against Bass and Davis's model of extracting repressed truths from the unconscious like so many bills from an automatic teller. Thus a classically trained psychoanalyst would hesitate to claim, as the memory therapists do, that a dream— supposedly a mosaic of infantile and diurnal residues, of wish and defense, of confession and concealment—could be regarded as a *direct* source of information about the dreamer's early history or the identity of her suspected molester.

Then, too, there is the saving fact that psychoanalysis, in continual retreat from its founding (but unfounded) therapeutic claims, has long since ceased advertising itself as curative in any straightforward sense of the term. That development minimizes the risk that Freudian patients will be devastated in the ways that once beset Freud's personal

215

practice[19] and that now beset the recovered memory profession. "Hysteria," of course, has vanished along with the doctors who battened on it; the psychic mysteries into which Freudian patients now get initiated are reassuringly universal, banal, and devoid of clear implications for changing behavior; and fastidious criteria of selection tend to weed out nearly all applicants who are suffering from anything more wrenching than a wish to know themselves better. Though many recovered memory clients, too, enter therapy with only vague and mild complaints, the incest stories that are forced upon them guarantee a more brutal jarring of their equanimity and identity than any Freudian patient can now undergo.[20]

When all this is said, however, there remains an important core of shared assumptions between psychoanalysis and its hyperactive young successor. These are:

1. To become mentally healthy, we must vent our negative feelings and relive our most painful psychic experiences. The deeper we delve, and the harsher and more bitter the truths that we drag to the surface, the better off we will be.

2. Through the aid of an objective therapist in whom we

---

19. To take an admittedly extreme example, Freud once treated a teen-age girl for what he called "an unmistakeable hysteria, which did in fact clear up quickly and radically under my care" (SE, 6:146n). But her abdominal pains had the ingratitude to recur, and two months later she was dead of cancer—a fact that caused Freud a rare access of chagrin but prompted no second thoughts about the correctness of his diagnosis. Today, the borderline psychotics, epileptics, and victims of Tourette's syndrome who used to fare so badly under psychoanalysis are safely steered into more appropriate regimens. But for a sense of the way Freudian treatment was still wreaking major havoc as late as the 1960s, readers could learn much from John Balt, *By Reason of Insanity* (Heinemann, 1963).
20. *Later:* This paragraph is now lamentably out of date. See pp. 15–29 above.

invest authority, trust, and love, we can not only arrive at an accurate diagnosis of our mental problems but also retrieve the key elements of our mental history in substantially accurate form, uncontaminated by the therapist's theoretical bias.

3. Our minds don't simply keep functioning when consciousness is absent; they feature an unconscious, a unique agency possessing its own special memories, interests, and rules of operation.

4. Everything that we experience is preserved in either conscious or unconscious (repressed) memory; "even things that seem completely forgotten are present somehow and somewhere..." (SE, 23:260).

5. The content of our repressions is preponderantly sexual in nature. Therefore, sexual experiences can be regarded as bearing a unique susceptibility to repression and can accordingly be considered the key determinants of psychic life.

6. The difficulty we meet in trying to recall our earliest years is attributable not, as neurologists believe, to the incomplete infantile development of our hippocampus and prefrontal cortex, but rather to extensive repression (see, e.g., SE, 7:174–176), which in some instances can be successfully lifted. Inability to recall any other part of our past may therefore be assigned to that same cause.

7. The repressed unconscious continually tyrannizes over us by intruding its recorded-but-not-recalled fantasies and traumas upon our efforts to live in the present. "A humiliation that was experienced thirty years ago acts exactly like a fresh one throughout the thirty years... " (SE, 5:578).

8. Symptoms are "residues and mnemic symbols of particular (traumatic) experiences" (SE, 11:16), and "dreaming is

217

another kind of remembering" (SE, 17:51). Consequently, a therapist's methodologically informed study of symptoms and dreams can lead (through however many detours) to faithful knowledge of an originating trauma.

9. Challenging though it may be, this work of reconstruction is made easier by the existence of a universally distributed store of unconscious equations between certain symbols and their fixed sexual meanings.

10. As a result of all these considerations, the most prudent and efficient way to treat psychological problems is not to address the patient's current situation, beliefs, and incapacities but to identify and remove the repressions that date from much earlier years.

All ten of these principles are, I believe, erroneous or extremely open to doubt. Yet they are so widely believed as to constitute what Richard Wollheim and Thomas Nagel, among others, regard as the psychological common sense of our era.[21] For Nagel, indeed, this popularity serves as actual proof that Freud must have been on the right track; if the Freudian revelation has convinced people as savvy as ourselves, Nagel thinks, there must be something to it.[22] He might entertain

---

21. See Wollheim, *The Mind and Its Depths* (Harvard University Press, 1993), and Nagel, "Freud's Permanent Revolution," *The New York Review*, May 12, 1994, pp. 34–38.

22. "I believe that the pervasive Freudian transformation of our modern working conception of the self is evidence of the validity of his attempt to extend the psychological far beyond its conscious base. Common sense has in fact expanded to include parts of Freudian theory. This in turn makes it credible that more extensive and systematic insights of the same type can be developed by analysts who probe far more deeply and uncover far more material for interpretation" (Nagel, p. 36).

second thoughts after realizing how the common sense of the 1990s, not unlike that of the 1690s, has run amok when taken literally by demonologists.

As Freud well appreciated when he chose as his epigraph for *The Interpretation of Dreams* Virgil's line about stirring up hell (SE, 4:ix), psychoanalysis is already demonology.[23] That is, it allegorizes the psychologically unknown as a dark power that must be coaxed forth, scrutinized, and kept in check by professionals who, incorruptible themselves by virtue of their faith and training, sniff out the hidden corruption of others. This sanctioned prurience is the thread that Mark Pendergrast traces from witch persecutions through mesmerism to hypnotherapy to psychoanalysis itself and, full circle, to the detection of Satanic abuse. Exactly that same compatibility between pre-industrial and modern forms of superstition, we may recall, proved the undoing of the Freudian Christian Paul Ingram, who wrote in his diary after conferring with his fundamentalist pastor, "John thinks several spirits are in me yet, still in control of my unconscious.... [It] may take someone like John to guide me around my defenses" (Ofshe and Watters, p. 172).

According to his confidant Sándor Ferenczi, the early Freud used to hurl himself body and soul against the forces that had invaded his patients' minds. He "worked passionately, devotedly, on the curing of neurotics," wrote Ferenczi in his diary, "(if necessary spending hours lying on the floor next to

---

23. Note Freud's question to Fliess in 1897: "Do you remember that I always said that the medieval theory of possession held by the ecclesiastical courts was identical with our theory of a foreign body and the splitting of consciousness?" (Freud–Fliess Letters, p. 224).

a person in a hysterical crisis)." Those were the work habits not of a fifty-minute psychoanalyst but of an exorcist. It was only after many therapeutic setbacks, Ferenczi reminded himself, that Freud came to call patients "a rabble," good for nothing but "to provide us with a livelihood and material to learn from."[24] Eventually, his private pessimism about ever being able to cast out our psychic demons crept over his whole affluent institution, which now, in the 1990s, stands suddenly naked before the only skeptics it can't ignore, the insurers who decide what is and isn't a reimbursable form of treatment. The exorcist's fervor has passed into coarser and more passionate hands such as those of Bass and Davis.

But this is not to say that psychoanalysis is doomed to stand by helplessly while young fanatics strut upon the stage that Freud built. Since every Freudian concept and commitment is revisable in a pinch, we may yet see the emergence of a hybrid psychoanalysis that has borrowed new vitality from the recovered memory movement. Portents of such an eventuality can already be found. The psychoanalyst Lawrence Hedges, for example, has recently proposed that therapeutically retrieved molestation scenes are not exactly false; they may be screen memories for inferrable bad experiences suffered "[i]n utero and in the earliest months of life."[25] In a new book from the Analytic Press, Lynda Share similarly proposes that the interpretation of adult

24. *The Clinical Diary of Sándor Ferenczi*, edited by Judith Dupont, translated by Michael Balint and Nicola Zarday Jackson (Harvard University Press, 1988), p. 93.
25. Lawrence E. Hedges, "Taking Recovered Memories Seriously," *Issues in Child Abuse Accusations*, Vol. 6 (1994), pp. 1–31. The quoted phrase is from p. 15.

dreams can give us detailed knowledge of real traumas from early infancy.[26] And in *Feminist Psychoanalytic Psychotherapy*, Charlotte Krause Prozan, who sensed which way the wind was blowing long ago, reports that whereas analysts used to be watchful for penis envy in women patients, today "we are looking for sexual abuse."[27]

In a follow-up book, Prozan offers a case history that dramatically embodies the blending of elements from standard psychoanalysis and therapy for repressed abuse. Prozan's treatment of "Penelope" was classically Freudian in its ground rules, in its heavy reliance on dream interpretation, and in its length—fourteen years. Although Penelope never did recall any molestation, Prozan wasn't fazed; as she reminds us, "[t]he phenomenon of not remembering...is in itself a symptom indicative of a severe traumatic experience."[28] As an appointed termination date loomed, the frantic Penelope surrendered at last to Prozan's thirteen-year insistence that her dreams—of setting fires, of a van crashing into a house, of being shot by a man, of sex with Prozan herself—admitted of no other explanation than the enduring of anal rape by a family friend when she was nine years old.

Exiting psychoanalysis at age forty-nine, Penelope was still smoking, drinking, and binge eating—the behaviors she had entered treatment to bring under control. Now, as well, she was estranged from her unbelieving mother and sister. But

---

26. Lynda Share, *If Someone Speaks, It Gets Lighter: Dreams and the Reconstruction of Infant Trauma* (Analytic Press, 1994).

27. Jason Aronson, 1992, p. 207.

28. Charlotte Krause Prozan, *The Technique of Feminist Psychoanalytic Psychotherapy* (Jason Aronson, 1993), p. 270.

she was glad, at least, to have puzzled out the identity of her abuser, "[t]hat SON OF A BITCH! It's totally his fault!" And she was eagerly looking forward to full-throttle survivorship in what she called "the days of being powerfully angry."[29]

The disapproval that most psychoanalysts would feel upon reviewing this case is less significant than their substantial sharing of Prozan's axioms about the repressed unconscious, its modus operandi, and its amenability to symbolic decoding. Their confidence about such matters stems from the same source that encourages writers like Bass and Davis to trust their own findings—once again, "clinical experience" and its replication by other members of their sect. As Thomas Nagel innocently puts it, each doubtful hypothesis "has to find its empirical support in countless other applications to other patients in other settings" (Nagel, p. 35). That is exactly the home-team approach to validation that produces abundant support for "facilitated communication," Satanic mind control, UFO abductions, previous incarnations, and telepathy—this last a favorite pastime of Freud's.

In a refreshingly sane essay, Paul R. McHugh, director of the Department of Psychiatry and Behavioral Sciences at the Johns Hopkins University School of Medicine, recently depicted a long-term struggle, within the mental health disciplines, between what he called empiricists and romanticists—between, that is, those who bind themselves to methodical study of facts and those who "rely upon feelings for evidence,

29. Prozan, *The Technique of Feminist Psychoanalytic Psychotherapy*, pp. 303, 308.

reality, on inspiration and myth for guidance."[30] The essay is especially pertinent because it relegates both psychoanalysis and recovered memory therapy to the romanticist camp, where they surely belong. But it also relegates them to history's ashcan. In McHugh's opinion, the empiricists are winning hands down, because their insistence on real-world testing allows them to deliver what they promise, proven remedies for specific complaints.

In the long run this victory does look inevitable. For now, however, I remain mindful of an earlier observation of McHugh's—that every ten years or so, "psychiatric practice has condoned some bizarre misdirection, proving all too often the discipline has been captive of the culture."[31] Out in the rough-and-tumble psychotherapeutic marketplace, to which our mental health associations discreetly turn their backs, Freudian clichés are breeding promiscuously with those of religious zealots, self-help evangelists, sociopolitical ideologues, and outright charlatans who trade in the ever seductive currency of guilt and blame. So long as "Freud's permanent revolution," as Nagel calls it, retains any sway, the voodoo of "the repressed" can be counted upon to return in newly energetic and pernicious forms.

*December 1, 1994*

---

30. Paul R. McHugh, "Psychotherapy Awry," *The American Scholar*, Vol. 63 (Winter 1994), pp. 17–30; the quotation is from p. 17.
31. Paul R. McHugh, "Psychiatric Misadventures," *The American Scholar*, Vol. 61 (Autumn 1992), pp. 497–510; the quotation is from p. 498.

# EXCHANGE

THERESA REID is the executive director of the American Professional Society on the Abuse of Children (APSAC). She writes, on behalf of APSAC's Board of Directors:

In his two-part article, "The Revenge of the Repressed," Frederick Crews offered a cogent critique of many aspects of the "recovered memory movement." Crews quite rightly denounces the naive use of diffuse "symptom checklists" and very broad definitions in the diagnosis of a childhood history of incest; reliance upon "therapeutic" modalities with no support in the empirical literature; insistence on unquestioning belief in patients' tentative emerging memories, no matter how bizarre; and the poor training and marshy theoretical basis of some practitioners in this field. Crews argues reasonably against the presumed therapeutic benefits of unearthing and "abreacting" all traumatic experiences, and trenchantly analyzes the shortcomings of the Freudian concept of repression, which authorizes the irresponsible assertion that the lack of memory for trauma is itself evidence of trauma.

Because we share Crews's belief in the necessity of a measured and well-informed response to adults' allegations of sexual abuse in childhood, we regret that Crews himself strayed so far from the empirical evidence on which he rightly insists we all rely, and reserved his skepticism for those who make or believe allegations of childhood incest. We wish to correct the misimpressions Crews's intemperate article may have left regarding (1) the criminal justice system response to allegations of sexual abuse in childhood, (2) the standard of therapeutic practice in this field, and (3) the concept of repression. First, however, we would like to point out how egregiously Crews commits the very sin he finds most damning in others: that of credulity.

Crews praises the False Memory Syndrome Foundation (FMSF)—most of whose members are parents who have been accused of incest by adult daughters—for making "steady progress in public enlightenment" on the issue of adult recollections of childhood incest. The cruel fact for all parties to such accusations is that both the wrongly accused and the rightly accused vociferously and convincingly deny the accusations against them. Crews acknowledges, "Pedophiles *will* undoubtedly try to portray any accuser as deluded by a trick of memory." When Crews refers to the members of FMSF as "slandered relatives of survivors," he claims an access to wisdom that Solomon himself would envy (not to mention the thousands of American judges who, according to Crews's caricature of the judicial system's response to child sexual abuse allegations, are doing so lamentable a job of adjudicating these cases).

Crews displays a similar credulity in bestowing lavish praise upon a forthcoming book by a Mark Pendergrast, both of whose grown daughters have accused him of incest. Crews lauds Pendergrast's 603-page compilation of interviews and lore (to be issued by the obscure "Upper Access" publishers) as "the most ambitious and comprehensive, as well as the most emotionally committed, of all the studies before us." While Pendergrast may be innocent of the charges against him, Crews applies very different criteria in assessing his work than in assessing that of "survivor" therapists. Whereas

Crews finds "confirmatory bias" in the beliefs of alleged survivors and their therapists, in Pendergrast's book he finds a thoroughly laudable emotional commitment.

Crews's credulity for one set of claims is reflected in significant bias throughout the article. Among the empirical knowledge Crews flouts is that regarding the operation of the criminal justice system in cases of child sexual abuse and adult recollections of incest. Certainly, we would all have a great deal to worry about were in fact accusations launched by "a vengeful or mentally unhinged adult...immediately believed by police and social workers," or "draconian sentences...being served and plea bargains...being coerced in the face of transparently clear signs that the charges are bogus." However, empirical data regarding the operation of the child protective services and criminal justice systems do not support these crude caricatures.

In fact, a large percentage of reports of child sexual abuse—up to 60 percent in some states—are not substantiated by child protective services workers. Only 42 percent of sexual abuse allegations that have been substantiated by child protection authorities or reported to the police are actually forwarded for prosecution, according to a study by the American Bar Association. Moreover, because sexual abuse is so frequently a crime without other witnesses or physical corroboration, and prosecutors are concerned about children's credibility, people arrested for sexual offenses against children are somewhat *less* likely to be prosecuted than are other violent offenders. One detailed study of allegations of sexual abuse in day care found that 82 percent of such allegations were dismissed by investigators. When prosecutions do occur, the majority—about 75 percent according to one study—result in convictions. However, most of these convictions (over 90 percent) result from guilty pleas and plea bargains. Sexual abusers are convicted somewhat more frequently than other violent offenders, probably because prosecutors are so selective in the cases they take to trial. Even when convicted, however, child sexual abusers receive light sentences. Three studies suggest that 32 percent to 46 percent of convicted child sexual abusers serve no jail time at all. Only 19 percent receive sentences longer than one year, which is about the same as those convicted of other violent crimes.

Crews's depiction of the standard of practice among therapists working with women who recall a childhood history of incest is similarly skewed. Crews cites with indignation the results of an unnamed "survey" indicating that "well over 50,000" of America's 255,000 licensed psychotherapists are now "willing to help their clients realize that they must have endured early molestation." Victims of childhood physical and sexual abuse are, not surprisingly, heavily overrepresented in clinical therapeutic populations. Since several empirical studies indicate that 40 percent to 85 percent of psychotherapy patients suffered abuse in childhood, we are somewhat distressed to learn that only 20 percent of psychotherapists may be willing to help their patients explore this possibility.

More important, Crews leaves the impression that modal practice in this field is carried on by wild-eyed zealots. Of course bad practice occurs in the field of child maltreatment, as in any other. We fully agree with Crews that bad practice in this field can have tragic results, and should energetically be opposed. But no empirical evidence suggests that the practice displayed on *Geraldo* is typical. Child interview guidelines distributed by such major organizations as the American Academy of Child and Adolescent Psychiatry (1985) and the American Professional Society on the Abuse of Children (1990) specifically recommend against the coercive and suggestive questioning practices that Crews suggests are the rule. The writers and lecturers on "adult survivor" therapy who are most admired and sought after by professionals in this field caution against the use of hypnosis and sodium pentothal, and against the tenet that remembering and "working through" all traumatic material is necessary or positive. Given this and other evidence that modal professional practice is thoughtful and responsible, Crews's vitriol against professionals is hard to understand, and his depiction of zealous incompetence as the rule is indefensible.

Finally, Crews very effectively demolishes the naive concept of repression in which memories are hermetically sealed and stored intact for future revelation. However, he fails to shed any light on the processes that are at work in the very well-documented phenomenon of imperfect recall of traumatic events. His categorical statement, "Reputable scientific research ... offers no support to the concept of repression even in its mildest form," is misleading. A vast scientific literature on memory offers no consistent definition of repression, but a great deal of information about variously defined memory lapses. Full or partial amnesia for traumatic events has been well-documented in combat veterans, people who have survived natural disasters and other traumas, and people who have experienced physical and sexual abuse in childhood. Saying that such amnesia does not conform to the naive depiction popularized on talk shows and in some books or to the very narrow, specific definition of repression used by Crews does nothing to explain how such amnesia does occur, how once-forgotten or faded memories reemerge, or how to assess the veracity of such memories.

The most conservative data available on the prevalence of father–daughter incest suggest that 1.3 percent of American women will experience it. These data are from upper-middle-class white college students in the Northeast responding to a paper-and-pencil questionnaire. Everything we know about differential prevalence rates and the efficacy of different methods of information-gathering suggests that this prevalence estimate is low. However, even at this low estimate, 1.6 million American girls and women are now or have been victims of father–daughter (or stepfather–daughter) incest. A number of factors have converged in the last several years to encourage these women to speak out about their victimization, including a greater attention to child sexual abuse generally and a feminist reinterpretation of father–daughter incest as, like rape, a victimization rather than a shameful secret.

These allegations challenge us intellectually and emotionally. Like many allegations of child sexual abuse, allegations by adult women of childhood incest often pit one person's word against another's. In response to such extraordinarily difficult epistemological situations, a natural impulse is to make a summary judgment in favor of the least painful alternative. For the vast majority of Americans, that alternative is to believe that adults do not victimize children in the ways now being alleged. It takes the greatest discipline for individuals and for the society to fairly weigh the veracity of these reports. Crews very effectively chronicles the failure of some people to maintain this discipline. We regret that he was not able to serve the readers of NYRB better by maintaining such discipline himself. ✳

Richard P. Gartner, Ph.D., and Dodi Goldman, Ph.D., both from the William Alanson White Institute in New York City, and twenty-seven cosigners, nineteen of them also members of that institute, wrote an 800-word letter to *The New York Review* that they did not wish to see republished here. Hence this summary.

Although they joined Frederick Crews in criticizing overly zealous recovered memory therapists who neglect the corrupting influence of suggestion and fantasy, Gartner, Goldman, et al. wrote that the existence of forgotten sexual trauma is well established. Psychiatrists working with confirmed cases of molested children, they reported, have found that a significant minority of them are indeed known to have lost all memory of their ordeals. In this connection, the correspondents cited a 1992 study by Linda Meyer Williams purporting to show that, in one instance, 38 percent of girls once hospitalized for sexual abuse subsequently lost their memory of that abuse.

Gartner, Goldman, et al. criticized not only Crews's apparent lack of compassion for people whose "loved caretakers" have betrayed them, but also his equation of psychoanalysis with the most objectionable features of recovered memory treatment. Modern analysts, they pointed out, do not "advocate traditional hypnosis or suggestion" or rely single-mindedly on abreaction (cathartic re-experiencing) when dealing with survivors of abuse. Thus, the writers alleged, Crews's apprehension of psychoanalytic theory and practice is drastically out of date.

According to this letter, one important sign of Crews's ignorance of developments in contemporary psychoanalysis is his failure to appreciate that victims of molestation typically resort to dissociation, not repression, as their chief means of managing trauma. The "emotional flooding and paralysis" brought on by molestation typically prevents the sufferer from taking cognizance of the act even while it is occurring. The result can be various dissociative reactions not only to the abuser—who may in fact be one of the child's parents—but also to the other parent, who is unconsciously blamed for having allowed the abuse to proceed. Not just suppressed memories, then, but also clashing feelings of love and rage produce in survivors "multiple experiences of self and others."

Gartner, Goldman, et al. suggested that Crews might improve his understanding of such matters by consulting "a growing and rich psychoanalytic literature" about the treatment of adult survivors, and in particular the following books:

Jody Messler Davies and Mary Gail Frawley, *Treating the Adult Survivor of Childhood Sexual Abuse: A Psychoanalytic Perspective* (Basic Books, 1994).

Darlene Bregman Ehrenberg, *The Intimate Edge: Extending the Reach of Psychoanalytic Interaction* (Norton, 1992).

234

Howard B. Levine, editor, *Adult Analysis and Childhood Sexual Abuse* (Analytic Press, 1990).

Leonard Shengold, *Soul Murder: The Effects of Childhood Abuse and Deprivation* (Yale University Press, 1989).

CHARLOTTE KRAUSE PROZAN is the author of *Feminist Psychoanalytic Psychotherapy* and *The Technique of Feminist Psychoanalytic Psychotherapy*. She is a licensed psychotherapist and therapist in San Francisco and Associate Director of the San Francisco Institute for Psychoanalytic Psychotherapy and Psychoanalysis. She writes:

The current significant discourse on the issue of repressed memory is not well served by the the snide, contemptuous tone of Dr. Crews's hit piece. Those of us who actually practice the professions of psychoanalysis and psychotherapy are also deeply concerned about the issues of truth and justice in this field, but polarizing the topic by vindictive, bitter, and emotional attacks against those who disagree with you serves to shed no light on these vital questions, but only to polarize and alienate and thereby divert our search for wisdom. I am currently editing a book on the subject which will be published in 1995, *Construction and Reconstruction of Memory*, in which my goal is to integrate the knowledge of a number of important writers and thinkers on this topic and hopefully further our understanding. I don't believe Dr. Crews's writing is a contribution to this much-needed integration.

Specifically in reference to his personalized attack on me, please allow your readers to see the full statement from which

Dr. Crews selected one phrase to quote: "we are looking for sexual abuse." This gives a very distorted view of my thinking, which actually supports some of Dr. Crews's concerns.

> In 1973 and before, analysts were looking for penis envy. In 1990, we are looking for sexual abuse. It is true that, now as then, we are more likely to find what we are looking for—the subjective component of our scientific investigation. It is common for therapists today to see a great number of women patients reporting sexual abuse, because that is what they are reading about and hearing about on radio and television. Women in the 1950's read and heard about happy housewives; they came to therapists distressed because they were unhappy and had concluded there must be something wrong with them. The analysts' answer was that they envied their husbands. Patient and analyst are living in the same culture, and are being formed by similar trends. They may collude in what they believe is an accurate diagnosis of the patient's problems. But because they are both culture-bound, the truth may elude them both. (1992, p. 207)

I hope this full quote will assure you and your readers that I am not the simpleton Dr. Crews would like you to believe I am.

But I am most disturbed by his vicious attacks on our patients, both my patient "Penelope" and Eileen Franklin Lipsker. His alleged concern for the welfare of all women and his specific concern for women patients is belied by his assaults on Lipsker and "Penelope." As authors and speakers we take upon ourselves the risk that by sticking our necks out, someone might find some cruel satisfaction in cutting them off. But why attack our patients? This, in my mind, is unconscionable. To dismiss Mrs. Lipsker's testimony by saying "as many observers perceived, she had a distinct taste for fame" is beneath contempt. And who are these "many observers"? Dr. Crews gives us no names or citations. And we then learn that Elizabeth Loftus, whom he so admires, as do I, appeared on a Faith Daniels talk show. Are we to conclude that Elizabeth Loftus is motivated solely by a "distinct taste for fame"? And what about writers who publish essays in *The New York Review of Books*, especially such highly controversial articles? Does that entitle me to question Dr. Crews's motives and dismiss his intelligence because he has a "distinct taste for fame"?

As to my patient Penelope, he is most unfair and mean-spirited in his characterization of her as "frantic" and as a simple pawn who "surrendered" to pressure from me. "Penelope" is a highly intelligent and thoughtful woman and I really resent Crews's insult to her. His disrespectful dismissal of me I can brush off as the product of a very bitter, unhappy, and angry man, but please leave my patients out of it. Of course she is incensed by it. But how can one have a dialogue with someone who totally dismisses the concept of repression? It is futile. He even manages to convince himself that Ross Cheit, the Brown University professor, simply "refocused" his attention and just happened to be reading a book on pedophilia. I mean after all, don't we all just happen to pick up books on pedophilia to read in our spare time? Might there have been just a touch of "suggestion" in the telephone conversation in which the no doubt surprised Dr. Cheit is questioned by Dr. Crews as to the source of his memory? I do wish to point out, however, that it is a lose–lose situation with these cynics. If I had made the diagnosis in the first weeks of therapy, I of course would be dismissed as a crank. But the fact that it took us fourteen years of work to be certain of the diagnosis means that my motive for this long treatment was "ideological or financial gain." Give me a break.

Crews was most dishonest in referring to Penelope's symptoms as overeating, drinking, and smoking. It stretches the imagination beyond limits to believe he simply forgot to mention that Penelope's most serious symptom, and the one that led to my suspicion that she may have been sexually abused, was severe promiscuity. This symptom was completely relieved by our analysis. He states she left analysis with the same symptoms with which she entered. Living in the San Francisco Bay area, Crews must know that being able to completely stop a lifelong pattern of picking up men in bars could easily have saved her life in this AIDS infested city.

There is only one reference in this entire piece to the concept of dissociation, which is perhaps even more important than repression in these cases, and that is in the reference to a book *Repression and Dissociation* edited by Jerome L. Singer. I am curious, since Dr. Crews apparently read the book, why he never once mentions dissociation. That, in my view, is one of the key questions for our field. We are at fault for not being clear enough about the differentiation between these two mechanisms and that is one contribution I hope my forthcoming book will make. Crews has omitted the most important issue for us to address now, because it is in fact dissociation and not repression which is at the heart of the memory dilemma.  ✳

"PENELOPE" is the pseudonym given Charlotte Prozan's patient, whose case is discussed above by both Frederick Crews and Prozan. She writes:

I am "Penelope," the patient whose case history Frederick Crews refers to in his mean-spirited comments regarding the work of my therapist, Charlotte Prozan, and her book *The Technique of Feminist Psychoanalytic Psychotherapy.*

  Mr. Crews paints a picture for your readers of a Penelope who did not exist. First, and most seriously distorted, is his image of me as a helpless creature subject to the whims of a therapist with a wild agenda of her own. I put a tremendous amount of myself into the therapy process over years and years, knowing even at the most difficult times that my responsibility to myself was to confront the realities that my dreams, my behavior and, finally, my memories were so clearly indicating. (Crews states erroneously that I don't recall any molestation. My memories leave me no doubt whatsoever of the fact that I was!) What is wrong with this man Crews that he must use belittling, sarcasm, and a snide, one-sentence summary of fifteen years of my hard work on my dreams in an attempt to convince your readers that my therapist (who of course was spending an equally arduous fifteen years) was only interested in being correctly aligned with the so-called prevailing winds. There could not be a better therapist than

Ms. Prozan. If your readers wish to see for themselves true scholarship and conscientious professionalism on the subject of repressed memories of sexual abuse, they will surely find them in Ms. Prozan's books.

Not only was I not helpless and misguided, I was not "frantic," as I terminated this successful fifteen-year therapy which truly saved my life. I was instead healing. Weight loss, exercise regimens I still adhere to, a major promotion and success as a supervisor at work, and a dramatic decrease in depression are all the proof I need to confirm the effectiveness of my final years in therapy, learning how to be angry at the right person (yes, the man who molested me is a son of a bitch, and yes, it is his fault).

The real tragedy, completely missed by Crews, is that the serious damage inflicted by the molestation and subsequent repression could not have been attended to earlier. There were few tools, few therapists, and no recognition of the long-lasting effects of this crime when I was growing up. I am glad there now are, but I am nevertheless a woman bereft of children, and one who still has to work at learning to trust men.   ✳

Janna Malamud Smith, C.S.W., declined permission to republish her 900-word letter. She, too, agreed with Crews that the recovered memory movement possesses an "extreme, fanciful, and destructive dimension." She maintained, however, that Crews's all-out attack had not sufficiently credited the prevalence of real molestation and its terrible effects. The incidence of sexual abuse, Smith wrote, is much higher than that of false memory formation.

Nevertheless, Smith argued, people are known to forget traumatic experiences under many circumstances. She cited the documented occurrence of traumatic amnesia—for example, that of the jogger who was brutally raped in Central Park several years ago but who failed to remember the experience. Alcoholic blackouts, Smith maintained, are also relevant in this regard. Smith has come across many such instances in her own experience as a social worker who has practiced psychotherapy. If the concept of "repression" is an unsatisfactory one, we must seek new explanations for the complex workings of memory.

Like Gartner, Goldman, et al., Smith found Crews apparently "oblivious to the terrible suffering of trauma patients." She wondered what Crews would recommend that she do with a hypothetical patient who exhibited a considerable number of the symptoms that would seem to suggest a history of molestation. Shouldn't the therapist at least look into the possibility that such a patient had been sexually abused?

In conclusion, Smith suggested that the battle over memory is connected to a number of important social issues, including "health care and money," animus against long-term psychotherapy, and "the fear men have of women becoming slightly more powerful." She regretted Crews's failure to explore those matters.


FREDERICK CREWS replies:
1. Each of these letters addresses part of my reasoning in "The Revenge of the Repressed" but necessarily loses sight of the whole. A précis, then, is in order.

Our country, along with several others, has recently been caught up in a plague of false charges based on "memories" that fit the expectations of therapists who believe that any number of grave or trivial adult symptoms are strongly indicative of long-repressed sexual abuse. That belief lacks credible empirical support. There are sound reasons to distrust the techniques by which therapists and patients have been forming and bolstering their convictions about previously unremembered events. Some of those techniques originated in early beliefs of Freud's that still flourish within psychoanalysis—beliefs, for example, in repression, the unconscious, the capacity of dreams and symptoms to disclose long-past traumatic events, and the need to lay primary therapeutic emphasis on a patient's reconstructed early years. My essay ends by predicting that until the unfoundedness of the Freudian system becomes generally known, we can expect to keep encountering new forms of therapeutic mischief in the name of recovering "the repressed."

Most of the letters above depict me as a callous person who lacks all compassion for victims of abuse. That is at best a misperception, at worst a smear. My essay does not focus on actual victims, except to acknowledge that some of them can indeed forget their abuse for long periods. I feel as much sympathy for them as my detractors do. But precisely because molestation is such a grave matter, we must condemn and rectify the casualness with which *false* accusations are now being generated within an ideologically inflamed therapeutic fad.

2. Theresa Reid is executive director of the American Professional Society on the Abuse of Children. Her letter is an adroit brief for her guild's rank and file, making a token

acknowledgment of improprieties by "some practitioners" (nonmembers, no doubt) but generally projecting a Panglossian contentment with the status quo. Our criminal justice system, she maintains, is doing a fine job of discriminating between innocent and guilty parties; the educational efforts of the False Memory Syndrome Foundation needn't be credited, since some of its members may conceivably be pedophiles; and existing practices in the interrogation of small children leave little to be desired. The only significant flaw in the system, according to Reid, is that *too few* therapists have dedicated themselves to smoking out perpetrators.

Where to begin? Since APSAC is committed to the welfare of children, let me turn first to the matter of child interrogations. Reid apparently thinks that if humane guidelines have been issued by her organization, and if most practitioners follow those guidelines, there is nothing to worry about. But it is still a common enough occurrence for both "child protection" workers and police to overreact as soon as an excitable adult has voiced a suspicion that a day-care worker or relative may have been molesting children. Attention is concentrated upon those children who reject the adult's hypothesis. Their punishment is to be subjected to frightening and humiliating physical poking and to repeated, relentless, prurient questioning. Both of those practices torment and corrupt initially truthful children, breaking down their sense of trust, arousing morbid fears about bodily invasion, and coaching them to confabulate.

Abusive practices of interrogation must be stopped altogether, not only because children are being psychologically damaged but because each case of coerced testimony bears the potentiality of condemning innocent adults to prison. One such case, that of the New Jersey day-care teacher Margaret Kelly Michaels, is in the news even as I write. Michaels had been convicted on 115 counts of sexual abuse after a three-year-old was heard to make a suggestive remark about her behavior, and the witch hunt got under way. She served five years of her forty-seven-year sentence before being released when an appellate panel of judges ruled that "her trial was full of egregious prosecutorial abuses, including questioning of the children that planted suggestions, tainting their testimony" (*The New York Times*, December 3, 1994).

That is progress, of course; and New Jersey's Supreme Court, unlike most others, has recently taken cognizance of the need for noncoercive questioning and for videotaped records of initial interviews with children in criminal cases. But Theresa Reid's near-perfect system clearly failed Margaret Kelly Michaels. So, too, it failed the Massachusetts school-bus driver Robert C. Halsey, who is serving *two consecutive life terms* for far-fetched misdeeds unwitnessed by any adults; and Frank Fuster, whom Janet Reno helped to put away for *165 years* in another bizarre and fantasy-ridden case in Florida; and Robert Fulton Kelly, Jr., who is serving *twelve consecutive life terms* in the North Carolina case whose fraudulence was exposed in the PBS documentary *Innocence Lost*. Kelly will be eligible for parole in 240 years.[1]

---

1. *Later:* On May 2, 1995, a three-judge panel of the North Carolina Court of Appeals ordered a new trial for Kelly and for Dawn Wilson, formerly a cook in Kelly's day-care center, who had received a life sentence for alleged acts of child sexual abuse.

It can be seen, I trust, that when Theresa Reid refers to the "light sentences" received by child abusers, she is mostly referring to the fate of actual sex criminals who are caught abusing a single child, and who are therefore eager to plea bargain. It is no coincidence that life terms tend to be reserved for the innocent, since, in a climate of rumor and panic, one false accusation against an individual easily breeds many others.

As for standards of therapeutic prudence, Reid expresses satisfaction that the "most admired" authorities caution against reliance on drugs and hypnosis to extract memories. The fact that other admired authorities say the opposite and that those tools continue to be widely employed does not appear to interest her.[2] Moreover, she misses the more crucial point that drugs and hypnosis are not needed for generating false memories; one needs only a vulnerable client, a therapist

---

2. In 1993, Debra A. Poole and D. Stephen Lindsay surveyed randomly chosen Ph.D.-level therapists (that is, the most scientifically sophisticated cohort) who treat a substantial number of female patients. Of 151 respondents, 75 percent admitted to using one or more aids to recovered memory, including hypnosis, "body memories," dream interpretation, guided imagery, and age regression. Again, 25 percent said not only that they place emphasis on recovering memories of abuse but that they have sometimes overridden their clients' initial denials and, indeed, that they have occasionally been able to form their conclusions after a single session. (Poole and Lindsay's paper is in press.) Another researcher, who distributed a questionnaire to over a thousand psychotherapists at conventions in 1992, found that 47 percent of the respondents believed that "psychotherapists can have greater faith in details of a traumatic event when obtained hypnotically than otherwise." In fact, 28 percent of them averred that hypnosis can produce accurate memories *of past lives*. This is the "modal professional practice" that Theresa Reid so admires. See Michael D. Yapko, *Suggestions of Abuse: True and False Memories of Childhood Sexual Trauma* (Simon and Schuster, 1994), pp. 57–58.

who is strongly predisposed to regard symptoms as "consistent with abuse," and a copy of *The Courage to Heal*—which is, *pace* Reid, overwhelmingly the most widely consulted and recommended book in the field.[3]

Reid sneers at Mark Pendergrast, an investigative journalist whose well-researched book she hasn't even seen, for his inability to find a mainstream publisher. When she does peruse *Victims of Memory*, she will find that it discusses the runaround Pendergrast was given by major houses, which wanted no part of an "accused perpetrator"—even though an earlier work of his was chosen by *The New York Times* as one of the "Notable Books" of 1993. Reid tries to incite Pendergrast's prospective readers to sustain that ostracism, just as she warns them away from the unsavory FMSF. But it is her own tactics that are truly unsavory. To slander cogent and important presentations of evidence by implying that the presenters may be sex criminals is the McCarthyism of the Nineties.[4]

---

3. As Paul Ingram's case among others illustrates, even less is required for confabulation to occur. See Maryanne Garry and Elizabeth Loftus, "Pseudomemories without Hypnosis," *International Journal of Clinical and Experimental Hypnosis*, Vol. 42 (1994), pp. 363–378.

4. To gather from Reid's letter, the gullible Crews believes that all members of FMSF are "slandered relatives of survivors." What I actually wrote is that most of them are. Does Reid wish to dispute that claim and maintain that a majority are active pedophiles? It must be puzzling to her that such non-shady figures as Martin Gardner, Rochel Gelman, Lila Gleitman, Ernest Hilgard, David Holmes, Philip Holzman, Paul McHugh, Ulric Neisser, Martin Orne, Thomas Sebeok, and Donald Spence are all represented on the FMSF board. I have recently joined that board myself.

For the record, Reid is in error when she writes that Mark Pendergrast's daughters have accused him of incest. One of them acquired in therapy a belief in some sexual misdeed that she has never specified—a belief that is rendered

Reid counts me among those naive people who refuse to believe that widespread child abuse occurs. My essay, however, makes repeated mention of that abuse, while continually seeking to emphasize the need to differentiate between real and ersatz cases. That Reid herself lacks any real concern to do so is manifested in her statement that as many as 85 percent of all psychotherapy patients were abused as children. Games with statistics are rife in this field, but it is safe to infer that a figure as wild as that one came from investigators who not only define abuse very broadly but also add questionable "repressed" cases into their totals. It is Reid who is credulous here; she is counting claims of abuse that are confided to importuning therapists as if they had been authenticated.[5]

On the issue of whether repression exists, Reid displays her taste for "measured" and "responsible" stands by implying that only a fanatic would want to reach any conclusions from the "vast scientific literature" out there. When generally accepted

---

suspect by plentiful evidence of her affection and trust up till then. For Theresa Reid, however, an accusation once made, even though it may have been generated by an illegitimate exercise of influence, becomes an indelible stain, and in Pendergrast's case she seems eager to make sure that the mud stays on.

5. Other figures cited by Reid are equally irrelevant and obfuscatory. There is no comfort to be found in her statement that up to 60 percent of reported molestations "are not substantiated by child protective services workers"; the question is whether a significant number of erroneous reports are "substantiated." The same objection applies to Reid's figures on dismissal of day-care charges. And why should we rejoice that 75 percent of prosecutions result in convictions, given that some significant proportion of those convicted may be innocent? What Reid's figures, taken together, actually imply is that baseless charges of molestation are now as common as rain. Moreover, she conveniently overlooks the permanently scarring effects of unproven allegations, especially when they are taken to trial.

criteria of scientific judgment are applied to that literature, however, the full-blown psychoanalytic concept of repression can be seen to lack appreciable *independent* support. And that fact is crucial for determining whether "expert witnesses" should be allowed to indoctrinate juries in the folklore of repression, to say nothing of the zanier "robust repression" that figures in most recovered memory cases.[6]

Reid beclouds the issue by invoking "variously defined memory lapses" that no one would dispute, including organically determined traumatic amnesia and imperfect recall of

---

6. New Hampshire Superior Court Justice William J. Groff recently issued a decision that could serve as a model for every jurisdiction:

> Before testimony of the victim's memory of the alleged assault may be admitted, a hearing shall be held at which the burden shall be upon the State to establish that the phenomenon of memory repression and the process of recovery through therapy have gained general acceptance in the field of psychology. The State must establish the validity of the phenomenon and process by demonstrating that the reasoning or methodology underlying the testimony is scientifically valid; and that it is capable of empirical testing and can properly be applied to the facts in issue. (*State* v. *Hungerford and Morahan*, State of New Hampshire Nos. 94-S-45 through 47 and 93-S-1734 through 1936, September 14, 1994)

*Later:* Justice Groff then conducted just such a thorough hearing in the case at hand, taking testimony from prominent expert witnesses on both sides of the recovered memory debate. His subsequent ruling of May 23, 1995, which is widely regarded as a legal milestone, declared trial testimony about recovered memory to be inadmissible. The heart of Justice Groff's thoughtful statement is this sentence: "The Court finds that the testimony of the victims as to their memory of the assaults shall not be admitted at trial because the phenomenon of memory repression, and the process of therapy used in these cases to recover the memories, have not gained general acceptance in the field of psychology; and are not scientifically reliable."

remembered events. The key question that she tries to obscure is whether therapeutically generated memories of *otherwise unknown and biographically anomalous* early events tend to get corroborated by hard evidence. The answer is: Never! That is why the seeming rationality of Reid's "moderate" position—some memories are true and some are false—is deceptive. In view of the facts, it amounts to middle-of-the-road extremism.

Reid's letter, approved by a forty-seven-member board of directors, is a disservice not only to truth and fair play but also to children, who suffer when family members are needlessly pitted against one another, and who can still be torn away from their parents, during rumor panics, by overzealous "child protection" functionaries and police.[7] I hope that those members of APSAC who actually care about the welfare of the helpless will hold their leadership accountable for Reid's whistle-while-you-work response to a national tragedy.

---

7. Consider the case of Andrew Myers, his young sister, and his baby brother, who were abruptly seized from Greg and Jane Myers in 1984 and placed in foster homes while the "Scott County sex case" played out in Minnesota. After three months of grilling, the eleven-year-old Myers, who had been issued a new name, began fabricating the demanded sex charges against his parents, who were indicted along with twenty-two other defendants. With the "help" of a county-appointed therapist, Myers came to half-believe that he had been molested by his innocent parents. Although the entire case resulted in only one conviction and Myers was allowed to return home after a year and a half, his relationship with his parents was poisoned thereafter by the lies that he had been forced to tell about them and others.

Myers still recalls what his mother screamed as the police and social workers were abducting him and his siblings: "This is America! This is America! You can't take my kids. This is America!" But it was the America of Cotton Mather, reincarnated as an incest bureaucrat. See *Minneapolis Star Tribune*, October 16, 1994, pp. 14A, 15A.

3. Richard B. Gartner, Dodi Goldman, and their twenty-seven cosigners write in the hope of putting maximum distance between the excesses of the recovered memory movement and their own psychoanalytically oriented practice. But they offer few clues to how that practice deals with issues of memory. Do they, for example, take pains to distinguish between real and false reports of abuse, and if so, on what basis? Have they renounced the traditional Freudian belief that childhood fantasies of incest are as pathogenic as actual rape? Do they concentrate on their patients' supposed infancy and early childhood, or do they address contemporary problems as such?[8]

And how long, and at what expense, do Gartner, Goldman, et al. typically treat an identified incest survivor? Without this last information, we have no way of knowing whether the therapy offered by Gartner, Goldman, et al. is a cost-effective and humane response to victims' unique needs or a hewing to the Freudian norm—namely, the subjecting of all patients, regardless of their complaints, to the same roundabout regimen on the couch.

Gartner, Goldman, et al. are surely disingenuous in chiding me for believing that "contemporary analysts...*advocate* traditional hypnosis or suggestion when treating abused individuals." My essay makes no such ridiculous claim. It does, however, emphasize suggestion in a quite different and more

---

8. An answer of sorts is suggested by one of the books in Gartner's bibliography, Darlene Ehrenberg's *The Intimate Edge*: "When massive dissociation and denial occur, patients often come for treatment with no memories of having been abused, so that it is only late in treatment that this comes to light" (p. 161). This looks like recovered memory therapy in its most reckless mode.

important sense: the subtly induced compliance of a subordinate party with a dominant party's wishes and beliefs. That is the epistemic flaw not only in recovered memory treatment but also within all "clinical evidence" gathered by psychoanalysts. Gartner, Goldman, et al. show no sign of even beginning to come to grips with it, and neither do the papers I have read that bear the imprimatur of the William Alanson White Institute.

I fail to see why Gartner, Goldman, et al. think they are refuting me by pointing to studies showing the noncontroversial fact that some people forget early incidents of molestation. Perhaps, however, the authors mean to insert a subliminal plug for repression, a concept that they otherwise manifestly shun. Since they raise the point, I will mention that the main account they cite, that of Linda Meyer Williams, fails to take adequate account of the difference between *second-hand knowledge about* abuse and *purported memory of* abuse, or between the significance of non-recall dating back to age twelve years and of that dating back to age ten months. And since nearly all of Williams's women who failed to remember one target incident did recall others, even the most sanguine construction of her results leaves the idea of chronic repression unsupported.[9]

---

9. On this point, see pp. 305–307 of Ofshe and Watters's *Making Monsters.* The authors cite a more recent report by Williams than the one mentioned by Gartner, Goldman, et al.: "Recall of Childhood Trauma: A Prospective Study of Women's Memories of Child Sexual Abuse." This was a paper delivered to the 1993 annual meeting of the American Society of Criminology in Phoenix. *Later:* It has been published in the *Journal of Consulting and Clinical Psychology,* Vol. 62 (1994), pp. 1167–1176.

The same point applies to another concept, dissociation, that Gartner, Goldman, et al., in concert with many other memory therapists, are suddenly finding more congenial than repression. That mechanism rests on no firmer scientific basis, but it comes with a record of medical overreaching that is considerably more lurid. In making mention of "the individual's multiple experiences of self and others," the signers would appear to be endorsing the latest folly countenanced by the American Psychiatric Association, "dissociative identity disorder." As I mentioned in my essay, that is just a cosmetic name for multiple personality disorder (MPD). However designated, MPD is a preponderantly or entirely iatrogenic (and now, in both senses of the term, telegenic) phenomenon whose main promoters constitute the Satan-fearing lunatic fringe of present-day psychiatry. If Gartner, Goldman, et al. are looking to shore up their scientific respectability, they have turned in exactly the wrong direction.

A propos, one of Gartner's recommended texts, Davies and Frawley's *Treating the Adult Survivor of Child Sexual Abuse*, places MPD at the far end of a dissociative continuum and, citing "the best psychiatric literature on the subject," passes along the ludicrous judgment that "between 88% and 97% of all multiple personalities have experienced significant sexual and / or physical abuse in childhood (Putnam, 1989; Ross, 1989)" (p. 76). Aficionados of MPD will recognize these "best" authorities as Frank Putnam, who uses hypnosis and age regression to locate "alters" in patients who weren't previously suspected of being MPD candidates, and Colin Ross, who is on record as believing that since the 1940s the CIA has been using drugs, electroshock, sensory deprivation, and "enforced memorization" to create Manchurian candidates whom he must deprogram. These are evidently the giants of "modern medicine" to whom Gartner, Goldman, et al. now wish to entrust the desperate fortunes of psychoanalysis.

4. To judge from her letter, Charlotte Krause Prozan, too, has recently become a fan of dissociation, an idea that is only glancingly mentioned in her 562-page book of 1993, *The Technique of Feminist Psychoanalytic Psychotherapy*. But that book does embody Prozan's enduring diagnostic and therapeutic principles, which now deserve a closer look. My essay argued that psychoanalysis stands closer to recovered memory theory and practice than its adherents will admit, but Prozan has actually managed to fuse the worst of both traditions, achieving, in the showcase example of "Penelope," an outcome whose significance neither Prozan nor Penelope herself now appears able to grasp.

Prozan's starting point is a desire to retain as much of psychoanalysis as can be reconciled with "feminism," which she construes not as a multifarious sociopolitical movement but as a unitary body of proven theory about the mind. On one side, she looks to Freud for her faith in repression, the unconscious, and the symbolic decoding of dreams. "Were it not for my knowledge of dream interpretation," she acknowledges, "I might never have known that Penelope had been sexually abused as a child by a trusted friend of the family...."[10] But the psychoanalytic Freud, of course, could not have spurred Prozan to pursue her hunch; for that purpose, "feminism"

---

10. Prozan, *The Technique of Feminist Psychoanalytic Psychotherapy*, p. 260. Subsequent parenthetic citations refer to this book.

came to the rescue. In 1977, Prozan relates, she read *one feminist article* dealing with the prevalence of consciously remembered abuse, and, presto, "the case of Penelope developed into an example of repressed sexual seduction and rape" (p. 248). Penelope thus became the guinea pig for a novice memory therapist who, in her own words, "had never been able to bring back an actual case of molestation . . . and so . . . had had to piece it together as best I could from symptoms, memory traces, screen memories, and dream analysis" (p. 262).

"The clinician," Prozan writes, "must be able to recognize symptoms of incest and have the emotional capacity to accept the patient and elicit the details" (p. 250). Needless to say, this is rather different from discriminating between reliable and specious signs of abuse. Prozan tells us that she takes direction, not from the prudent authorities alluded to by Theresa Reid, but from the "incest survivors' aftereffects checklists" provided in E. Sue Blume's *Secret Survivors* and, predictably, in the early editions of *The Courage to Heal* (Prozan, pp. 310–311). Indeed, she regularly commends Bass and Davis's work to her patients, and she told Penelope about *Secret Survivors* just as soon as it appeared in 1990, while Penelope was in her fourteenth and final year of trying to remember the molestation scene that Prozan continually urged upon her (p. 280).

These facts bear upon Prozan's charge that I quoted her out of context when I had her saying that analysts today "are looking for sexual abuse." To be sure, that phrase was plucked from a paragraph in which Prozan displayed a momentary realization that diagnoses are subject to fashion. But in the larger context of her two books and her self-described "leading the witness" (p. 267) in Penelope's case, the quotation accurately reflects her policy. Indeed, to say that Prozan merely "looks for" abuse would be a considerable understatement.

Penelope herself now informs readers of *The New York Review* that she did remember being anally raped at age nine, but Prozan cannot bring herself to endorse that claim. How could she, when her book is explicit about Penelope's acquisition of "insight into her emotional state as a child *without specific memory*" (p. 308; italics added)? If by now Penelope has turned her "insight" into visions, that proves only that she has persisted in the work of self-deception so strenuously facilitated by Prozan.

Prozan chides me for failing to grant that Penelope's "most serious symptom," sexual promiscuity, was "relieved by our analysis." That behavior did indeed abate, whether or not through Prozan's ministrations. But readers who study the case history will discover that Penelope's sexual habits receive minor emphasis, and for a good reason. She picked up men in bars only "in the beginning of her therapy," thereafter progressing to a still troubling "married-man syndrome" that she was unable to overcome (pp. 23–24). If Prozan had turned this modest gain into the centerpiece of her case, as she now belatedly attempts to do, she would have had to explain why the hunt for the missing memory of rape had to continue for another dozen years or so.[11]

---

11. Note, by the way, how the matter of promiscuity in this case fails to jibe with Freudian expectations. Prozan's letter states that it was Penelope's sexual conduct that first alerted her to the likelihood of molestation. Presumably, then, Penelope would need to "derepress" her rape memory, or at the least to accept its buried existence, before overcoming her symptom. Just the opposite occurred: the symptom vanished and the struggle to induce belief went on and on and on.

Now Penelope declares that she was "healing" for all of her fifteen years under Prozan's care. Again, however, the book tells a different story. Not only were Penelope's highlighted behavioral problems still in evidence at termination, but Prozan's narrative is a saga of thwarted efforts on Penelope's part to overcome an emotional bondage (alias "transference") that was *preventing* meaningful advances. Penelope "acknowledged that at times her smoking, drinking, and overeating were done with a sense of secret rebellion in relation to me and made her feel free and independent" (p. 27); and

> I made many interpretations that Penelope was afraid I would be angry if she lost weight, was successful with men, and left me. At other times she expressed the wish for termination at points in the therapy when she still had considerable work to do on her molestation, saying she believed that if she left therapy she could lose weight. This idea was both an avoidance of the frightening subject of her sexual molestation and also a recognition that the dependency tie to me required, in her mind, that she remain overweight. (pp. 187–188)

Prozan and Penelope both criticize me for saying that Penelope turned frantic as termination approached. But Prozan's case notes for the period show Penelope weeping frequently both in therapy sessions and at home, worrying about her ability to be self-possessed on her own, repeatedly feeling "very distressed" (pp. 303, 305), and telling Prozan that "I'm afraid to stop therapy, I might lose control" (p. 303). In the same period, however, she ceased doubting Prozan's diagnosis

256

and began interpreting her own dreams in Prozan's single-minded style. That is what Prozan in her case notes proudly calls "working independently" (p. 293). Instead, as I maintained, it seems to have constituted an intellectual surrender in the face of prospective abandonment.

None of this is meant to dispute the fact that Penelope is now feeling better and conducting herself more self-assertively than she did under Prozan's tutelage. Indeed, according to Prozan's book, a dramatic improvement commenced *just as soon as the therapy was over*—resulting, for example, in a thirty-pound weight loss within Penelope's first six months of freedom (p. 309). Neither Prozan nor Penelope can detect the irony in that fact—although, as we have seen, there were prior signs of Penelope's well-founded belief that "if she left therapy she could lose weight."[12]

---

12. Even if Penelope had made impressive progress over a fifteen-year period, the question would remain whether the credit for that progress belonged to her therapist. The gains could have been made despite Prozan's efforts rather than because of them. In fact, Prozan's case notes hint at some responsibility on her part for two of the ongoing debits in Penelope's psychic ledger, her lack of success with men and her alienation from her mother. When Penelope, clinging at age forty to a frayed strand of self-esteem, expressed a stubborn faith that "there was a man for her out there," Prozan intervened to convince her that the man in question was only her oedipally desired but long-dead father. "Her realization of the source of this fantasy was a crushing blow," we are told (p. 260). And Prozan's interpretations hammered home the point that Penelope's by then elderly mother was "selling her out," that she was "insensitive," that she "put you in a vulnerable position," and so on (pp. 265, 304, 306). More basically, it was Prozan who widened the chasm between Penelope and her family by burdening her with the tale of molestation that both her mother and her sister found so unbelievable and offensive.

As I suggested in my essay, experienced psychoanalysts will deplore this case history, but it is less parodic of their own work than they might wish. Like Penelope, many an orthodox Freudian patient finds in the "transference" a tar baby rather than a clear path to independence and relief. And what is there to choose between mining dreams for knowledge of abuse and for standard oedipal content? In either case the "unconscious meaning" is produced through circular operations that lack even a semblance of empirical authorization.

Two other points raised in Prozan's letter remain to be clarified. First, I have never phoned Ross Cheit; he surprised me with a call after I had sent him a letter posing a number of questions. And second, Eileen Lipsker's "taste for fame" (and money) expressed itself variously and was often remarked around the time of the George Franklin trial; see pages 173–175, 181–182, 184, 216, 328–329, and 478 of Harry N. MacLean's *Once Upon a Time*. If Prozan recognizes no moral difference between writing an article that denounces a horrendous epidemic of malpractice and getting a Hollywood agent to negotiate the book and movie rights to one's adventures shortly before obtaining a questionable murder verdict against one's father, I am at a loss to help her.

5. Janna Malamud Smith falls into a number of traps that may look familiar by now. She confounds the immediately detected molestation of children with recovered memory cases; she fails to distinguish between inaccurate or incomplete memory and the full obliteration of a painful incident; she fails to note how the organically accountable amnesia of an alcoholic or of a severely battered victim of mugging differs from the alleged repression of entire years' worth of habitual

fondling or rape; and she puts a glib political gloss on an issue that is ultimately ethical and practical—namely, whether psychotherapists shouldn't finally begin making due allowance for human suggestibility and for their own role in exploiting it, however inadvertently and with whatever benign intentions.

Smith does raise one issue that must be on many readers' minds: What should a therapist do with a patient who shows every sign of having been abused? First, there are no empirically established behavioral patterns that point unambiguously to abuse; the recovered memory literature on this topic consists of reckless speculation. Even the extremely disturbed patient conjured by Smith would not automatically qualify as a survivor. Thus, to assume the contrary and begin probing for memories of molestation would be to risk heading down the path of mutual error and misplaced vengefulness.

And second, no one, either in the psychoanalytic tradition or in the newer school of Bass and Davis, has shown that the exhuming of distant memories is psychologically beneficial *at all*, much less that it is a treatment of choice—and there is much evidence that it can prove destructive, even to the point of inducing suicide. I would hope that Smith could address her patient's current symptoms, feelings, attitudes, and ideas in the hope not of "reconstructing" a dubiously accurate early history but of fortifying the patient to deal with the challenges lying directly before her.

I should add that psychotherapists rarely meet an *initial* cluster of symptoms as drastic as the one Smith portrays—unless, of course, the patient has already been damaged by other recovered memory therapists and is being handed down toward the movement's hell, the MPD ward. The stories of brutal antipsychiatry that are beginning to reach us from that quarter will, I predict, launch the wave of public nausea and outrage that will finally put a stop to "therapy" surrounding so-called repressed memories.

Ellen Bass and Laura Davis, coauthors of *The Courage to Heal*, declined to allow their 600-word letter to be published here. That letter alleged many inaccuracies in "The Revenge of the Repressed," of which only a few would be mentioned.

Bass and Davis denied that *The Courage to Heal* is about clinging to victimhood. Rather, it is a compassionate effort to promote healing and "moving on." It deals less with memory than with self-esteem, self-trust, intimacy, grief, and other topics of direct usefulness to survivors. Bass and Davis also denied holding a belief that repressed abuse is more prevalent than remembered abuse. Some of the book's informants had indeed forgotten some or all of their traumatic experience, but even those victims, when they regained their memory, rarely did so with the assistance of a therapist or a support group. And others had always remembered their abuse.

*The Courage to Heal*, said Bass and Davis, is not anti-male, as Crews maintained. They were mystified by Crews's assertion that "women's collectives" provided the reports on which the book is based, and they declared that the problem of child abuse is not gender specific. *The Courage to Heal* discusses female as well as male abusers, and the authors expressed pleasure that it has proved useful to male as well as female survivors.

The authors expressed regret that Crews did not examine the positive achievements of their book, and that he chose instead to indulge in the "mean-spiritedness" characteristic of "backlash" literature, which creates a hostile atmosphere that discourages the abused from coming forward with their stories. As for themselves personally, however, Bass and Davis are not made nervous by the backlash; nor, more particularly, are they fearful of lawsuits, as Crews had inferred.

FREDERICK CREWS replies:
In their letter, Ellen Bass and Laura Davis present themselves as innocents who are unaware of any social damage caused by *The Courage to Heal.* Their chapters, after all, consist mostly of tender advice and instructive stories and testimonials, all designed to comfort and guide victims of sexual molestation. Where, they want to know, is the harm in that?

The catch is that, by and large, the "survivors" to whom their book makes its strongest appeal are not women who have always remembered early sexual abuse. Most such women have long since forged their individual strategies for coping with painful memories and emotional wounds. By contrast, those who desperately cling to Bass and Davis's counsel are struggling to convince themselves or to stay convinced, in opposition to everything they have previously believed or re-called, that they were chronically raped in childhood, usually by their fathers and/or other related males. The active core of *The Courage to Heal* is precisely its "supportive" encour-agement of that belief. The authors' exhortations to self-esteem are thus quixotically premised on a *shattering* of their readers' prior sense of identity and trust. And the recom-mended path to healing is strewn with tragic confrontations and with the civil or criminal prosecution of heartbroken relatives.

Despite Bass and Davis's protestation to the contrary, very little "moving on" is to be found in their survivor narratives. As they admit, "Some women...go through an emergency stage that lasts several years.... [T]hey still feel suicidal, self-destructive, or obsessed with abuse much of the time" (Bass and Davis, p. 76). The authors can't comprehend that this suffering is typically brought on by their own suggestions and by those of the reckless therapists whom they have urged, in their words, to "believe the unbelievable" about their patients' histories (second edition, p. 345).

Bass and Davis now insist on the "compassionate" character of their book. Among accused parents, however, *The Courage to Heal* is known with good reason as *The Courage to Hate*. "First they steal everything else from you," it says, "and then they want forgiveness too? Let them get their own.... It is insulting to suggest to any survivor that she should forgive the person who abused her" (p. 161). Instead, the authors prescribe a cultivation of rage:

> A little like priming the pump, you can do things that will get your anger started. Then, once you get the hang of it, it'll begin to flow on its own.... You may dream of murder or castration. It can be pleasurable to fantasize such scenes in vivid detail. Wanting revenge is a natural impulse, a sane response. Let yourself imagine it to your heart's content.... Suing your abuser and turning him in to the authorities are just two of the avenues open.... Another woman, abused by her grandfather, went to his deathbed and, in front of all the other relatives, angrily confronted him right there in the hospital. (pp. 135, 139)

263

Bass and Davis's compassion, it seems, extends only to the women whom they have helped to wall off from the solicitude of their grieving families.

The authors dispute my account of the "knowledge base" underpinning *The Courage to Heal*, but they misrepresent both my argument and the known sources of their movement. In the early 1980s, both Bass and Judith Herman, who says that her intellectual home for the past two decades has been the Women's Mental Health Collective in Somerville, Massachusetts,[1] belonged to an informal Boston-area network of militant feminists who were gathering (always recalled) molestation stories from workshops, patient surveys, and support groups. By the mid-1980s, influenced in part by such writers as Alice Miller, Diana Russell, and Jeffrey Masson, those theorists of trauma were adding repression and dissociation into the mix, with the result that virtually any unhappy woman, with a little effort and assistance, could now lay claim to full membership in the corps of survivors.

In her recent book *Trauma and Recovery*, Herman notes the contribution of social pressure in the eliciting of previously unconscious material:

> As each group member reconstructs her own narrative, the details of her story almost inevitably evoke new recollections in each of the listeners. In the incest survivor groups, virtually every member who has defined a goal of recovering memories has been able to do so. Women who feel stymied by amnesia are encouraged to tell as much of their story as they do remember.

---

1. Judith Lewis Herman, *Trauma and Recovery* (Basic Books, 1992), p. ix.

Invariably the group offers a fresh emotional perspective that provides a bridge to new memories.[2]

One might say that the recovered memory movement was born when Herman, along with Bass and other anti-patriarchal activists, failed to greet such "new memories" with appropriate skepticism.

Bass and Davis's latest edition does show a dawning awareness that some of the accused and reviled may be innocent after all. Meanwhile, however, the authors display an ominous new interest in supposed women perpetrators and boy victims (p. 14). As their gender bias thus becomes less prominent, the net of their inquisition continues to widen. And their fallacious diagnostic reasoning—epitomized in one quoted survivor's rhetorical question, "Why would I be feeling all this anxiety if something didn't happen?" (p. 92)—remains as virulent as ever.

The authors of *The Courage to Heal* profess themselves indifferent to the threat of damage suits. I will take their word for it. Along with the False Memory Syndrome Foundation, I disapprove of prosecuting writers for the content of their ideas; the only proper response to Bass and Davis is to show how they have deceived themselves and others. No one, however, should underestimate the reverberating havoc they have unleashed upon vulnerable women and their families.

---

2. *Trauma and Recovery*, p. 224. For further insight into the movement's origins, see Chapter 3 of Mark Pendergrast's *Victims of Memory*.

MATTHEW HUGH ERDELYI is a professor in the Department of Psychology at Brooklyn College and the Graduate School of City University of New York. He is the author of *Psychoanalysis: Freud's Cognitive Psychology*. He writes:

Frederick Crews has tried to correct one "folly" by countering it with the opposite folly. Just because many of the so-called recovered memories in the modern literature turn out to be "false recollections" (to use Freud's terminology), it is not logical to assert that recovered memories and the phenomenon of repression are therefore false. Just because many apples are demonstrably not green, it does not follow that Granny Smiths are a "myth."

Within about one decade, and working by himself, without the benefit of an army of funded researchers, cowriters, and special conferences, Freud reached today's cutting-edge position on recovered memories: He concluded that recollections in therapy were typically distorted and emphasized, as any mainstream memory scientist would today, that the recollection of complex events from the past is a pastiche of fact and fantasy. Freud also advanced, already in 1895, the empirical (note, not romantic) observation, confirmed by experimental research in the past decade, that hypnosis is not memory enhancing.

Also, although one would not suspect it from Crews's treatment, Freud's stance against the credulous acceptance of witness testimony is completely in keeping with the position that memory scientists—and Crews himself—advocate. In 1906, around the time Freud was withdrawing his infantile-seduction hypothesis of hysteria (note, not denying childhood sexual abuse), he published a brief article, "Psychoanalysis and the Ascertaining of Truth in Courts of Law."[1] "There is," he begins, "a growing recognition of the untrustworthiness of statements made by witnesses, at present the basis of so many judgments in Courts of Law..." (p. 115). He comments later on cases where the witness is actually testifying against himself —persons like Crews's "Freudian Christian Paul Ingram":

> You may be led astray in your examination by a neurotic who reacts as though he were guilty even though he is innocent—because a lurking sense of guilt already existing in him assimilates the accusation made against him on this particular occasion... and it is indeed a question whether your technique will succeed in distinguishing such self-accused persons from those who are really guilty. (p. 124)

As for false witnessing, I was surprised to read in Crews's reference to my work:[2] "Remarkably, Erdelyi welcomes Freud's unclarity as providing a sound basis for integrating the 'dynamic' with the cognitive unconscious." This is, perhaps, a false memory of Crews's, not my position.

Crews also misrepresents the status of memory recovery and repression in the scientific literature. He embraces the

---

1. *The Collected Papers of Sigmund Freud*, 10 volumes, translated by E. B. M. Horford (Collier Books, 1963), Vol. 1, pp. 115–125.
2. Matthew H. Erdelyi, "Repression, Reconstruction, and Defense: History and Integration of the Psychoanalytic and Experimental Frameworks," in *Repression and Dissociation: Implications for Personality Theory, Psychopathology, and Health*, edited by Jerome L. Singer (University of Chicago Press, 1990), pp. 1–32.

notion "that memory always fades with the passage of time," when a huge literature shows that recall can progressively improve over periods of minutes, days, weeks, months, and probably years. Several scientific reviews of the recent experimental literature have been published over the past decade.[3] My in-press book, *The Recovery of Unconscious Memories: Hypermnesia and Reminiscence* (University of Chicago Press) reviews and integrates a century of clinical and experimental work on the phenomenon of upward-trending memory. The Diagnostic Statistical Manual of the American Psychiatric Association (DSM-IV) includes *dissociative amnesia*, "an inability to recall important personal information, usually of a traumatic or stressful nature... which may resolve spontaneously. ... Some individuals with chronic amnesia may gradually begin to recall dissociated memories" (pp. 478–479).

Crews himself, in another section, seems to accept the phenomenon he has elsewhere disclaimed, as when he states, while criticizing repression: "Ross Cheit, a Brown University professor, has recently proved beyond question that his suddenly recovered 1968 molestation by a music camp administrator was real."

---

3. For some of these reviews, see, in addition to the work cited in footnote 2: Matthew H. Erdelyi, "The Recovery of Unconscious (Inaccessible) Memories: Laboratory Studies of Hypermnesia," in *The Psychology of Learning and Motivation: Advances in Research and Theory*, Vol. 18, edited by Gordon Bower (Academic Press, 1984), pp. 95–127; David G. Payne, "Hypermnesia and Reminiscence in Recall: Historical and Empirical Review," *Psychological Bulletin*, Vol. 101 (1987), pp. 5–27; Henry L. Roediger III, Mark A. Wheeler, and Suprana Rajaram, "Remembering, Knowing, and Reconstructing the Past," in *The Psychology of Learning and Motivation: Advances in Research and Theory*, Vol. 30, edited by Douglas L. Medin (Academic Press, 1993), pp. 97–134.

Ignoring for the moment the question of repression, which is a vast red herring in Crews's article, Cheit's recovered memory suggests that memory need not invariably decay over time. Even if, for the sake of argument, we chose to deny the existence of repression as Freud defined it—the exclusion of some memory or impulse from consciousness—inaccessible memories, forgotten *for whatever reason*, are still subject to recovery.

Although repression is not material to the existence of delayed recall, this does not mean that repression does not exist nor that what Crews suggests about repression is accurate—for example, that repression needs to occur "abruptly and completely." Repression can be laborious and imperfect.

Jerome Singer's edited book, *Repression and Disassociation*, includes a range of positions by mainstream scholars. By highlighting the quote of David Holmes, probably the most constant critic of repression in psychology, Crews is not accurately conveying psychology's stance on the issue, which is mixed. In my own cited chapter I suggest that a large part of the problem is that the field has confused Sigmund Freud with Anna Freud. Unlike his daughter, Sigmund Freud did not insist that repression needed to be unconscious (he actually warned his readers that repression did not have to be always conscious) and used, as I show in this and later publications, the terms repression and suppression interchangeably, along with "inhibition," "dissociation," "thought avoidance," among others. I do not know of an experimental psychologist who would dispute the phenomenon of conscious repression or suppression. Experiments show[4] that avoiding thinking

---

4. See the work cited in footnote 2.

about a complex event leads to the classic memory "decay" function of Ebbinghaus. Some of the "decayed" memories, however, can be recovered by the simple expedient of refocusing thought upon the forgotten material.  ✳

FREDERICK CREWS replies:
If Matthew Erdelyi had carefully read "The Revenge of the Repressed," he could have spared himself some of the effort displayed above. Erdelyi has me saying, for example, that Freudian repression is simply "false." What I actually wrote was that repression may conceivably occur but that it remains undemonstrated by controlled studies—a point that Erdelyi himself has often conceded.[1] My full position, ignored by Erdelyi, is that the idea of repression is too speculative and inflammatory to be harmless in the hands of impressionable patients, therapists, and juries.

Again, Erdelyi thinks he has caught me asserting that no memories are ever recovered, thanks to the fact that "memory always fades with the passage of time." I am allegedly contradicting myself, then, when I discuss an authentic case of recovered memory. My statement about decay, however, was specifically addressed to what I called "the retrievers' notion that 'videotaped' records of events are . . . yielded up to perfect recall." Erdelyi has failed to grasp my dual point that (a) more mundane processes than repression and derepression can

---

1. See, e.g., "Issues in the Study of Unconscious and Defense Processes: Discussion of Horowitz's Comments, with Some Elaborations," in *Psychodynamics and Cognition*, edited by Mardi J. Horowitz (University of Chicago Press, 1988), pp. 81–94. There Erdelyi grants that "the laboratory evidence has failed to provide viable proof for the existence of repression" (p. 84).

account for the occasional instance of belated recall, and (b) the mere retrieval of a memory does not establish the pathogenic character of the recalled event.

Erdelyi is that rarity, an experimental psychologist who clings to a prior Freudian faith. The contortions necessitated by such divided loyalty are on view not only in the letter above but also in the article I originally cited, "Repression, Reconstruction, and Defense." My brief account of that article's strange logic, Erdelyi claims, sounds like the product of a "false memory" on my part. Let us see.

Erdelyi maintains that Freud, thanks to his "tendency toward self-contradiction" (p. 13) and to "the impalpability of the referents" (p. 10), held only a vague and unstable idea of what repression entailed. The concept, Erdelyi shows, answered to "a vast sprawl" of characterizations, from mere "neglect" through "pushing [the unbearable idea] away" (p. 9). Yet Erdelyi is undaunted by this sloppiness. Brazenly, he takes the lowest common denominator of Freud's many "repressions"—namely, the mere "intentional not-thinking of some target material" (p. 4)—and claims that it has been vindicated by rigorous experiments on diminished recall:

> The essential point is that not-thinking/repressing/dissociating/cognitively avoiding/leaving to itself/warding off some to-be-remembered material for whatever reason—psychological poverty, defense, experimental exigencies, or what have you—can result in amnesia. (p. 11)

It seems, then, that Freud was right after all: when we cease thinking about something, it becomes harder to remember!

Erdelyi's article thus salvages repression by radically trivializing its function in Freud's psychodynamic system. Now a pea-sized repression, purged of oedipal, etiological, and therapeutic implications, can be reintroduced as a conscious cognitive skill, "an obvious and ubiquitous device" (p. 14) whose general recognition can lead at last to "the integration of psychoanalysis and experimental psychology" (p. 14). Erdelyi then wills this integration into being by executing a neat pirouette. He adds back in the classic defensive role of repression that he has just finished belittling, and concludes by declaring that academic psychology must now embrace "conflict-fraught" repression as the needed corrective to its "overemphasis of the merely intellective" (p. 27).

Crucial to Erdelyi's special pleading is his claim that, on the whole, Freud conceived of repression as a conscious rather than an unconscious mechanism. Readers may wonder why, after nearly a century of study by hundreds of investigators, only Erdelyi has perceived that fact. The answer is that he has jumbled the *decision* to repress, which Freud sometimes treated as conscious, with the *continuous work* of repression as a supposed blocker of access to consciousness. Pathogenic traumas, Freud consistently maintained, "are never present in conscious memory, only in the symptoms of the illness" (SE, 3:166). Otherwise, the rationale for protracted psychoanalytic treatment would have immediately collapsed.[2]

---

2. If repression works unconsciously, moreover, Freud's and Erdelyi's idea of a conscious decision to repress becomes incoherent. Since the subject subsequently fails to perceive that he is repressing, he must also have repressed the memory of his decision to repress. So, too, this latter conscious choice must have undergone

Erdelyi's remarks above about the prophetic Freud are a throwback to the worshipful tradition of Ernest Jones. One would never know from reading Erdelyi that it was Freud's own rashness—first in prematurely declaring his "seduction theory" proven, then in using even wilder guesswork to keep in play the gratuitous idea of repression—that made his notion of memory appear so complex. Nor would one suspect that it was precisely Freud's credulity about feats of hypnotism that inclined him toward repression in the first place. Freud gave up hypnotism not (as Erdelyi urges) because he had exposed its unreliability but simply because he was no good at it. "I soon began to tire of issuing assurances and commands," he confessed, "such as: 'You are going to sleep!... sleep!' and of hearing the patient... remonstrate with me: 'But, doctor, I'm *not* asleep'" (SE, 2:108).

More tellingly, Freud never questioned the fateful inference he had drawn from others' dexterity with hypnotism, namely, "that my patients knew everything that was of pathogenic significance and that it was only a question of obliging them to communicate it" (SE, 2:110). This was the central mistake that turned Freud into both a bullying therapist and a feverish speculator about the buried infantile past. And his favorite wild card of repression enabled him to trump all empirical challenges, ensuring that psychoanalysis would remain a body of dogma rather than a science.

---

repression, and so on ad infinitum, with increasingly implausible homunculi effacing their predecessors' work within the psyche. It is, I suspect, Erdelyi's uneasiness about this dilemma (Zeno's paradox) that inclines him toward the heterodox view that repression itself operates consciously.

Erdelyi draws our attention to a 1906 paper (SE, 9:103–114) in which Freud warns against "neurotic" self-incrimination by innocent suspects. Actually, this was a lecture delivered to a class of Vienna law students, encouraging them to make forensic use of C. G. Jung's word association tests—the value of which Freud was later to deprecate. He does address false confessions but characteristically overlooks their most likely source, coercive and deceptive means of interrogation. As always, Freud emphasizes the enduring determinism of "the unconscious" while remaining blind to compliance with the expectations of an interested inquirer.

Sealed within the analytic bell jar, Erdelyi cannot perceive the obvious Freudian underpinnings of our present recovered memory movement.[3] Nor can he comprehend that his own experimental work on memory enhancement has no bearing on the credibility of that movement. Erdelyi's studies favor the likelihood of some improved recall, mixed with error, when occasions for rehearsal of previously presented

---

3. As my article maintained, the "scientific" pretensions of that movement derive from a number of unwarranted beliefs that were directly propagated by Freud: that repression is the normal human response to trauma; that experiences in infancy produce long-term memories that can be accurately retrieved decades later; that adult psychological difficulties can be reliably ascribed to certain forgotten events in early childhood and not others; that sexual traumas are incomparably more susceptible to repression and the formation of neurosis than any other kind; that symptoms are themselves "memories" that can yield up the story of their origin; that dream interpretation, too, can disclose the repressed past; that memory retrieval is necessary for symptom removal; and that psychotherapists can confidently trace their clinical findings to the patient's unconscious without allowing for the contaminating influence of their own diagnostic system, imparted directly or through suggestion.

images, words, or stories are repeatedly supplied. That finding dovetails with my own acknowledgment that cueing can remind us of forgotten though unrepressed events. But it fails to come anywhere near the key question surrounding our recent epidemic of dire accusations. This is whether we ought to grant credence to highly anomalous "memories" of multiple sexual violations that were previously unremarked by the subject or anyone else—memories, moreover, "recovered" with the aid of hypnotism, sodium amytal, trance writing, and/or other leading procedures administered by therapists who have acquired a faddish belief that many adult symptoms are likely indicators of childhood molestation.

In short, *pace* Erdelyi, the question is not whether memory can ever be enhanced but whether otherwise incredible tales, produced in a climate of suggestion, should be allowed to ruin people's lives. Erdelyi's misconceived quibbles over repression will only lend encouragement to quacks whose "therapeutic" depredations ought to be halted at the earliest possible moment.

MARCIA CAVELL is the author of *The Psychoanalytic Mind: From Freud to Philosophy*. She will be a visiting professor of philosophy at the University of California, Berkeley, in the spring of 1996. She writes:

I hadn't been moved to protest Frederick Crews's handling of psychoanalysis until his piece on the "recovery" movement, which midway turns into yet another occasion for him to criticize Freud's theories about repression. This is not the basis of my quarrel, since I think Freud built a theory around a relatively homely notion of repression, a theory that has little to recommend it. I have in mind his views about "primary process," a "system Unconscious" that works according to its own special laws, and "primary" (versus "secondary") repression.

What moves me are, first, Crews's extremely mis-leading picture of psychoanalysis (he never troubles to distinguish between Freud and psychoanalysis now, but it is the latter of which he presumably speaks); and then, related to that, his inaccurate account of Richard Wollheim's and Thomas Nagel's defense of Freud in these pages.

Crews lists what he calls "an important core of shared assumptions between psychoanalysis and its hyperactive young successor" (the "recovery" therapists). Of the ten assumptions he comes up with I'll mention only the first two, since what is wrong with them suggests the sort of thing that is wrong with all the rest.

1. To become mentally healthy, we must vent our negative feelings and relive our most painful psychic experiences. The deeper we delve, and the harsher and more bitter the truths that we drag to the surface, the better off we will be.

2. Through the aid of an objective therapist in whom we invest authority, trust, and love, we can not only arrive at an accurate diagnosis of our mental problems but also retrieve the key elements of our mental history in substantially accurate form, uncontaminated by the therapist's theoretical bias.

Probably there are some psychoanalysts who believe these things, but I don't know any. Even Freud thought some bitter truths best left in the dark. One of the marks distinguishing well-trained psychoanalysts (for Crews this must be an oxymoron) from "psychic healers" who are less well-trained and less responsible is the care the former take not to attack defenses that are perhaps better left in place. And a great many psychoanalysts have been so impressed by the currently fashionable denigration of objectivity that they have traded in the ideas of diagnosis and truth-telling for the idea of coherent narrative. I think this is unfortunate. But one might as well get one's misfortunes straight.

So while I agree with Crews that these along with the other eight "shared assumptions" are "erroneous or extremely open to doubt," so, I believe, would most of the psychoanalytic establishment.

Crews goes on to say: "Yet they [these ten erroneous principles] are so widely believed as to constitute what Richard Wollheim and Thomas Nagel, among others, regard as the psychological common sense of our era." I would bet my bottom dollar that neither philosopher accepts any one of these principles, nor regards them as any part of "psychological common sense." It would be fun to try to articulate what that is.   ✳

FREDERICK CREWS replies:

Marcia Cavell starts to go wrong as soon as she complains that I never "distinguish between Freud and psychoanalysis now." I have done so frequently—for example, in my reply to several letters responding to "The Unknown Freud," when I pointed out that "merely by refraining from reliance on such backward ideas as inevitable female masochism and the fateful consequences of masturbation, any contemporary therapist would have a head start over Freud." The question I went on to raise, though, is how we are expected to choose *on scientific grounds* between Freud's notions and those of his improvers. Since all parties accept his question-begging principle that "unconscious ideas, unconscious trains of thought, and unconscious impulses [are] no less valid and unimpeachable psychological data than conscious ones" (SE, 7:113), all are playing the knowledge game with the same loaded dice. In their own writings about psychoanalysis, Richard Wollheim, Thomas Nagel, and Cavell herself have traced elegant philosophical orbits around this point without ever meeting it squarely.

Cavell now maintains that, on the whole, today's "psychoanalytic establishment" would not subscribe to any of the ten principles which, I claimed, the recovered memory movement derived from Freudian precedent. If so, the retreat of psycho-analysis from its original therapeutic and theoretical pretensions has gone farther toward unconditional surrender than I had thought. In any event, my ten points were drawn not from the dwindling and demoralized "establishment" but from the Freudian revelation as it colonized the West, bequeathing to psychotherapy at large its main agenda of symptom decoding, memory retrieval, and purgation of the repressed.

Whether she realizes it or not, Cavell herself has bought shares of that agenda; on no other grounds could she be so certain about what she calls, in her recent book *The Psycho-analytic Mind*, the "momentous discoveries of psychoanalysis." Thus when Cavell counterintuitively asserts that a man typically retains his repressed childhood wish to be "buggered by his father" and that Little Hans's famous horse phobia was brought on by castration fear rather than by the actual horse that had fallen down in his presence, she is willy-nilly ratifying Freud's key premises and the alleged catharses, cures, and recovered memories that underwrote them.[1]

But Cavell wants to lay her bottom dollar on a different proposition: that neither Thomas Nagel nor Richard Wollheim accepts a single one of my ten Freudian points about the meaning of symptoms and dreams, the operation of the unconscious, its predominantly sexual content, the tyranny of the repressed, and so forth. This is a dumbfounding claim, since both Nagel and especially Wollheim have argued vigorously for the gener-

---

1. Cavell, *The Psychoanalytic Mind: From Freud to Philosophy* (Harvard University Press, 1993), pp. 77, 191, 182–185.

al correctness of the classic Freudian outlook. Although Nagel, for example, keeps his detailed affirmations to a minimum, he must have had some standard tenets in mind when he recently declared that "there is now, in advance of all [definitively probative] experiments, substantial reason to believe in the unconscious and psychoanalytic explanations which refer to it."[2]

Cavell's appeal to Richard Wollheim is odder still. Wollheim is a Freud idolator of the old school who has characterized his hero as having done "as much for [humanity] as any other human being who has lived."[3] His trust in Freud admits no impediment. Unsurprisingly, then, his texts not only show explicit support for most of the items I named but cast the net of faith far beyond them. Not content with defending the entirety of Freud's "discoveries" and "clinical findings," Wollheim also looks favorably on the whole assortment of constructs, including even the death instinct,[4] that Freud supposedly derived from them.

Thus, whereas Cavell doubts that Wollheim or any other modern Freudian holds that a psychoanalyst can accurately retrieve a patient's infantile past, that is exactly what Wollheim proclaims. "A line can...be traced," he writes, "from certain adult or adolescent activities to certain infantile experiences." He is disposed to accept at face value, for example, Freud's recon-

---

2. Thomas Nagel, letter to *The New York Review*, August 11, 1994, pp. 55–56.
3. Richard Wollheim, *Sigmund Freud* (1971; reprinted by Cambridge University Press, 1981), p. 252. In outward form, this book is a mere exposition of Freud's ideas. In fact, however—as the quoted sentence manifests—it is a sustained act of advocacy for those ideas.
4. Richard Wollheim, *The Mind and Its Depths* (Harvard University Press, 1993), p. 58.

struction of the Wolf Man's having defecated on the floor, at age one and a half, when he supposedly saw his parents copulating from the rear—all this and much more having been deduced from a dream allegedly experienced at age four but reported to Freud only in adulthood.[5] No practitioner of recovered memory therapy could lay claim to sharper gnostic vision than that.

Moreover, Wollheim still affirms the unique "processes and modes of operation" of the unconscious, the preeminent role of sexuality in causing neurosis, the interpretability of dreams and symptoms as symbolic expressions of the repressed, and the practical efficacy of such interpretations in removing symptoms.[6] All of these points appeared in my list of root psychoanalytic assumptions, along with still another that Wollheim appears to approve—that the fixed meanings of universal sexual symbols can come to the aid of clinical interpretation.[7]

According to Cavell, my passing references to Nagel and Wollheim constitute an "inaccurate account of [their] defense of Freud." Incomplete, yes; inaccurate, no. Nagel and

---

5. Wollheim, *Sigmund Freud*, p. 172; *The Mind and Its Depths*, p. 99; and Sigmund Freud, *The Case of the Wolf-Man: From the History of an Infantile Neurosis*, introduction by Richard Wollheim, etchings and woodcuts by Jim Dine (Arion Press, 1993).

6. Wollheim, *Sigmund Freud*, pp. 183, 86, 88, 203, 146, 149–150, 172, 231, 166–167; introduction to *The Case of the Wolf-Man*, p. 11.

7. Thus, according to Wollheim, Freud "interpreted without difficulty" a schizophrenic's habit of squeezing blackheads "as representing in the first instance masturbation, and secondly castration where this is consequential upon masturbation. Accordingly, the blackhead represents the penis, and the squeezed-out cavity represents the vagina in the sense of that which is left when the penis has been lopped off" (*Sigmund Freud*, p. 190). The effortlessness of detection cited here is surely ascribable to the standard meanings of protuberances and concavities as expounded in *The Interpretation of Dreams*.

Wollheim seek to prop up Freud in more ways than I indicated, but none of them could impress a reader who hadn't already decided that psychoanalytic truths are unassailable.

Thus Nagel and Wollheim bow to the pretension of analysts to be uniquely situated, in Nagel's words, to "probe far more deeply and uncover far more material for interpretation" than others, garnering "extensive and systematic insights"[8] that we ought to believe. "It is impossible," declares Wollheim, "to have access to the mass of clinical evidence that a given hypothesis [of Freud's] subsumes," and hence we cannot know "how the match of one case to a hypothesis is enhanced by a consideration of all parallel cases."[9] Consequently, Wollheim hands a blank check to the master without pausing to worry that "parallel cases" might reflect a parallel methodological extravagance. And as I mentioned in my article, Nagel displays the same laxity, averring that each Freudian hypothesis or interpretation will "find its empirical support in countless other applications to other patients in other settings."[10]

Both thinkers minimize the besetting epistemic problem of suggestion, maintaining that we needn't concern ourselves with that well-authenticated phenomenon until its dynamics are better understood. Moreover, both of them urge that because Freudian notions are hard to test experimentally, they are therefore exempt from the necessity of such testing.[11] (As an example,

8. Thomas Nagel, "Freud's Permanent Revolution," *The New York Review*, May 12, 1994, p. 36.
9. Wollheim, *Sigmund Freud*, p. 237.
10. Nagel, "Freud's Permanent Revolution," p. 35.
11. Wollheim, *The Mind and Its Depths*, pp. 102–111, and Nagel, "Freud's Permanent Revolution," p. 35.

Nagel cites the supposedly illuminating idea that melancholia features "abuse by the ego of the internalized object.") Thus psychoanalysis, in the charitable view of Wollheim and Nagel, deserves special indulgence for what other observers consider to be its worst vice, the proliferation of concepts and entities that stand at several removes from experience.

Again, one might expect two keen philosophers to be troubled by the fact that the "insights" produced by all schools of analysis amount to a tangle of contradictory propositions. Doesn't that fact suggest an epistemic flaw in the fundamental method of knowledge acquisition—the study of free associations —that those schools share? But Wollheim and Nagel allow the point to escape them. And this lapse is doubly remarkable in view of the fact that *they themselves* favor different versions of the Freudian gospel. Thus, Nagel dissents from what Wollheim calls Melanie Klein's "proper continuation" of Freud's thought,[12] whereby, for example, every nursling reportedly "seeks to destroy the inside of the mother's body, and uses its urine and faeces for this purpose."[13] In this instance, Nagel's doubts appear to rest on legitimate empirical considerations. One waits in vain, however, for him to acknowledge that similar considerations vitiate mainstream Freudian dogma.

Finally, Wollheim and Nagel alike attempt to shield psychoanalysis from criticism by assimilating it to a bland-looking intuitive "form of understanding"[14] that is said to

---

12. Wollheim, *The Mind and Its Depths*, p. 52.
13. Klein, quoted in *The Mind and Its Depths*, p. 58; cf. Nagel, "Freud's Permanent Revolution," p. 36, and Nagel's letter, p. 56.
14. Nagel's letter, p. 56.

characterize psychological explanation in general. This tactic serves a joint strategy of claiming that Freud, rather than having derived eccentric dogmas from overzealous guesswork, merely "added to the commonsense conception" of the mind so as "to accommodate new mental phenomena that he had discovered."[15] Unfortunately, Wollheim and Nagel offer no reason for us to agree that Freud did discover new mental phenomena, much less that his explanations of them deserve to be believed.[16] Their oversubtle arguments, like Cavell's own, boil down to special pleading for a tradition whose waywardness has by now become generally apparent.

---

15. Wolheim, *The Mind and Its Depths*, p. 92; see Nagel, "Freud's Permanent Revolution," p. 34.
16. Nagel adds that in any given act of interpretation, "what is unintelligible to naive common sense may be seen as 'justified,' after all, from a concealed aspect of the subject's point of view" (Nagel's letter, p. 56). But once again the argument is circular, since the question at issue is precisely whether or not people "conceal" motives of a Freudian kind. The fact that patients can be maneuvered into acquiescence to an analyst's surmises about such motives hardly warrants the assumption that the motives inhabited the patients' preexisting "point of view."

# AFTERWORD:
# CONFESSIONS OF A
# FREUD BASHER

In its issue of November 18, 1993, *The New York Review of Books* published a review essay of mine, "The Unknown Freud," to which the adjective "controversial" hardly seems adequate. The article attracted, and continues to attract, more attention than all of my previous writings combined, dating back to my fledgling literary-critical efforts in 1957. For several ensuing months, an unprecedented number of protesting letters to the editor poured in, mostly from psychoanalysts outraged by the indignities I had heaped on their honorable profession and its founder. Two rounds of published exchanges, the first of which alone consumed more ink than *The New York Review* had ever devoted to the aftermath of an article, left the overwhelming majority of complainants fuming on the sidelines.

---

This essay originally appeared, in slightly different form and with the editors' preferred title, "Cheerful Assassin Defies Analysis," in *The* [London] *Times Higher Education Supplement*, March 3, 1995, pp. 20–21.

As several correspondents remarked in injured tones, the main burden of "The Unknown Freud" could have been predicted from several earlier writings of mine. In my essay "Analysis Terminable" of 1980, and in several following, I had made a similar two-pronged argument: that Freud's scientific and ethical standards were abysmally low and that his brain-child was, and still is, a pseudoscience.[1] Why, then, did this recent essay prove so upsetting?

A number of answers come to mind. For one thing, Freudian loyalists were shocked to find my judgments aired in the pages of *The New York Review*, where Freudian issues are often discussed but only rarely with such negative adamancy as mine. Thus the editors of *The New York Review* appeared almost like pet owners who had negligently or maliciously consigned their parakeet to the mercies of an ever-lurking cat. My essay also contained some disturbing biographical information which, though known to Freud scholars, either was new to most analysts—for example, the story of Freud's greedy and fatal meddling in the life of his disciple Horace Frink—or had been discounted by them as atypical and insignificant, such as the infamous sequel to Emma Eckstein's nasal surgery, when Freud made so bold as to accuse that unfortunate woman of "bleeding for love" of himself.

Then, too, there was my report of what a number of scholars have independently discovered about the birth of psychoanalysis—namely, that Freud, amid the ruins of his untenable "seduction theory," peremptorily and gratuitously saddled his patients with a repressed *desire for* the incestuous

---

1. See Chapters 2–5 of *Skeptical Engagements* (Oxford University Press, 1986).

acts that he had until then been unsuccessfully goading them to remember. (His later contention that *they* had told *him* about having been molested in early childhood characteristically reshaped facts to comply with theory.) My readers were thus invited to confront the unsettling fact that psychoanalysis arose from nothing more substantial than a confused effort on Freud's part to foist his explanatorily worthless hobbyhorse of repression onto the fantasy life of his patients— patients who, moreover, far from being cured by his revised ministrations as he would eventually claim, had for the most part already lost faith in him and abandoned his practice. My essay left a plain impression that such opportunistic improvising, which was to become Freud's chronic reaction to theoretical crises, could not have been the work of a genuine scientific pioneer.

Beyond those provocations, however, a more general factor must have swelled the uproar over "The Unknown Freud": the gradual but accelerating collapse of psychoanalysis as a respected institution. The "fear and rage" that one analyst (David S. Olds) noted among his colleagues when my essay appeared would not have spread so rapidly without a preexisting sense that Freudianism could ill withstand another setback. Indeed, one sign of that desperation pervaded the very letters disputing the conclusions of my article. Whereas those who objected to "Analysis Terminable" in 1980 had flatly denied my entire case against psychoanalysis, these recent statements mostly took the plaintive form of "yes, but...." Although virtually all of my charges were conceded in one letter or another, each correspondent clung to some mitigating factor that might justify the continuation of psychoanalytic business as usual.

Yes, one analyst conceded, Freudian grand theory is a mess, but some of its lower-level formulations still prove helpful when patients invest belief in them (Herbert S. Peyser). Yes, the idea of repression remains undemonstrated, but can't we acknowledge that it possesses "heuristic value in generating research and further theory-building" (Morris Eagle)? Yes, "Freud's tendentious arguments...were extremely harmful to some of his patients and to the field he tried so hard to establish," but "psychoanalytic scholars continue to study Freud's theories and case histories as part of the ongoing effort to...widen knowledge about a still largely 'unknown' psychological universe..." (Marian Tolpin). Yes, Freud was a bit of a scoundrel, but at least "he did not sleep with his patients, nor found a lucrative ashram" (David S. Olds). And yes, American psychoanalysis is in decline, but the blame can be laid entirely on tight-fisted insurance companies that fail to appreciate the need for lengthy treatment (Lester Luborsky). To judge from such temporizing, psychoanalysis appears destined to end not with a bang but with a querulous whine.

Meanwhile, many Freudians who were stung by my article answered it with a tactic that Freud himself had developed in combat with such defectors as Fliess, Jung, Adler, Rank, and Ferenczi. Instead of addressing my criticisms, they treated them as symptoms of my own dysfunctional state. "I wonder," wrote one unpublished correspondent, "if Frederick Crews was aware when he wrote his vitriolic attack on Freud, that he laid himself bare to Freudian interpretations that would be numerous enough to fill as much space as his article." Another agreed: "We are all post-modern enough to understand the writing of his review as an *act*, an act about himself and not...about psychoanalysis itself." These and other writers, though they usually deem years of daily clinical inquiry to be scarcely sufficient for grasping a patient's deep unconscious structures, did not scruple to diagnose my own fixations by return mail.

Crews, wrote one petitioner to *The New York Review*, cannot see "that he is trapped in a transference which began as an idealization of [Freud], and which proceeded in normal fashion to hostile rejection.... [Thus] he is stuck on Freud-bashing." Peter Aspden said much the same thing in *The Times Higher Education Supplement.*[2] Eugene Goodheart, mounting a cautious endorsement of psychoanalysis in *Dissent*, summarily dismissed my criticism of Freud as an act of "parricide"—as opposed, say, to one of consumer protection.[3] My old student Murray Schwartz explained in sorrow to *Lingua Franca* that the problem is indeed oedipal: Crews is "after the sins of all the fathers."[4] And the psychoanalyst and sociology professor Jeffrey Prager, writing in *Contention*, depicted me as a "jilted lover" with an irrational vendetta against my erstwhile soulmate, Freud. By persecuting Freud, Prager divined, I am attempting to repress my Freudian past—"to pretend that it never happened."[5]

---

2. Peter Aspden, "Oedipus, the Final Act?," *The* [London] *Times Higher Education Supplement*, May 20, 1994, pp. 13, 21.

3. Eugene Goodheart, "Freud on Trial," *Dissent*, Vol. 42 (Spring 1995), pp. 236–243; the quoted word appears on p. 236.

4. Adam Begley, "Terminating Analysis," *Lingua Franca*, Vol. 4 (July/August 1994), pp. 24–30; the quotation is from p. 29.

5. Jeffrey Prager, "On the Abuses of Freud: A Reply to Masson and Crews," *Contention*, Vol. 4 (Fall 1994), pp. 211–25; the quotations are from pp. 217 and 218.

Other Freudians looked beyond my individual sickness to that of the age. Critiques like mine, said Eli Zaretsky in *Tikkun*, "are continuous with the attack on the Left that began with the election of Richard Nixon in 1968.... They continue the repudiation of the revolutionary and utopian possibilities glimpsed in the 1960s...."[6] Paul Williams, writing in *The Sunday Times*, took a slightly different tack, noting "the return of the (literally and militarily) repressed" after the fall of communism in 1989:

> So let's get Freud. He brought up all this stuff. He said that civilisation was a veneer over polymorphous perversity, incest, rapaciousness, man as a wolf to other men. . . . The analysts and therapists are held responsible for evoking all these things *that I cannot bear to know about my friends, my family and myself* [italics as found].[7]

In short, then, according to Williams, "Freud-baiting is above all a *political* activity. Those who wish to smear and dismantle Freud's work seek opportunities to define and manage what the rest of us think and believe about the way our minds and bodies function" (Williams, p. 18). (Does anyone besides me hear an echo of *Dr. Strangelove* in this last sentence?)

Whatever their specific hypotheses about my motives,

---

6. Eli Zaretsky, "The Attack on Freud," *Tikkun*, Vol. 9 (May/June 1994), pp. 65–70; the quoted words are from p. 67.
7. Paul Williams, "It's All in the Mind," *The* [London] *Sunday Times*, June 26, 1994, pp. 18–19; the quotations are from p. 19.

most Freudian commentators agreed that "The Unknown Freud" had been composed in a state of bitter anger by a malcontent with a vicious disposition. Indeed, this assumption was so common that Adam Begley, writing a profile of me in *Lingua Franca* some months later, considered it newsworthy to report that I am "quiet, unassuming, the kind of guy you just have to call mild-mannered," and that my academic associates consider me "a kind and gentle man."[8] Am I a Jekyll–Hyde, or could it be that taking an uncompromising line toward Freud and Freudianism is actually consistent with human decency?

Even Begley, to be sure, added that Crews "really hates Freud" (Begley, p. 24)—but he was wrong. Rather, I am *completely lacking in respect* for Freud, a very different matter. I don't hate Freud any more than, say, Karl Popper hated him, or than Ralph Nader hated General Motors. In each case the skeptical writer feels prompted to denounce a combination of unsubstantiated claims, inflated reputation, and deleterious practical consequences. The act of denunciation can be cheerful and confident as well as public-spirited. That was my mood, I clearly recall, during the writing of "The Unknown Freud."

In theory at least, Freudians ought to have been well equipped to guard against mistaking their anger for my own. Their pertinent doctrine of projection, after all, lay ready to hand for acts of ironic self-scrutiny. In failing to make use of it, however, my adversaries were being loyal to the Freudian tradition in a more fundamental sense. Despite Freud's own self-analysis and the training analyses that came later,

8. Begley, "Terminating Analysis," pp. 24, 29.

psychoanalysis has always been tacitly employed as a psychology *for the others*, not for the interpreter him- or herself. As Ernest Gellner has shown, Freudianism rests on an outlook of "conditional realism" whereby psychological truth is thought to be monopolized by, and fully available to, those who have removed their deeply programmed barriers to clarity. The analyzed and the doctrinally faithful are thus exempt from their own otherwise remorseless hermeneutic of suspicion. Since the quintessential Freudian assertion is, in Gellner's words, "I am freer of inner veils than thou," recourse to ad hominem argument becomes all but irresistible.[9] This is why the numerous slurs on my personality that circulated in the wake of "The Unknown Freud" were not deviations from but typical instances of the Freudian way with dissenters.

In rendering their diagnoses-at-a-distance, my critics appear to have been guided by a principle that struck them as too obviously warranted to bear articulating—namely, that "Freud bashing" is itself a sign of mental illness. They simply *knew*, after all, that Freud, despite some occasional missteps and out-of-date assumptions, had made fundamental discoveries and permanently revolutionized our conception of the mind. As three of the unpublished *New York Review* correspondents put it, Freud had proved once and for all that our behavior owes a great deal to unconscious emotions and ideas, that the mind can prove extraordinarily devious, and that humans fall ill when the real and the ideal, or desire and necessity, or the rational and the irrational are out of harmony.

---

9. Ernest Gellner, *The Psychoanalytic Movement: Or The Coming of Unreason* (London: Paladin, 1985), p. 97.

These and similar formulations were noteworthy for their high quotient of generality and vagueness, approaching, in thinness of atmosphere, the perfect vacuum achieved by the historian and Freud apologist Peter Gay, who has characterized Freud's "central idea" as the proposition that "every human is continuously, inextricably, involved with others...."[10] It is hard to dispute any of these statements about "humans," but it is also hard to see why they couldn't be credited as easily to Shakespeare, Dostoevsky, or Nietzsche—if not indeed to Jesus or Saint Paul—as to Freud. Was it really Freud who first disclosed such commonplaces? Or, rather, has the vast cultural sway of Freud's system caused us to lose focus on his more specific, highly idiosyncratic, assertions, to presume that a number of them must have been scientifically established by now, and to transform him retrospectively into the very personification of "human" complexity and depth?

Freud bashing begins to look less self-evidently pathological when we lower our sights to Freud's actual, far from modest, claims to discovery in four major categories of knowledge:

1. *The causes and cure of neurosis*. We needn't pause over Freud's pretensions in this realm, since scarcely anyone, including Freudian practitioners, can now be found who takes them seriously. The "oedipal repression etiology" of neurotic complaints is a dead letter, and mainstream psychoanalysis has backed away from its original boast of curative power.

---

10. Peter Gay, *Freud for Historians* (Oxford University Press, 1986), pp. 147–148.

2. *The meaning of symptoms, dreams, and errors.* Freud's greatest novelty lay here, in his widening of intentionality to cover phenomena that had been thought to lack expressive content or, in the case of dreams, to be expressive only in random flashes. When we get down to the details, however—for example, Freud's attribution of "Dora's" asthmatic attacks to her once having witnessed an act of parental intercourse, or his explanation of her coughing as an allusion to her desire to suck her father's penis—we find that the symptomatic interpretations rest on nothing more substantial than vulgar thematic affinities (heavy breathing in coitus=asthma; one oral function=another) residing in Freud's own prurient mind. So, too, the heart of his dream theory, the contention that every dream expresses a repressed infantile wish, was merely an extrapolation from his etiology of neurosis; it is counterintuitive and has never received an iota of corroboration. As for the theory of errors, Sebastiano Timpanaro among others has shown that it suffers from Freud's usual overingeniousness and wanton insistence on universal psychic determinism and that it is unsupported, in its emphasis on *repressed* causes of slips, by any of the examples provided in *The Psychopathology of Everyday Life*.[11] Having serially applied the same style of license to the decoding of symptoms, dreams, and errors, Freud was able to imagine that the resultant "convergence of findings" had proved him correct in all three areas. All it really proved is that the imperiousness of Freudian interpretation knows no bounds.

---

11. Sebastiano Timpanaro, *The Freudian Slip*, translated by Kate Soper (Humanities Press, 1976).

3. *Methodological principles for investigating the mind.* Chief among these, in Freud's view, was free association, the correct management of which can supposedly allow us not merely to discover the meaning of a dream but also to trace a symptom to its traumatic source in childhood. As Ludwig Wittgenstein suspected and as Adolf Grünbaum and Malcolm Macmillan have shown in laborious detail, the claim is hollow. A patient's ramblings, which Freud took to be a direct window on the invariant repressed unconscious, are channeled and contaminated by the psychoanalytic exchange itself, and instead of establishing the causes of earlier events, they merely show what is on the patient's contemporary mind as she strives to meet (or thwart) the analyst's expectations.

Of greater intuitive appeal are the numerous "mechanisms of defense" that Freud invoked for retracing the psychic compromises behind a given expression or symptom. (I have already mentioned one of them, projection.) Here, too, however, the prospect of reliable hermeneutic insight turns to dust. The so-called mechanisms are merely a lavish set of options for creating, not detecting, thematic links. In the absence of any guidelines for knowing which "mechanism" (if any) shaped a given phenomenon, the application of these tools by different interpreters yields a cacophony of incompatible explanations—and, ultimately, an indefinite proliferation of squabbling sects.

4. *The structure and dynamic operation of the mind.* Even when he sounded most tentative in this realm, Freud's speculations about conscious, preconscious, and unconscious mental systems, or about the ego, the superego, and the id, or about instincts of self-preservation and sex, or of life and

death, went far beyond any data that he could legitimately claim to have unearthed. On close inspection, the Freudian "dynamic unconscious" turns out to be not only a morass of contradictions between primitive and sophisticated functions but also an ontological maze peopled by absurd homunculi possessing their own inexplicable sets of warring motives. To be sure, Freud was occasionally willing to admit that his "metapsychological" constructs were speculative, even mythological. Nevertheless, he persisted in endowing them with quasi-physical energies and seemingly precise functions, and most of his disciples have followed suit. The result has been a legacy of utter conceptual murk.

Where, then, are Freud's authenticated contributions not to ethics or mores or literary criticism but to actual knowledge of the mind? So far as I am aware, no distinctively psychoanalytic notion has received independent experimental or epidemiological support—not repression, not the Oedipus or castration complex, not the theory of compromise formation, nor any other concept or hypothesis. Nor is this negative result anomalous in view of the reckless, conquistadorial manner in which psychoanalytic theory was launched and maintained in the teeth of rational criticism. What passes today for Freud bashing is simply the long-postponed exposure of Freudian ideas to the same standards of noncontradiction, clarity, testability, cogency, and parsimonious explanatory power that prevail in empirical discourse at large. Step by step, we are learning that Freud has been the most overrated figure in the entire history of science and medicine—one who wrought immense harm through the propagation of false etiologies, mistaken diagnoses, and fruitless lines of inquiry.

Still, the legend dies hard, and those who challenge it continue to be greeted like rabid dogs. A year after "The Unknown Freud" appeared, I published another long article in *The New York Review*, this one attacking the pernicious "recovered memory movement" and detailing its rather obvious origins in some of the most fundamental premises of Freudianism. The first of many lamentations—seven grandiloquent pages, signed by a psychoanalyst—arrived by fax on the very day that the first half of my two-installment essay hit the newsstands. Having been "made physically ill" by my earlier effort, the writer thought it best to quit this time "after reading less than a full page." Thus restored to equanimity, he set about the task of refutation.

This book's text was set in the Adobe Type Foundry's version of Garamond, originally designed by Claude Garamond (French, ca. 1500-61). Based on the roman letters of Aldus Manutius, Garamond had become the standard European type by the end of the sixteenth century and has been revived in this century, with several versions existing under the Garamond name. Garamond's first roman appeared in the 1530 edition of *Paraphrasis in Elegantiarum Libros Laurentii Vallae* by Erasmus, and the 1545 *Pia et Religiosa Meditatio* of David Chambellan used a new Garamond Italic cut in two sizes. The titling display type is Mantinia, designed by Matthew Carter of Carter and Cone Type Foundry.

Cover and book design by Bethany Johns Design, New York
Printed and bound by RR Donnelley & Sons Company